DOCTOR STRANGE AND PHILOSOPHY

The Blackwell Philosophy and Pop Culture Series
Series editor William Irwin

A spoonful of sugar helps the medicine go down, and a healthy helping of popular culture clears the cobwebs from Kant. Philosophy has had a public relations problem for a few centuries now. This series aims to change that, showing that philosophy is relevant to your life—and not just for answering the big questions like "To be or not to be?" but for answering the little questions: "To watch or not to watch *South Park*?" Thinking deeply about TV, movies, and music doesn't make you a "complete idiot." In fact it might make you a philosopher, someone who believes the unexamined life is not worth living and the unexamined cartoon is not worth watching.

DOCTOR STRANGE AND PHILOSOPHY

THE OTHER BOOK OF FORBIDDEN KNOWLEDGE

Edited by

Mark D. White

WILEY Blackwell

Registered Offices
John Wiley & Sons, Inc., 111 River Street, Hoboken, NJ 07030, USA
John Wiley & Sons Ltd, The Atrium, Southern Gate, Chichester, West Sussex, PO19 8SQ, UK

Editorial Office
9600 Garsington Road, Oxford, OX4 2DQ, UK

For details of our global editorial offices, customer services, and more information about Wiley products visit us at www.wiley.com.

Wiley also publishes its books in a variety of electronic formats and by print-on-demand. Some content that appears in standard print versions of this book may not be available in other formats.

Library of Congress Cataloging-in-Publication Data

Names: White, Mark D., 1971– editor.
Title: Doctor Strange and philosophy : the other book of forbidden knowledge / edited by Mark D. White.
Description: Hoboken : Wiley, 2018. | Series: The Blackwell philosophy and pop culture series | Includes bibliographical references and index. | Identifiers: LCCN 2018004197 (print) | LCCN 2018010034 (ebook) | ISBN 9781119437918 (pdf) | ISBN 9781119437925 (epub) | ISBN 9781119437949 (pbk.)
Subjects: LCSH: Doctor Strange (Motion picture) | Motion pictures–Philosophy.
Classification: LCC PN1997.D (ebook) | LCC PN1997.D D537 2018 (print) | DDC 791.43/72–dc23
LC record available at https://lccn.loc.gov/2018004197

Cover images: Spell Ring © Shutterstock/TAW4, Firework Traces © iStock.com/RMAX, Blue Satin © iStock.com/gmutlu, Red Satin © iStock.com/LOVE_LIFE
Cover design: Wiley

Set in 10.5/13pt Sabon by SPi Global, Pondicherry, India

Printed in the UK by Bell & Bain Ltd, Glasgow.

10 9 8 7 6 5 4 3 2 1

Contents

Contributors
The Philosophers Supreme

Philipp Berghofer is a Ph.D. candidate and lecturer at the University of Graz, Austria. He works primarily on phenomenology, epistemology, and the philosophy of physics, focusing on the concept of evidence. He is a recipient of a DOC Fellowship of the Austrian Academy of Sciences. Recently, he acquired the Eye of Agamotto at a local gift shop, and since then he has made many bargains.

Armond Boudreaux is the only assistant professor of English at East Georgia State College with a Captain America shield on his office wall. He has published three books, including *Titans: How Superheroes Can Help Us Understand a Polarized World* (with Corey Latta). He often regales his four children with tales of the superheroics of his youth—and they believe every word. Really.

Matthew William Brake is a graduate student at George Mason University pursuing a dual master's degree in philosophy and interdisciplinary studies, and has a Master of Divinity degree from Regent University. He has published numerous entries in the series *Kierkegaard Research: Sources, Reception, Resources*, volumes 15–18, from Ashgate, and blogs at www.popularcultureandtheology.com. Like Doctor Strange at Kamar-Taj, he banged on Mark White's door for hours to be allowed into this volume.

Skye C. Cleary teaches at Columbia University, Barnard College, and the City College of New York. She is the author of *Existentialism and Romantic Love*, managing editor of the Blog of the American Philosophical Association, and an advisory board member of Strategy of Mind. Her work has been published with *TED-Ed, Los Angeles*

Review of Books, Aeon, Huffington Post, The Conversation, Business Insider, New Republic, The New Philosopher, The Philosophers' Magazine, and others. While her favorite power of Doctor Strange is being able to pop into the library and borrow books without having to do the whole check-out thing, she wouldn't turn down the ability to fold time and space, especially when writing and grading deadlines loom over her like dark dimensions.

Paul DiGeorgio is an adjunct professor at Duquesne University in Pittsburgh. He researches and writes on existentialism and phenomenology, and is very upset they've changed the wifi password at Kamar-Taj.

Sarah K. Donovan is an associate professor of philosophy at Wagner College in New York City. Her teaching and research interests include community-based, feminist, social, moral, and continental philosophy. She was one of the top three candidates for the position as Doctor Strange's new librarian, but was rejected for not tempering her philosophy with science. The position was eventually taken by Zelma Stanton.

George A. Dunn is a writer on philosophy and popular culture. In addition to contributing essays to numerous books in the Wiley-Blackwell series, he has edited or co-edited six books on philosophy and pop culture, most recently *The Philosophy of Christopher Nolan* (Lexington Books, 2017) with Jason Eberl. George shares with Stephen Strange the fact that both have visited Mount Everest, though George made it only as far as base camp, and he only got that far as a passenger in an older van that was ill-equipped to absorb all the shocks of those winding, gravel-covered Himalayan roads, all the time wishing he had packed his sling ring.

Christopher P. Klofft is an associate professor of theology at Assumption College Worcester, MA. He is the author of *Living the Love Story: Catholic Morality in the Modern World* (Alba House, 2008) and lectures widely on issues of Catholicism and culture as well as marriage, family, and sexual ethics. He blogs at www. christopherklofft.com. Christopher prefers the *Summa Theologiae* to the Book of the Vishanti, but he might be willing to trade a copy of his dissertation for the Darkhold.

Dean A. Kowalski is professor of philosophy at the University of Wisconsin-Waukesha, and regularly teaches philosophy of religion,

Asian philosophy, and ethics. He is the author of *Classic Questions and Contemporary Film* (2nd edition, 2016) and *Moral Theory at the Movies* (2012). He is the editor of *The Big Bang Theory and Philosophy* (2012), *The Philosophy of The X-Files*, revised edition (2009), and *Steven Spielberg and Philosophy* (2008), and the co-editor of *The Philosophy of Joss Whedon* (2011). He marvels at all the classic tomes he could read by mystically dislodging his astral form from his body, but he (sheepishly) admits he would probably just watch more Marvel movies.

Corey Latta is a writer, teacher, and public speaker who has written on subjects such as C.S. Lewis, philosophy, and the intersections of religion and literature. Corey holds master's degrees in religion and English as well as a Ph.D. in 20th Century Literature. He is the author of *C. S. Lewis and the Art of Writing*, *When the Eternal Can Be Met: The Bergsonian Theology of Time in the Works of C. S. Lewis, T. S. Eliot, and W. H. Auden*, and co-author of *Titans: How Superheroes Can Help Us Make Sense of a Polarized World* (with Armond Boudreaux). Corey is currently Writer-in-Residence at Kamar-Taj, but he refuses to tell Paul DiGeorgio the new wifi password.

Sander H. Lee is professor of philosophy at Keene State College in New Hampshire. He is the author of *Woody Allen's Angst: Philosophical Commentaries on his Serious Films* (McFarland, 2013). Sander's essay, "Primo Levi's Gray Zone: Implications for Post-Holocaust Ethics," appeared recently in the journal *Holocaust and Genocide Studies*. He has also written numerous additional essays on issues in aesthetics, ethics, Holocaust studies, social philosophy, and metaphysics. He has Doctor Strange's persistence but, unfortunately, none of his mystical abilities.

Michael Lyons is a Ph.D. candidate in philosophy at Trinity College Dublin. His work is predominantly in ethics, focusing on questions and problems of the more theoretical and fundamental variety. Having seen the 2016 film *Doctor Strange*, he thought it would be wonderful if he were able to say that Wong won a Wand of Watoomb.

Daniel P. Malloy teaches philosophy at Aims Community College in Greeley, Colorado. He has published numerous chapters on the intersections of philosophy and popular culture, including chapters on

Spider-Man, the Avengers, Iron Man, Batman, Green Lantern, and Deadpool. He tried to join the Hoary Hosts of Hoggoth, but failed the physical.

Tuomas W. Manninen earned his Ph.D. in philosophy in 2007 from the University of Iowa, and is presently a senior lecturer at Arizona State University, where he teaches courses in critical thinking, philosophy of mind, political philosophy, and other assorted topics. Although he doesn't think he knows how the world works, he has internalized the lesson that not everything has to make sense. While he is not too keen about breaking the laws of nature, he thinks that learning about astral projection could help him immensely with his grading.

Carina Pape teaches at the University of Flensburg, Germany, and writes on moral philosophy, especially on gender and race, indignation, diversity, and philosophy of education. Instead of heading for Kathmandu to open her mind and change her reality, she decided to go to Kyoto University, Japan, where she's been doing research on cultural diversity as a visiting fellow. She grew up with four male cousins and one brother—from whom she snatched her first comic books—and realized early on that women make pretty good fighters too. Her role models are Socrates, Gamora from the Guardians of the Galaxy, O-Ren Ishii from *Kill Bill*, and of course, the (female) Ancient One, even though the latter conflicts with the Kantian within her from time to time.

Konstantin Pavliouts has a Ph.D in philosophy and works at Krasin Moscow State Vocational School, Russia. He is interested in the philosophy of space and time, and has published on the specific Indian comprehension of space and time problematics, as well as the philosophical foundations of social space and time categories in Western philosophy. He is also interested in the philosophical ideas in the literature of Tolstoy and Dostoyevsky. He'd like to experience Doctor Strange's spiritual transformation in Kamar-Taj as a philosopher, but would rather not become Sorcerer Supreme of the Earth, thank you very much.

Edwardo Pérez is an associate professor in the Department of English at Tarrant County College Northeast Campus in Hurst, Texas. When he's not teaching, he's writing essays, blogs, stories, poetry, and the occasional orchestral composition. When he's not writing, he's thinking about philosophy, rhetoric, politics, and the infinite possibilities of the multiverse. Edwardo spends his free time studying the Book of Vishanti and practicing with the Axe of Angarruumus, the Ebony Blade, and Dragonfang (because you can never have enough magical weapons).

Nicholas Richardson is a professor in the Department of Physical Sciences at Wagner College in New York City, where he teaches general, advanced inorganic, and medicinal chemistry. He was one of the top three candidates for the position as Doctor Strange's new librarian, but was rejected for not tempering his science with philosophy. The position was eventually taken by Zelma Stanton.

Brendan Shea teaches philosophy at Rochester Community and Technical College in Minnesota, and is also a Resident Fellow at the Minnesota Center for Philosophy of Science. His teaching and research interests include the philosophy of science, biomedical ethics, logic, and the philosophy of religion. He's contributed over a dozen chapters to books on popular culture and philosophy, including volumes on *Alice in Wonderland*, *The Princess Bride*, and *Ender's Game*. He's studied Doctor Strange's work carefully in the hopes of picking up some magical skills, but his sorcerous talents (so far) are limited to an uncanny ability to make his socks disappear.

Chad William Timm is an associate professor of education at Simpson College in Indianola, Iowa. He teaches courses on the history and philosophy of education and specializes in examining ways to use pop culture as a vehicle to teach complex concepts. His work also appears in Wiley Blackwell volumes on *The Girl with the Dragon Tattoo*, *Game of Thrones*, *Ender's Game*, and *The Hunger Games*. While writing his chapter for this volume, he sought to embody the Socratic heroism of Doctor Strange, leading him to periodically blurt out exclamations in class like "By the Hoary Hosts of Hoggoth!" and "By the Mystic Moons of Munnopor!" Unsurprisingly, his students gave him the highest course evaluations of his career.

Andrew T. Vink is a Ph.D. candidate in systematic theology at Boston College. He holds master's degrees in philosophy and theology from Marquette University in Wisconsin, and his research interests include philosophical theology, political theology, liberation theology, and the thought of Bernard Lonergan. When not buried under a pile of books in the libraries of Kamar-Taj, Andrew sits patiently waiting for the next Marvel Cinematic Universe film with popcorn in hand.

Mark D. White is chair of the Department of Philosophy at the College of Staten Island/CUNY, where he teaches courses in philosophy, economics, and law. He has edited or co-edited six other volumes in the Blackwell Philosophy and Pop Culture Series, including ones on Iron Man and the Avengers; contributed chapters to many more; and authored books on Captain America and *Civil War*. Someday he hopes to find a woman wearing Clea's awesome leggings, for then he will be sure he has found the one.

Bruce Wright is Regional Associate Dean of the Island Medical Program at the University of British Columbia, and Head of the Division of Medical Sciences at the University of Victoria. He has a research interest in medical education which has led to over fifty peer-reviewed publications in the areas of medical student career choice and medical school curriculum development. Of the many teaching awards he has received over the years the ones he cherishes most are those bestowed on him by medical students. He is trained in family medicine and has a special interest is geriatrics. He aspires to be like Doctor Strange and not simply strange, which appears to be what others think, while rockin' a perfectly coiffed Doctor Strange beard.

E. Paul Zehr is an award-winning science communicator, professor, author and martial artist at the University of Victoria. His popular science books *Becoming Batman*, *Inventing Iron Man*, *Project Superhero*, and *Chasing Captain America* use superheroes as metaphors exploring the science of human potential. In 2015, he won the Science Educator Award from the Society for Neuroscience, and *Project Superhero* won the Silver Medal for Juvenile fiction from the Independent Book Sellers of North America. He secretly wishes he had a real life Sanctum Sanctorum within which he could train with Wong.

Acknowledgments
By the Glorious Grandiloquence of Gratitude!

I would like to thank Sian Jones at Wiley-Blackwell for guiding this book up the snowy mountains to the promised land of publication; the Series Editor Supreme, William Irwin, whom I would never dare call the Ancient One if he weren't so slow; and the contributors to this volume, without whom it would simply be a list of clever names of spells I made up while sculpting my goatee in the mirror on a Saturday night.

In all seriousness, I wish to thank all the brilliant creative minds that gave us this fascinating character and his world, including Stan Lee, Steve Ditko, Roy Thomas, Gene Colan, Steve Englehart, Frank Brunner, P. Craig Russell, Peter B. Gillis, Brian K. Vaughan, Marcos Martin, Brian Michael Bendis, Jonathan Hickman, Devin Grayson, Robbie Thompson, Javier Rodriguez, Jason Aaron, and Chris Bachalo. Thanks also go to everyone involved in making the 2016 film that brought this marvelous world to life, including Scott Derrickson, Kevin Feige, Jon Spaihts, C. Robert Cargill, Benedict Cumberbatch, Tilda Swinton, Benedict Wong, Chiwetel Ejiofor, Rachel McAdams, and all the other talented people in front of and behind the camera.

Introduction
Opening the Book of the Vishanti

In 1963, comics legends Stan Lee and Steve Ditko added a unique figure to the expanding Marvel Universe: Doctor Stephen Strange, a brilliant neurosurgeon turned Sorcerer Supreme, who stood as the Earth's sole defender against mystical threats from strange dimensions. (Their other famous creation, Spider-Man, was just a warm-up.) Combining Lee's affection for astonishing alliteration—"By the Mystic Moons of Munnopor!"—with Ditko's psychedelic panoramas, Doctor Strange was unique in a growing stable of heroes mostly based on the promise of science and the fear of radioactivity.

Since then, Doctor Strange has been a mainstay of the Marvel Universe, if not often a featured player, an appropriate position for a loner who prefers to serve his role in thankless solitude. With faithful Wong always at his side, and occasionally teaming up with Defenders, Avengers, and fellow mystics such as Clea and Brother Voodoo, Strange added a welcome maturity and stability to a world full of superpowered teens, impetuous Norse gods, and gamma-fueled rage machines.

In 2016, audiences outside the strange realm of comic book conventions and Wednesday pull-lists were exposed to a cinematic vision of Doctor Strange, deftly portrayed by Benedict Cumberbatch alongside Benedict Wong, Chiwetel Ejiofor, Rachel McAdams, and the enigmatic Tilda Swinton as the Ancient One. Ditko's startling visions of alternate universes were reflected in dazzling color and three dimensions in front of our very eyes, and Lee's arrogant doctor came to life

Doctor Strange and Philosophy: The Other Book of Forbidden Knowledge,
First Edition. Edited by Mark D. White.
© 2018 John Wiley & Sons Ltd. Published 2018 by John Wiley & Sons Ltd.

on the big screen where he was brought down a few pegs before being rebuilt as a noble self-sacrificing hero.

Fifty-plus years of comics adventures and a brilliant feature film provide us not only with tales of mind-bending mysticism and self-sacrificing heroics, but also a wealth of philosophical inspiration. How does Doctor Strange reconcile his belief in hard-boiled science with his mystical training? What does he mean when he tells the Ancient One they're just "tiny momentary specks within an indifferent universe"—and why was he wrong? What does his astral self say about the relationship between mind and body? And why is he always so alone? Two dozen of our dimension's Philosophers Supreme stand ready to help answer these questions and many more.

So don your Cloak of Levitation, light the Flames of the Faltine, and travel with us to the strange and marvelous world of magic, wonder ... and philosophy! (And despite the subtitle, there is no forbidden knowledge here, we promise!)

Part I
"YOU'RE JUST ANOTHER TINY, MOMENTARY SPECK WITHIN AN INDIFFERENT UNIVERSE"

Bargaining with Eternity and Numbering One's Days

Medicine, Nietzsche, and Doctor Strange

George A. Dunn

From the standpoint of modern medicine, death is a failure—and one of the first things that we learn in the 2016 movie *Doctor Strange* is that Stephen Strange does not like to fail. In fact, at the time of the automobile accident that brought his brilliant career as a neurosurgeon to a tragic end, Stephen Strange and failure had apparently never yet crossed paths. He had a "perfect record," as he casually reminded Nurse Billy in an offhand boast when Billy proposed that he help a "68-year-old female with an advanced brain stem glioma." Such a diagnosis predicted a poor outcome that he would prefer not to have sully his résumé. At the same time, though, he doesn't want to build his reputation on easy victories. He declines to help "a 35-year-old Air Force colonel who crushed his spine in some sort of experimental armor," dismissing it as the surgical equivalent of child's play: "I could help but so can fifty other people."[1]

So it's no surprise that after Stephen's catastrophic accident that crushes his hands, his world collapses. Physical therapy alone can never restore his hands to what they were before and—ironically, in light of his own practice of rejecting patients who might ruin his perfect record—another doctor rejects him as a candidate for a cutting-edge experimental treatment lest it fail and ruin the doctor's reputation. Stephen's entire professional life, outside of which he seems to have little else, has been about undoing damage and defying death. His own research has focused on the stimulation of neurogenesis in the

Doctor Strange and Philosophy: The Other Book of Forbidden Knowledge, First Edition. Edited by Mark D. White.

central nervous system, restoring damaged neural tissue through a process that promises to save thousands of lives. His experience in the operating room is one of snatching patients from the jaws of death or, in at least one instance, restoring to life a patient who had already been declared brain dead. If death is failure for Stephen, the converse is also true after his accident—the failure to restore his hands is tantamount to death, the end of the only life that holds any meaning for him.

Heading East

"This isn't the end. There are other things that can give your life meaning," his friend and colleague Christine Palmer urges. "Like what? Like you?" he snaps backs. Christine tries to shake Stephen of his obsession with reversing the irreversible and get him to accept that "some things just can't be fixed." But because he's unable to envision a new life for himself, he clings to the unrecoverable past with mounting desperation and anger. That desperation finally drives him to Nepal, high in the Himalayas, in search of a miracle, to Kamar-Taj, where he becomes a student of the Ancient One. Though he hopes to learn the secret to restoring what was lost, he instead learns to surrender his attachment to the past and embrace transformation and mortality. As it turns out, that was the very same lesson that Christina was trying to teach him, but maybe Stephen first needed to travel to the other side of the world, to the exotic East, to sink to the absolute nadir of desperation, and then encounter that same truth wrapped in saffron robes before he could truly hear it.

Since at least the nineteenth century, it has become something of a cliché to view the East—the Indian subcontinent, the Himalayan regions, and the Far East in particular—as the repository of wisdom and spirituality, while the West has been depicted as an abode of soulless materialism where an ever-increasing store of scientific knowledge is coupled with a paucity of wisdom about how to use it well. Stephen Strange in many ways epitomizes the unflattering picture that these stereotypes paint of a spiritually desolate West. He's a vain egoist engaged in a self-defeating attempt to control every facet of his world, a believer only in what's given to his senses, trusting only in reason and science and living like an existential orphan in a universe that's barren of any meaning or purpose except what we impose on it. "We are made of matter and nothing more," he lectures the Ancient

One, reciting the creed of scientific materialism. "You're just another tiny, momentary speck within an indifferent universe."

Obviously, not every resident of Western civilization shares this worldview, which is at once bleak in its assessment of our existential plight and madly optimistic in its faith in our ability to bend this particular corner of our indifferent universe to our will through science, technology, and medicine. Still, it does represent an attitude that is at least native to the West, one that often claims as its warrant the tremendous power over nature that it has allowed us to achieve. We witness the bounty of this power in the early scenes of the movie that take place in the hospital, where Stephen deploys the most advanced medical technology, knowledge, and skill in the service of saving lives. Yet when he begins his training at Kamar-Taj, the Ancient One admonishes him, "Your intellect has taken you far in life but it will take you no further," following that up with an instruction to "silence your ego." If the West is hyper-rationalist and obsessed with subduing the forces of nature, the East of popular imagination is where one goes to gain the wisdom that begins with surrendering control and accepting the limits of reason.

Kamar-Taj is a Westerner's dream of exotic Asian culture, an Orientalist pastiche of incongruous elements from diverse traditions that variously evoke an idea of the mystical, spiritually enlightened East. The Ancient One, who is not a Buddhist, wears the saffron robe of a Buddhist monk and shows Stephen a book containing diagrams of both Indian chakras (tantric centers of spiritual energy) and Chinese acupuncture points. Denizens of Kamar-Taj wear Japanese-inspired clothing and engage in martial arts training, while the Ancient One mouths various mystical-sounding clichés with sage-like solemnity ("At the root of existence, mind and matter meet; thoughts shape reality"). The Ancient One is obviously not of Asian heritage herself, however— we're told that she's Celtic, which vaguely associates her with a certain New Age image of occult wisdom and intimacy with nature drawn from the pre-Christian West. In the popular imagination, the Celts represent something like a remote outpoint of Eastern wisdom in the West, one that is long gone, trampled under by the advance of Christianity. But what this imaginary, hybrid, trope-laden Asian landscape signifies is not so much the reality of Asian civilizations, but rather a sense that, despite the manifold successes of Western science and technology, something vital has been lost along the way, something that this fantasy imagines still exists elsewhere. As Stephen tells Christine upon his return, "After Western medicine failed me, I headed East."

"Matter and Nothing More"

Stephen speaks of Western medicine, but it might be more accurate to refer to modern medicine, since the kind of medical practice in which Stephen was engaged is bound up with a set of ideas and aspirations regarding humanity's place in nature that emerged only in the seventeenth century in tandem with the scientific revolution. Among the intellectual guiding lights of this revolution were two great philosophers: Francis Bacon (1561–1626) and René Descartes (1596–1650). Because Bacon came first, the project that he and Descartes initiated is often referred to as the Baconian project.

This project, which came to shape Western civilization and then in due course the emerging civilization of global modernity, was guided by the imperative to reduce human suffering—"to subdue and overcome the necessities and miseries of humanity," as Bacon put it—and to expand the realm of human freedom through the technological conquest of nature.[2] Descartes was even more blunt about the aims of this project: the new technology enabled by a proper science of the natural world promised to make us "the masters and possessors of nature," which was

> desirable not only for the invention of an infinity of devices that would enable us to enjoy trouble-free the fruits of the Earth and all the goods found there, but also principally for the maintenance of health, which is the first good and the foundation of all the other goods in this life.[3]

Consequently, for Descartes, the indefinite lengthening of human life was to be the crowning achievement of modern science. "The preservation of health has always been the principal end of my studies," he wrote.[4] Whereas the goal of pre-modern medicine was to care for the sick and the dying, in full awareness that not every ailment could be cured and that death was inevitable, within the context of the Baconian project, any limitation on human powers is an insult to our autonomy, a challenge to be overcome, and a summons for us to reclaim control of our existence. For Descartes, as for Doctor Stephen Strange, death is an enemy to be subdued.[5]

It's more than a little ironic, then, that, as contemporary philosopher (and physician) Jeffrey Bishop points out, the human body as conceived within the Baconian project is essentially a dead body, as opposed to the living, suffering, fully animated body of someone with a particular identity, history, hopes, fears, and loved ones.[6] It's not just that, for most medical students learning the techniques of surgery, "their first patient is dead [a cadaver], literally patient beneath the dissecting knife."[7] Rather, it's that the body is approached as a machine, albeit one of dazzling intricacy, to be studied, manipulated, and repaired in ways that are analogous to how a mechanic fixes an inanimate contraption that is broken. Stephen's belief that we are matter and nothing more simply reflects the way medicine approaches the human body.

The anesthetized body on Stephen's operating table at Metro-General Hospital is for all practical purposes indistinguishable from a corpse. Indeed, it would have been treated no differently than a corpse, its organs harvested while the heart was still beating, if Stephen had not overruled the treating physician's misdiagnosis of brain death. Hospitals are places of efficient operations and high tech instruments, where bodies are objects whose inner workings are skillfully manipulated to produce the desired effects. It is no accident that the medical art turns living bodies into passive objects, since otherwise it would be impossible to make reliable predictions about them and gain some measure of control over their machinery. As Bishop observes, "Life is in flux, and it is difficult to make truth claims about matter in motion, about bodies in flux. Thus, life is no foundation upon which to build a true science of medicine."[8]

Looking Beyond Death

Of course, to say that doctors relate to their patients' bodies as machines to be repaired, rather than as the bodies of living beings, doesn't mean that doctors don't care for their patients. Christine Palmer obviously cares a great deal about her patients in the Metro-General emergency room. And in a certain way the exclusive focus on the machinery of the body to the neglect of the "whole person" makes medicine a highly ethical discipline, strictly impartial and fundamentally egalitarian. Unlike Stephen, Christine doesn't believe it's beneath her to come into work just to save the life of a "drunk idiot with a gun" or "another dreg of humanity," as Stephen describes her patients. The mission of a doctor is to save lives, not to make judgments about the worth of those lives, a restricted mission that coincides with the doctor's restricted sphere of competence. Doctors can keep our bodies alive, often for a very long time, but they can't tell us what our lives are good for and, consequently, they can't tell us when it would be best to gracefully—and gratefully—let go of life. The goal is no longer living out a natural lifespan, whatever that could mean once the Baconian project has persuaded us that natural limits are given to us only to be surpassed, but simply more and more life—like the Ancient One stealing centuries of life from the Dark Dimension until she's finally defeated by an external power. For modern medicine, too, death is always a defeat, a failure to deliver on its implicit promise of a cure.

And that's one of the problems with the Baconian project. When the paramount passion of our civilization becomes the conquest of nature, it's hard to imagine on what basis we could assign any non-arbitrary limits to that conquest. So our expectations of medicine, as well as our expectations of human power and ingenuity more generally, grow to be increasingly immodest. Any limitation of our powers becomes an affront, an intolerable absurdity in a universe that should be made to bend to our will, which is precisely how Stephen experiences the news that even the most advanced medicine can't undo the damage done to his hands. Such news is world-shattering for him—and not just in the sense that it marks the end of the life he had made for himself as an acclaimed surgeon at the pinnacle of success in his field. It also represents a crisis in his Baconian worldview, its shipwreck on the shoals of harsh, unalterable reality.

The Ancient One chides Stephen for his "overinflated ego," discerning that he wants "to go back to the delusion that you can control anything, even death, which no one can control. Not even the great doctor Stephen Strange." Though apparently referring to Stephen's peculiar personal shortcomings, her words are really an indictment of the entire Baconian project that had captured his imagination—and that of the modern West—and shaped his view of the world before failing him and leading him to the brink of despair. And whether Stephen fully realizes it or not, recoiling from the failure of that project was what his journey to the East was really all about.

"The World Is Not What It Ought to Be"

We don't need to head east in order to find a critique of the aspirations of the modern West. The philosopher Friedrich Nietzsche (1844–1900) believed that the goal of the Baconian project to overcome "the necessities and miseries of mankind," its twofold ambition of eliminating suffering and forestalling death, sought objects that were neither possible nor desirable. Nietzsche had harsh words for those who wanted to abolish suffering, since he believed that only by passing through adversity and enduring life's brutal necessities was it possible for human beings to make something worthwhile of themselves.

Nietzsche himself was intimately acquainted with suffering. He was afflicted with chronic bad health, digestive problems, poor eyesight, and crippling migraine headaches, all of which made his life in many ways one of constant torment. These physical infirmities forced him into early retirement from his initial profession as a professor of classical studies at the University of Basel in Switzerland, which gives him something in common with Stephen Strange, whose illustrious career in medicine was also cut short by physical disability. But unlike Stephen, Nietzsche did not rage against his fate as though it were some terrible injustice for which the universe must be held accountable. Recovering from one of his many protracted bouts of illness, he wrote:

> I want to learn more and more to see what is necessary in things as what is beautiful in them—thus I shall be one of those who make things beautiful. *Amor fati* [love of fate]: let that be my love from now on! I do not want to wage war against what is ugly. I do not want to accuse; I do not even want to accuse the accusers! Let *looking away* be my only negation. And, all in all and on the whole: some day I want only to be a Yes-sayer![9]

For Nietzsche, the challenge is not to remake the world to our liking, but rather to learn to love the world as it is, which includes affirming both our capacity to suffer and the unalterable fact of our mortality.

According to Nietzsche, becoming this sort of Yes-sayer meant standing against the dominant traditions of Western religion and philosophy, both of which he believed were motivated by a subterranean animus against the conditions of life as we know it, its suffering, hardship, and finitude—or, as we say today, the fact that life's a bitch and then you die. It was in order to make life more tolerable that human beings constructed the fantasy of another, better world beyond this one, a changeless metaphysical realm immune from the flux of time, a heaven where all our wounds are healed and our tears wiped away. He calls the fabricators of these phantom worlds the "hinterworldly"—in German, *Hinterweltler*, literally "believers in a world behind the world"—and says, "It was suffering and incapacity that created all hinterworlds."[10]

The sorcerer Kaecilius, rogue disciple and nemesis of the Ancient One, also aspires to "a world beyond time, beyond death," where mortal beings can enjoy "eternal life as part of the one." However, unlike the fabrications of Nietzsche's *Hinterweltler*, the timeless realm of Dormammu that Kaecilius wants to bring to Earth is (at least within the Marvel Cinematic Universe) horribly real. Although Nietzsche is no believer in worlds beyond time, he would almost certainly have applauded the movie's depiction of Dormammu, the lord of the eternal realm, as a ravenous, beady-eyed monster whose promise of "eternal life" masks the fact that everything about his realm is the antithesis of life. His arrival on Earth arrests the flow of time and turns the living into lifeless effigies of themselves. Nietzsche would undoubtedly say that the movie's depiction of Dormammu and the nightmarish consequences of inviting him into this world reveal the hope for eternity to be grounded in a hatred of life. Kaecilius really should have read to the end of the book ("the warnings come after the spells")—or at least read Nietzsche, whose writings are also full of warnings about the dangers of putting our faith in hinterworlds.

Whither the Hinterworlds?

In the modern world, however, with the advance of scientific materialism—typified by saying that "we are matter and nothing more"—belief in these hinterworlds has become harder and harder to sustain. That does not mean that the antipathy toward life that motivated human beings to construct them has vanished, though. It is simply taken the form of the Baconian project to vanquish suffering in *this* world, since, being merely "tiny, momentary specks within an indifferent universe," we no longer have the consolation of belief in another world to help make our suffering bearable.

Those, of course, were Stephen's words to the Ancient One, describing what he takes to be our forlorn existential status. Surprisingly, he later hears those same words spoken to him by Kaecilius. This verbal coincidence suggests that there may be significant overlap in the worldviews of these two ostensible opponents—or at least between the views of Kaecilius and the Stephen Strange who first showed up at Kamar-Taj, bitter at how fate had treated him and desperate to regain the control he had lost. At that time, the Ancient One expressed concern over his "stubbornness, arrogance, ambition," prompting Mordo to say that Strange reminded her of Kaecilius. Mordo hinted further that Kaecilius' downfall, which could become Stephen's as well, resulted from their seeking "power" in order to defeat their "enemies" rather than for the purpose of using it, as Mordo says he had, to defeat their "demons." Nietzsche helps us to see that, for both Kaecilius the *Hinterwelter* and callow Stephen Strange, the Baconian foot soldier, the enemies and the demons are the same.

Their common enemy is time and their shared demon is what Nietzsche calls the spirit of revenge against time. "The world is not what it ought to be," declares Kaecilius. "Humanity longs for the eternal, for a world beyond time because time is what enslaves us. Time is an insult. Death is an insult." Time brings suffering due to the impermanence of all the things we cherish, while our inescapable advance toward our ultimate destination in the grave promises to deprive us of what we cherish most, our lives. "Time kills everything," bemoans Kaecilius. The passing away of our lives and the lives of our loved ones, the flux and fluidity of all things, the irreversibility of time with the irretrievable loss it brings—these are sources of our pain and distress.

Stephen may not share Kaecilius' hinterworldly ambition to transcend time altogether—Stephen is a Baconian, after all, intent on controlling this world, not escaping it—but he does suffer the passage of time as an insult, clinging desperately to an unrecoverable past in a quixotic hope to reverse what time has done to him. The anguish that leads him to sell everything he owns and finally to journey halfway around the world to Kamar-Taj is nothing other than his refusal to come to terms with the death of his old life. Both men are, in Nietzsche's words, sick with "revenge" against time. His description of the vengeful human will fits the demon that torments Stephen especially well: "Impotent against that which has been—it is an angry spectator of everything past."[11] The spirit of revenge, "the will's unwillingness toward time and time's 'it was,'" must be overcome if we are to embrace the *amor fati*, the love of fate, that Nietzsche believes is indispensable for living joyfully in the world.[12]

"Pain Is an Old Friend"

Attempting to arrest the flow of time and its unceasing process of transformation is futile, according to Nietzsche, but that is no reason to rage against our mortality or to succumb to otiose fantasies about sloughing off our mortal coil and ascending to a higher form of existence that is not susceptible to death and decay. Change, even the ultimate change we call death, is something we must affirm as part of the natural ebb and flow of existence. Impermanence is a feature, not a bug, of human existence, as can be seen when we look at the so-called salvation brought by Dormammu, an existence that is lifeless and frozen.

For Nietzsche, the antidote to the poisonous spirit of revenge against time is what he called the affirmation of "eternal return," an idea that he first introduced as a thought experiment in the same work in which he declared his allegiance to *amor fati*:

> What, if some day or night a demon were to steal after you into your loneliest loneliness and say to you: "This life as you now live it and have lived it you will have to live again and innumerable times again ..." Would you not throw yourself down and gnash your teeth and curse the demon who spoke thus? Or have you once experienced a tremendous moment when you would have answered him: "You are a god and never have I heard anything more divine." ... Or how well disposed you would have to become to yourself *to long for nothing more fervently* than this eternal confirmation and seal?[13]

To become so well disposed to existence that you would be willing to live this self-same life, with all of its pain and suffering, its disappointments and loss, its inevitable decline and inescapable demise, over and over again for all eternity—that is, according to Nietzsche, the ultimate formula for *amor fati* and the overcoming of revenge. But for those for whom our frail and mortal existence is simply not good enough, "not what it ought to be," the prospect of living forever in this eternal "time loop" would be absolutely intolerable.

Because Nietzsche believes that this thought of eternal return will be a tonic to some but toxic to others, he thought of it as a weapon that could be used defeat those who, like Kaecilius but also like Stephen at the beginning of his journey, were rebelling against the conditions of our mortal existence. There's no reason to suppose that Stephen ever read Nietzsche—after all, if he had, he might have been able to reconcile himself to his loss of his medical career without having to sell everything he owned to seek answers in the East. But he did learn something about "time loops" at Kamar-Taj and was astute enough to figure out on his own how to weaponize them against Dormammu himself, the very apotheosis of enmity toward transient existence.

Ascending to the Dark Dimension, Stephen took his stand on the surface of a giant sphere, announcing, "Dormammu, I've come to bargain." In response, Dormammu entered the negotiations with a predictable overture—he disintegrated Stephen with a blast of energy. But like Nietzsche's eternal return, this self-same scene began replaying itself over and over, with Stephen restored to confront Dormammu once again, only to suffer yet another death at the hand of the enraged god. Stephen explains to an angry and confused Dormammu exactly what he's doing:

STEPHEN: Just as you gave Kaecilius powers from your dimension, I've brought a little power from mine. This is time. An endless looped time ... This is how things are now. You and me, trapped in this moment, endlessly.

DORMAMMU: Then you will spend eternity dying.

STEPHEN: Yes, but everyone on Earth will live.

DORMAMMU: But you will suffer.

STEPHEN: Pain's an old friend.

DORMAMMU: You will never win.

STEPHEN: No, but I can lose again and again and again and again forever.

Dormammu finally has no choice but to discontinue his assault on the Earth and abandon his plan to ensnare humanity in an eternal prison of lifeless stupor. It's unclear whether Dormammu has teeth, but, if he does, we can certainly imagine him gnashing them like the first individual in Nietzsche's thought experiment, as horrified at being imprisoned in time as we might be at being locked forever in the Dark Dimension.

A Strange Realization

Even more striking is what this exchange tells us about the transformation that Stephen has undergone since the beginning of his journey. The proud doctor for whom death is always a failure—and who *really* hated to fail—is now willing to embrace suffering, death, and endlessly repeated failure in order to fulfill his new role as a sorcerer tasked with protecting his world from mystical threats. More than simply surrendering his impotent rage against the past and futile efforts to reverse it, he now looks back on what he has suffered with gratitude, as an "old friend." And as we noted earlier, a good friend is a good teacher.

Still, even recognizing that death is an inevitable part of life and that life is given to us only on condition that we consent to give it back when the days allotted to us have run their course, to be fully alive is to love our lives and to be reluctant to let them go. In the last moments of her life, the Ancient One confesses to Stephen, "I'm not ready. No one ever is. We don't get to choose our time." Yet, she adds, "Death is what gives life meaning. To know your days are numbered, your time is short." The necessity of death adds to the preciousness of our existence, giving weight and urgency to our choices. Death isn't an "insult." It's the reason we care so deeply about life.

Notes

1. All quoted dialogue is from the 2016 film *Doctor Strange*.
2. Francis Bacon, *The Philosophical Works of Francis Bacon* (New York: Routledge, 2011), 251.
3. René Descartes, *Discourse on Method and Meditations on First Philosophy*, 4th ed., trans. Donald A. Cress (Indianapolis: Hackett Publishing, 1999), 35. These two goals, relief from the pain of labor and the conquest of death, amount to an attempt to overcome two of the curses the biblical God placed on humanity when he expelled Adam and Eve from the Garden of Eden (Genesis 3:17–19).
4. René Descartes, *The Philosophical Writings of Descartes*, Vol. III: *The Correspondence*, trans. Anthony Kenny (Cambridge: Cambridge University Press, 1991), 275.
5. For a further discussion of the Baconian project that situates it within the context of medical ethics, see Gerald McKinney, *To Relieve the Human Condition: Bioethics, Technology, and the Body* (Albany, NY: SUNY Press, 1997), 25–38.
6. Jeffrey Bishop, *The Anticipatory Corpse: Medicine, Power, and the Care of the Dying* (Notre Dame, IN: University of Notre Dame Press, 2011), 14–23.
7. Ibid., 14.
8. Ibid., 21.
9. Friedrich Nietzsche, *The Gay Science: With a Prelude in German Rhymes and an Appendix of Songs*, trans. Josefine Nauckhoff and Adrian Del Caro (Cambridge: Cambridge University Press, 2001), 276 (Section IV.276).
10. Friedrich Nietzsche, *Thus Spoke Zarathustra: A Book for All and None*, trans. Adrian Del Caro (Cambridge: Cambridge University Press, 2006), 21 (Section I.3: "On the Hinterworldly").
11. Ibid., 111 (Section II.20, "On Redemption").
12. Ibid.
13. Nietzsche, *The Gay Science*, 194 (Section IV.341).

Death Gives Meaning to Life

Martin Heidegger Meets Stephen Strange

Sander H. Lee

How should we deal with the realization that all of us will eventually die? The rogue sorcerer Kaecilius argues that time and death are the real enemies of humanity and the fact of our inevitable death makes life meaningless; only by entering the Dark Dimension can one conquer death and live forever. Doctor Strange and his ally Mordo oppose Kaecilius, but they soon discover that their teacher, the Ancient One, has used dark and unnatural forces to extend her own life. She tells Doctor Strange that this was necessary because there was no one powerful enough to defend humanity. Once she realizes that Doctor Strange can replace her, she welcomes death, arguing, contrary to Kaecilius, that it is death that gives meaning to life.

It should come as no surprise that philosophers also discuss these issues. In this chapter, we will focus on one in particular, Martin Heidegger (1889–1976), who describes our lives as "indifferent" until we experience *angst*, the genuine fear resulting from the realization that death is inevitable.[1] There are many ways to experience *angst*. It could result from a near-death experience (like Doctor Strange's car accident), the death of a loved one, or even from exposure to a work of art—such as the film *Doctor Strange*. Once you have experienced *angst*, you can never go back to indifference; you must make a choice either to live authentically or to hide your true self from others by wearing a mask of inauthenticity. Heidegger refers to this experience as the Call.[2] Not everyone is called, but once it happens to you, as it does to Doctor Strange, life is never the same.

Doctor Strange and Philosophy: The Other Book of Forbidden Knowledge, First Edition. Edited by Mark D. White.
© 2018 John Wiley & Sons Ltd. Published 2018 by John Wiley & Sons Ltd.

The Brilliant Doctor Strange

Our introduction to Doctor Strange shows him to be very much like Sherlock Holmes, another character played by Benedict Cumberbatch: both are brilliant, impatient, and arrogant. (It is no accident that Arthur Conan Doyle, himself a doctor and the creator of Holmes, based the character on his mentor, Dr. Joseph Bell.) Strange is not only supremely knowledgeable about medicine, he displays amazing skills of surgical dexterity. His abilities are so far beyond the average surgeon that he can win a music trivia contest with an assistant while performing difficult surgery.[3] We meet his former lover, Dr. Christine Palmer, also a very capable surgeon, who recognizes Strange's brilliance. When her colleague Dr. West prematurely declares one of her patients to be dead, she knows that only Strange has a chance to save him. Strange instantly diagnoses the patient with a treatable condition and operates "freehand," a practice that the film tells us is extraordinary. In his humiliating treatment of Dr. West, we see that Dr. Strange, like Holmes, does not suffer fools lightly.

We can better understand Strange by using Heidegger's distinction between the *ontic* and the *ontological*.[4] Someone choosing to live his life ontically, like Strange, will interact with the world as though he is a neutral scientific observer, treating other people like objects and their illnesses as no more than intriguing problems to be solved. Strange doesn't see his patients as actual persons like himself. Healing them is simply a way to enhance his own reputation as a great doctor. Heidegger urges us to view our lives as inseparable from all that is around us. In the ontological way of living, instead of merely observing the world as spectators, we choose to become part of it. We throw ourselves into life, caring about others, and working to make the world a better place.

According to Heidegger, the experience of dread or angst (a realization of one's genuine mortality) presents us with the choice of either becoming authentic or inauthentic.[5] The authentic person chooses to fulfill his true caring nature, even though this means exposing the vulnerable parts of himself to a world of others who can sometimes treat him harshly. On the other hand, the inauthentic person chooses to hide his real nature behind a mask designed to superficially avoid the demands of others without exposing his true self to the inspection of the world.

Strange has lived his whole life ontically, denying the ontological implications of his acts. He cuts himself off from the rest of the world and classifies everyone (including himself) in terms that deny the genuine, ongoing connections between them. He hides his true feelings behind a mask, epitomized by his reaction to West's mistaken diagnosis and Strange's inability to accept a hug from a relative of the man whose life he saved.

Strange's talent and intelligence have won him wealth and luxury, but his superiority and smugness end up costing him much more. While driving his impressive sports car much faster than necessary, Strange consults over speakerphone with a nurse named Billy about possible cases. Tellingly, he rejects one surgery because there's a risk of failure and he doesn't want to "screw up his perfect record." Strange cares nothing about patients as people; to him, they are just problems to be solved. He pursues success not to help people but to further enhance his reputation as a brilliant surgeon. As Dr. Lane tells him, "Everything is always about you."

The Accident and Kamar-Taj

Moments later, Strange has the car accident that will change his life forever. Strange experiences Heideggerian *angst*, an emotional realization not only of his inevitable physical death, but of the death of his sense of self. The nerve damage to his hands destroys his career as a surgeon. He can no longer live his life as an uncaring miracle man whose superiority justifies his arrogance. He exhausts all conventional medical avenues for recovering his dexterity, including a failed appeal to a fellow brilliant surgeon who, like Strange before, does not want to risk his perfect record. Finally, Strange approaches Jonathan Pangborn, a paraplegic who miraculously regained the use of his legs thanks to the mystic teachings he learned in the Asian city of Kamar-Taj.

Strange follows Pangborn's example and travels to Kamar-Taj, where he meets the Ancient One and her follower, the sorcerer Mordo. Strange admits that he is desperate, yet he struggles at first against the possibility that mystic beliefs are any more than useless superstitions. Having lived his life as a doctor and scientist, he rejects claims of spiritual healing as nonsense peddled by hucksters who exploit the naïve desires of the masses for easy answers. He dismisses the charts shown to him by the Ancient One as the kind of junk found in touristy gift shops. When she asks him why, as a seeker of knowledge, he is unwilling to look through a wider keyhole into the nature of reality, Strange responds:

I reject it because I don't believe in fairy tales about chakras or energy or the power of belief. There is no such thing as spirit. We are made of matter and nothing more. We're just another tiny momentary speck in an indifferent universe.[6]

Strange will never be healed as long as he maintains his materialist belief in an indifferent world without the possibility of genuine meaning. In fact, later in the film we hear Kaecilius express a similar position. Materialists believe all that exists is what we can perceive and measure using our senses; they reject all belief in the spiritual or mystical as the pathetic babbling of weak fools. The Ancient One responds by pushing Strange's astral form out of his physical form. Still unconvinced, he asks if the tea contained a hallucinogen like LSD. She throws him into the astral dimension, a place where the soul exists apart from the body. We hear her ask,

What is real? What mysteries lie beyond the reach of your senses? At the root of existence, mind and matter meet. Thoughts shape reality. This universe is only one of an infinite number. Worlds without end. Some benevolent and life-giving; others filled with malice and hunger. Dark places where powers older than time lie ravenous and waiting. Who are you in this vast multiverse, Mr. Strange?

Finally convinced, Strange begs her to train him in the mystic arts. She refuses and throws him out; it is only after Mordo convinces her that they will need Strange if they are to beat Kaecilius that she agrees to train him (despite her fears that he might turn out to be like Kaecilius). We watch as Strange develops his abilities, proving himself to be just as adept in the mystic arts as he once was in the medical arts. He discovers that he must surrender his ego, silence his intellect, and learn to flow with the river of being. Strange thus experiences Heidegger's "call of conscience."[7] Once you experience the Call, you may no longer live a life of indifference. You must choose either to mask your feelings or accept the challenge and reveal your vulnerabilities to the world.

Tiny Momentary Specks within an Indifferent Universe

When Strange first meets the librarian Wong, he teases him by comparing his use of a single name to that of pop stars like Adele or Beyoncé. But he might also have mentioned the ancient philosopher

Aristotle (384–322 BCE), who is known for his belief that there is a natural order to things and that we should fulfill our potentialities to maintain that order by relying on our virtues.[8]

Aristotle distinguishes between *moral* and *intellectual* virtue. Moral virtue is the ability to follow rational commands and reject those that are obviously irrational. Everyone has the ability to be morally virtuous, although some people, like Kaecilius, reject morality and choose to become evil. In contrast, Aristotle believes that some people, perhaps very few, have the potential to become intellectually virtuous as well and can actually construct rational commands and develop practical wisdom that allows them to better understand reality and solve moral dilemmas. Fittingly, Mordo and Wong have committed themselves to maintaining the natural law against those, like Kaecilius and Dormammu, who violate it in order to fulfill their unnatural desires for power and immortality.

Kaecilius explains his goals to Doctor Strange during their fight at the Sanctum Sanctorum in New York City. After Strange captures Kaecilius in the Cloak of Levitation, the rogue sorcerer takes this opportunity to try to turn Strange to the Dark Side... oops, I mean the Dark Dimension. He tells Strange that it is the beginning of "the many becoming the few becoming the One," and explains that we can go beyond natural law and even beyond time.

KAECILIUS: This world doesn't have to die, Doctor. This world can take its rightful place alongside so many others as part of the One, the great and the beautiful One. We can all live forever ... Life, eternal life. People think in terms of good and evil when really time is the true enemy of us all. Time kills everything.

STRANGE: What about the people you killed?

KAECILIUS: Tiny, momentary specks within an indifferent universe ... The world is not what it ought to be. Humanity longs for the eternal, for a world beyond time, because time is what enslaves us. Time is an insult; death is an insult. Doctor, we don't seek to rule this world—we seek to save it, to hand it over to Dormammu, who is the intent of all evolution, the why of all existence.

Notice that he uses the same language as Strange in describing others as "tiny momentary specks within an indifferent universe," showing that Kaecilius and Strange once shared this pessimistic, ontic view of life.

Will Strange be tempted to join forces with Kaecilius and reject both natural law and morality? Kaecilius, like the philosopher Friedrich Nietzsche (1844–1900), thinks he can go "beyond good and evil."[9] Kaecilius claims that time is the real enemy because it is time that condemns us all to death. His response to *angst* is not to choose authenticity but to delude himself into believing that death can be defeated. Rather than accepting death as a natural end to life, he sees it as an "insult." Kaecilius thus denies that Dormammu is a "destroyer of worlds" and worships him as a benevolent savior who will give his followers eternal life in a heavenly realm, the Dark Dimension.[10]

Dark Powers

Like Kaecilius, Heidegger was also tempted by an evil force. In the early 1930s, Heidegger became a vocal supporter of Adolf Hitler and the Nazi Party. He accepted an appointment in 1933 as Rector of the University of Freiburg and betrayed his mentor Edmund Husserl (just as Kaecilius betrays the Ancient One). In 1934, Heidegger resigned his position, although he never quit the Nazi Party or apologized for his actions.[11] Philosophers have argued for decades about Heidegger's affiliation with the Nazis, some claiming that we should not read his philosophy because of this taint.

A similar issue also arises when Strange discovers that the Ancient One had been drawing power from the Dark Dimension to extend her life. As Kaecilius tells him, "We came to her to be healed, but the real magic she keeps for herself. You ever wonder how she managed to live this long?"[12] When Strange confronts the Ancient One over this and begins to question their mission, she tells him that he must nonetheless continue to fight against Kaecilius. Strange argues that he is a doctor and doctors should save lives, not take them—as he was forced to do already. But the Ancient One responds that Strange still has an over-inflated ego, telling him, "You want to go back to the delusion that you can control anything, even death, which no one can control, not even the great Doctor Stephen Strange."

After this conversation, Strange tells Mordo about the Ancient One's apparent hypocrisy, informing him that "she draws power from the Dark Dimension to stay alive." Once Mordo is convinced of the Ancient One's violation of the natural law, he rejects her. Showing himself to be a man of absolutes, Mordo refuses to accept any violation of principle. But, with a little help from the Ancient One, Strange is flexible enough to understand that the world is more complex than this.

In their last conversation, as her astral body experiences the final moments before death, the Ancient One tells Strange that "arrogance and fear still keep you from learning the simplest and most significant lesson of all," which is: "It's not about you." She explains, "I've hated drawing power from the Dark Dimension, but, as you well know, sometimes one must break the rules in order to serve the greater good." With no one powerful enough to replace her, the Ancient believed she had a duty to stay alive as long as possible to protect the world against its many enemies. She used the powers from the Dark Dimension, not because she feared death as Kaecilius does, but as a compromise that permitted her to serve the world until her replacement could be found. Thus, the Ancient One illustrates that acceptance of one's own death can lead to becoming an authentic person who cares about others.

Death Gives Meaning to Life

Kaecilius and Dormammu choose an inauthentic existence in which life is artificially prolonged to no purpose. When Strange uses his ability to create a time loop to trap Dormammu, it forces Dormammu to realize that he will relive the same moment endlessly, after which he accepts Strange's terms and abandons Earth. Dormammu's torment at the thought of repeating the same tasks endlessly is reminiscent of the tale of Sisyphus, as recounted by the French philosopher, Albert Camus (1913–1960).[13] Sisyphus was punished by the Greek god Zeus, who forced him to roll a heavy boulder up a steep hill only to see it roll down each time, condemning him to a life of endless frustration and meaningless despair. Strange traps Dormammu in a similar cycle so that he will do anything to escape, even give up his plans to conquer Earth.

What Dormammu (and Kaecilius) failed to appreciate is that eternal life is a similar trap: it is "not paradise," as the Ancient One tells Strange, but "torment." As Dormammu came to realize, though, with no ending to give our lives meaning, we would be reduced to endless repetitions of the same moments. The Ancient One echoes Heidegger when she says, "Death is what gives life meaning. To know your days are numbered, your time is short."[14] Once the Ancient One recognizes that Doctor Strange could replace her, she is ready to accept death, even though she prolongs the final moment to enjoy her last sight of snow: "You'd think after all this time I'd be ready, but look at me stretching one moment out into a thousand just so I can watch the snow." Even those who appreciate the true nature of death can be forgiven for putting it off, if only for a moment.

Notes

1. Martin Heidegger, *Being and Time*, trans. Joan Stambaugh (New York: State University of New York Press, 2010); see also Hubert Dreyfus, *Being-in-the-World: A Commentary on Heidegger's Being and Time, Division I* (Cambridge, MA: MIT Press, 1990), 289. On angst, see Steven Luper, *Existing: An Introduction to Existential Thought* (Palo Alto, CA: Mayfield Publishing Co., 2000), 203–206.
2. William Lawhead, *The Voyage of Discovery: A Historical Introduction to Philosophy*, 4th ed. (Stamford, CT: Cengage Learning, 2015), 553–555.
3. The character of Doctor Strange has much in common with Doctor Jack MacKee (played by William Hurt) in the 1991 film, *The Doctor*. Both doctors start their films as arrogant and uncaring men. Dr. MacKee is also shown playing music and joking with his colleagues as he performs surgery, and when he contracts cancer, he too experiences *angst* and becomes a more caring person.
4. Dreyfus, *Being-in-the-World*, 20.
5. Lawhead, *Voyage of Discovery*, 552–554.
6. All quoted dialogue is from the 2016 film *Doctor Strange*.
7. Lawhead, *Voyage of Discovery*, 553–554.
8. Aristotle, *Nicomachean Ethics*, 350 BCE, trans. W.D. Ross, available at: http://classics.mit.edu/Aristotle/nicomachaen.html
9. Friedrich Nietzsche, *Beyond Good and Evil: Prelude to a Philosophy of the Future*, trans. Walter Kaufmann (New York: Vintage, 1989).
10. Here he is referring to a quote from J. Robert Oppenheimer, the father of the atomic bomb, who told the reporters after witnessing the first atomic explosion that he was reminded of a passage from the sacred Hindu text, *The Bhagavad Gita*: "Now I am become Death, the destroyer of worlds." The quote is from Chapter 11, verse 32, of *The Bhagavad Gita*, available in English translation at http://www.bhagavad-gita.org/index-english.html. For more on Oppenheimer and the *Gita*, see Kai Bird and Martin Sherwin, *American Prometheus: The Triumph and Tragedy of J. Robert Oppenheimer* (New York: Vintage, 2006) and James Hijiya, "The *Gita* of J. Robert Oppenheimer," *Proceedings of the American Philosophical Society* 144(2000): 123–167.
11. Lawhead, *Voyage of Discovery*, 546.
12. This explains why Kaecilius calls the Ancient One a hypocrite during their fight in London at the beginning of the film.
13. Albert Camus, *The Myth of Sisyphus*, trans. Justin O'Brien (New York: Vintage, 2012).
14. The philosopher Bernard Williams (1929–2003) wrote similarly: "Immortality, or a state without death, would be meaningless, I shall suggest; so, in a sense, death gives the meaning to life" ("The Makropulos Case: Reflections on the Tedium of Immortality," in *Problems of the Self: Philosophical Papers, 1956–1972*, Cambridge: Cambridge University Press, 1973, 82–100, at p. 82).

3

"Time Will Tell How Much I Love You"

A Nietzschean *Übermensch*'s Issues with Love and Friendship

Skye C. Cleary

In the 2016 film *Doctor Strange*, the Ancient One says the title character is stubborn, arrogant, and egotistical. She's right. Strange is charming and witty, but he also has trouble loving anyone but himself. For example, his medical colleague and former girlfriend, Christine Palmer, maintains a somewhat affectionate friendship with him, but their romantic relationship obviously didn't last. Do these observations suggest that Strange is doomed to eternal loneliness in which he never enjoys a meaningful love relationship?

To help us understand Doctor Strange's relationship challenges, we'll turn to the German philosopher Friedrich Nietzsche (1844–1900), who wrote a great deal on sexual love and friendship. Nietzsche thought that sexual love is a distraction from more important things, like being a superhero. Nevertheless, for Strange, it's actually his narcissism that is holding him back the most. Christine Palmer saved Strange's life, but his other friendships—particularly with the Ancient One, Wong, and Mordo—challenge him in ways that he is not, at least initially, ready for, and which end up being exactly what he needs to reach his potential and become this dimension's Sorcerer Supreme.

Doctor Strange and Philosophy: The Other Book of Forbidden Knowledge, First Edition. Edited by Mark D. White.
© 2018 John Wiley & Sons Ltd. Published 2018 by John Wiley & Sons Ltd.

Doctor *Übermensch*

Nietzsche was an "aristocratic radical" and is most famous for his criticisms of traditional morality, Christianity, society, politics, love, and women.[1] Basically, he was critical of pretty much everything and everyone. (Sounds familiar?) Nietzsche is also known for his description of the *Übermensch*, often translated as "superman" but more accurately as "overman," someone who overcomes themselves.[2] We can interpret the *Übermensch* as an ideal rather than an end goal because it is about challenging oneself, combatting obstacles, being courageous, and creatively and passionately striving for greatness. While Nietzsche knew his philosophy would not be for everyone, he hoped that a few brave people would understand the virtues of striving toward the ideal of the *Übermensch*.[3]

Doctor Strange might see the appeal. He is a brilliant neurosurgeon at the top of his field—and he knows it. We know it too because he flaunts his intelligence by dropping complicated names of procedures, and he brags with a swagger about being able to perform surgeries that others find impossible. As he tells Palmer, he has been interviewed on CNN and is often celebrated at fancy dinners and invited to speaking engagements at events such as the Neurological Society dinner. Moreover, he constantly strives to be better—for example, by coming up with innovative techniques (often with Palmer) and only taking on the most interesting and intellectually challenging cases—even if only to increase his reputation and wealth.

Strange's situation is similar to that of Zarathustra, Nietzsche's fictional protagonist in *Thus Spoke Zarathustra*. Zarathustra is a sage who comes down from the mountain, where he has been living as a recluse, to teach. Without friends, he has become lonely, and so he goes in search of human interaction. While Zarathustra descended from his lofty heights by choice, Strange was thrown from his lofty intellectual heights by a car accident caused by his reckless behavior. Both men are hungry for wisdom, but whereas Zarathustra wants to be generous with his wisdom and share it, Strange's motivation is not so magnanimous: he wants knowledge about how to use his hands again so he can go back to his former lifestyle, career, and status. As the Ancient One points out, Doctor Strange became a doctor to save himself, not to help others.

It's not only Strange's brilliance and passion for wisdom that are reminiscent of Nietzsche's *Übermensch*, but also his flirtation with nihilism. For example, at one point in the film, he says, "We are just a tiny momentary speck within an indifferent universe," a nihilistic view that suggests nothing really matters because human life is so insignificant as to be meaningless.[4] Nietzsche is well known for proclaiming, "God is dead," meaning that we live in a world where science has taken over religion, leaving us without meaningful values with which to replace Christianity, resulting in a moral void of decadence, hedonism, and immorality.

Nietzsche wanted to find an antidote to this—but not a religious one. He thought we should overcome nihilism through creative action and striving toward the ideal of the *Übermensch*. It's possible that Strange realizes this when Kaecilius makes the same point about being specks within an indifferent universe to justify his deal with Dormammu: sacrificing the Earth and everyone on it to the Dark Dimension to achieve immortality for him and a few of his zealous best friends. The Ancient One is, as usual, the voice of wisdom when she tells Strange that "you think too little of yourself"—an odd thing to say to a narcissist, perhaps, but not one who is also a bit of nihilist! The Ancient One's comment serves as a reminder that humanity is much more meaningful than a fleeting speck of space dust and is worth fighting to save, certainly from evil demonic lords.

Problems with Love

There is another problem that Doctor Strange, Nietzsche, and Zarathustra all face: forming meaningful loving relationships. Nietzsche never had a girlfriend and he never married. It was not for lack of trying, though: He proposed to at least two women, and lamented in his letters about longing for a wife. Perhaps it was his giant bushy moustache that kept women at bay. Perhaps it was Nietzsche's obsession with milk and fruit. Or perhaps women were turned off by his tendency—and Zarathustra's—to make outrageously misogynistic comments. (To be fair, he said provocative things about everyone. It was his style.)

Stephen Strange does not have quite the same issues as Nietzsche—he did enjoy an intimate relationship with Christine Palmer, at least. But it's telling that she is the only one (other than his therapist) who helps him. Other colleagues hang up the phone on him, and there are no family members that we know of. His giant and lavish apartment is mostly empty, except for a desk, a laptop, and a brief visit from Palmer.

To put a more positive spin on it, we could say that Strange is a free spirit, preferring to be independent. As Nietzsche wrote, "Like the prophetic birds of antiquity, as present-day representatives of true thinking and truth-telling they must prefer *to fly alone.*"[5] This could explain why Doctor Strange is so frustrated that he needs to ask other people to help him repair his hands. The problem with intimate relationships is that they can become suffocating with their habits and rules; Nietzsche likens relationships to spider webs that one must tear off.[6] Specifically with respect to sexual love, Nietzsche says, "Perhaps our trees fail to grow as high on account of the ivy and the vines that cling to them."[7] It's painful but necessary to emancipate oneself from being too comfortable, from anything that threatens to hold one back from striving for the ideal of the *Übermensch*, including other people. For Nietzsche, freedom is measured "by the resistance that needs to be overcome, by the effort that it costs to stay on *top.*"[8]

When Christine Palmer brings Strange snacks after his accident, he lashes out at her for what seems like an innocent gesture of kindness: "No, don't pity me." When she tells him that she's not pitying him, he goes into a rant:

> Oh, yeah, then what are you doing here, bringing me cheese and wine like old friends going for a picnic? We are not friends, Christine. We were barely lovers. You just love a sob story, don't you? Is that what I am to you now? Poor Stephen Strange. Charity case. Finally needs me. Another dreg of humanity. Patch him up and send him back into the world. Heart's just humming. You care so much, don't you?

Palmer tries to make his life slightly more comfortable, but our would-be *Übermensch* rejects that: "the free spirit wants not to be served and in that he discovers his happiness."[9] They prefer obstacles to challenge them, to assert themselves and their striving for greatness. According to Nietzsche, "In every kind of womanly love there also appears something of motherly love"—and he didn't mean this in a nice way.[10] Nietzsche resented his mother, and many scholars (especially Freudians) blame Nietzsche's issues with women on his relationship with his mother.[11] Though we don't know anything about Stephen Strange's relationship with his parents, a psychoanalyst might see indications of problems there, given his excessively hostile reaction to Palmer.

Nietzsche hated pity at least as much as Strange because he thought it to be a virtue of herd morality: It negates life by glorifying and defending failure and misery, and is a function of the Christian virtue of "loving thy neighbor" that hands out love to those who don't deserve it.[12] Nietzsche thought that pity accepts and enables people's weaknesses instead of encouraging them to be better and stronger. This seems to be Strange's problem with Palmer's gesture, too. Doctor Strange believes her to be treating him as she treats her patients in the emergency room—to him, the weakest and lowest people in society— the same way she would treat a "drunk idiot with a gun" in what he calls her "butcher shop." Strange avoids the ER (except on special invitation from Palmer), refuses to take pity on patients, and rejects cases that will not help his career, including Jonathan Pangborn, the man who later told Strange about Kamar-Taj.

Noble Virtues

Overcoming pity is, according to Nietzsche, a *"noble* virtue" because one avoids being lured away from oneself, remains in control, and keeps "the *height* of your task free from the many lower and short-sighted impulses that are at work in supposedly selfless actions."[13] Palmer insists that she doesn't feel pity for Strange, and there's no reason to doubt her. Bringing him wine and cheese doesn't mean she's pitying him or treating him as a charity case; she's just doing what any normal person would do for a friend in a car accident. Moreover, working on saving the lives of whoever walks into the ER and doing it brilliantly, while being a decent person, is no less noble than Doctor Strange's work. The real problem is that Strange, like Nietzsche, mistakes love for pity because he's unfamiliar with both.

Nietzsche also pointed out that although free spirits *prefer* to fly alone, it doesn't mean they *should*. Nietzsche was a big fan of love and thought it to be a vitally important part of life. Without love, he says, "our soul becomes dry and unsuited even to understanding the tender inventions of loving people," and when one stops loving others, one forgets how to love oneself—something that could certainly apply to Strange. Nietzsche also wrote about how great it is to be loved by an intelligent person, and suggested that "Men who are too intellectual have great need of marriage, though they resist it as they would a foul-tasting medicine."[14] Without specifically saying why this is the case, he implies that it's helpful to have a great partner to challenge oneself. We see that Palmer does challenge Strange, such as when she tells him that life without his work "is still life. This isn't the end. There are other things that can give your life meaning," though he is not yet ready to hear this.

The reason he is not ready is that he's narcissistically attached to his former life, which Nietzsche would likely find problematic. Before talking about narcissism, however, it's worth mentioning that Nietzsche wouldn't have any qualms with Doctor Strange's egoism. Nietzsche proposed that egoism is a prerequisite for love: "You have to be firmly grounded in *yourself*, you have to stand bravely on your own two feet to be *able* to love at all."[15] Palmer and Strange seem entirely capable of love by this definition: they both seem grounded in themselves. They're both brilliant and rational; they don't get swept away with passionate swooning or look to one another to fill voids in their lives. They don't get caught up in possessive power games, nor do they use each other as means to other ends. For all these reasons, they would seem to have the makings of a great relationship. (Emphasis on "would seem.")

Narcissism

Unfortunately, Stephen Strange is so firmly grounded in himself that he struggles to change as his circumstances change. His narcissism holds him back: Strange is so in love with the image of himself as a neurosurgeon that he cannot envision his life any other way. Palmer challenges him to consider new ways of being, to look elsewhere for meaning in life, but he resents her for suggesting it. Nietzsche would have agreed with Palmer: according to Zarathustra, "You must be ready to burn yourself in your own flame: how could you become new, if you had not first become ashes?"[16] Strange isn't ready to burn his neurosurgeon-self—yet, to be an *Übermensch* requires it. Zarathustra says, "I love those who do not wish to preserve themselves. I love with my whole love those who go down and perish: for they are going beyond."[17] Though Strange is ready to "go beyond" with respect to trying experimental techniques to fix his hands, his goal is to restore his former self, not to create himself anew.

Narcissism is at the root of Doctor Strange's car accident, too. He thought himself to be invincible and superhuman. It's not unreasonable that he would think this, given his brilliance and ability to perform complicated procedures. He was so confident of his talents that he threw all caution to the wind when driving and thought it perfectly acceptable to review medical files while speeding in his Lamborghini Huracán Coupé. Yet, he made an all-too-human error, and crashed. He lost control of the car, of his life, and of his temper.

Zarathustra proclaims, "Man is something that should be overcome."[18] When Palmer suggested this to Strange (albeit in different words), he wasn't interested. Before entering Kamar-Taj, Mordo warned him to forget everything he knows, but Strange was not ready to listen to him either. When the Ancient One told him that she could help him "reorient the spirit to better heal the body," he again wasn't interested. It wasn't until she hurled him through a few space-time dimensions, and then out on the street for five hours with nothing but a smashed watch, that he was willing to listen to her—even if it was due to a lack of other options.

Nietzsche thought that the best friends are those who are challenging and inspiring. To be a good friend, Zarathustra advises, "You should be to him an arrow and a longing for the *Übermensch*."[19] Friends push us in ways that we could not have imagined without them, toward greater achievements and ambitions. A friend should be so challenging that he is also an enemy when needed: "If you want a friend, you must also be willing to wage war for him: and to wage war, you must be *capable* of being an enemy."[20] A friend should also be as careful as possible not to show pity: "Let your pity for your friend conceal itself under a hard shell; you should break a tooth biting upon it. Thus it will have delicacy and sweetness."[21] The Ancient One shows that she understands this (better than Palmer did) when she takes Strange to Mount Everest and leaves him there in the freezing weather to either die or save himself. It seems harsh, but it turns out to be exactly the sort of challenge that Strange needs to overcome the limitations that he imposes on himself.

What Doesn't Kill Me Makes Me Strange

Perhaps Nietzsche's best-known line is: "What doesn't kill me makes me stronger."[22] While this may not a useful mantra for everyone, it certainly suits Strange. The car crash didn't kill him, but it started a chain of events that led him to Kamar-Taj. He didn't die in the snow on Mount Everest, but he learned how to make a fire portal with his sling ring. Nietzsche faced physical challenges too: he was often sick with with seizures, vomiting, and paralysis. He said his existence was "a terrible burden" and yet he embraced his fate, telling his doctor that

I'd long ago have chucked it were it not for my having done the most illuminating psychological and moral research in just this state of suffering and almost absolute renunciation. My joyous thirst for knowledge brings me to heights where I can triumph over all torment and despair.[23]

In another letter he wrote: "My illness has been my greatest boon: it unblocked me, it gave me the courage to be myself."[24]

Strange isn't quite so enthusiastic about the state of his hands, but he seems to be well on the way to some sort of enlightenment, especially when he finds out that he could draw on dark matter to fix his hands and go back to his previous life. But still he chooses not to, and instead stays with fellow sorcerers to help fight Kaecilius and Dormammu. This certainly helps him avoid awkward questions about how his hands "miraculously" healed, or it could be simply that he realizes that unless he does stay and help, the world will be plunged into the Dark Dimension and there will be no neurosurgery job to go back to. Perhaps he's starting to think that neurosurgery isn't that great after all—at least in comparison to being Sorcerer Supreme. Hopefully, he's starting to realize that there are other things that can give his life meaning, such as choosing to use his abilities to help others rather than simply himself.

The Ancient One is a good friend to Strange in Nietzsche's sense, but the other main characters have similar qualities, especially in terms of challenging the neophyte sorcerer. Mordo takes on the role of enemy when he tells Strange that he must fight as if his life depends on it, because Mordo knows that one day it will. Wong refuses to laugh at his jokes, challenging Doctor Strange to question whether he is as witty as he thought. When Strange says, "People used to think that I was funny," Wong simply responds, "Did they work for you?"

In different ways, all of Strange's newfound friends are helping him, as Zarathustra urges, to overcome himself and his narcissism, and to "*Become hard!*"[25] Part of being a great friend is being able to share uncomfortable truths. Great friends help you to reflect on dimensions of your being, to see things about yourself that you may not see otherwise. Palmer doesn't specifically tell him he's a jerk, but she does imply that he's an egoist when she says, "Stephen, everything is about you," and doesn't tolerate it when he lashes out at her. Instead, she throws her keys to his apartment on his kitchen bench as she walks out the door. The Ancient One, too, has no qualms about telling him that he has an "overinflated ego" and that his narcissism is holding him back from true greatness, telling him that "arrogance and fear still keep you from learning the simplest and most significant lesson of all," which is that "it's not about you."

It isn't until the Ancient One shows him that there is much he doesn't know, and that there are things more important than he is, that Strange begins to annihilate his former self and create himself anew. He isn't only going to leave behind a legacy of techniques to save a few thousand people, but he will also be a warrior who is going to save the Earth and the billions of people on it. The film is ambiguous as to whether that idea feeds Strange's megalomania or if he actually learns that it's not all about him. Nevertheless, perhaps the lesson is that he can help himself best by helping others in a much broader sense than he could ever have imagined.

A Shared Higher Thirst

For Nietzsche, great friends help one another to become better people through "a *shared* higher thirst for an ideal above them."[26] The shared desire for a higher ideal to protect humanity is what unites Strange with his friends new and old. The Ancient One advises Strange to "silence your ego and your power will rise," and his power does rise when he focuses outwards—that is, less on himself, and more on protecting the Earth. At the end of the film, Strange seems to have come to the realization that Christine Palmer was right. As he tells her, "You said that losing my hands didn't have to be the end. That it could be the beginning," to which she adds, "Yes. There are other ways to save lives." Then she kisses him on the cheek and he leaves—for now. Nietzsche was skeptical that sexual lovers could also be great friends, and yet Palmer and Strange do have the potential. If only they could take time out from saving the world to go on a proper date—now there's a great idea for the sequel!

Notes

1. Peter Fuss and Henry Shapiro (eds.), *Nietzsche: A Self-Portrait from His Letters* (Cambridge, MA: Harvard University Press, 1971), 104.
2. Friedrich Nietzsche, *Thus Spoke Zarathustra* (London: Penguin Books, 1969), 41.
3. Fuss and Shapiro, *Nietzsche: A Self-Portrait from His Letters*, 99.
4. All quoted dialogue is from the 2016 film *Doctor Strange*.
5. Friedrich Nietzsche, *Human, All Too Human* (Cambridge: Cambridge University Press, 1996), 158.
6. Ibid.
7. Friedrich Nietzsche, *Daybreak* (Cambridge: Cambridge University Press, 1982), 205.
8. Friedrich Nietzsche, "Twilight of the Idols," in Aaron Ridley and Judith Norman (eds.), *The Anti-Christ, Ecce Homo, Twilight of the Idols and*

Other Writings (Cambridge: Cambridge University Press, 2005), 153–229, at p. 213.

9. Nietzsche, *Human, All Too Human*, 159.
10. Ibid, 151.
11. For example, Kelly Oliver, "Nietzsche's Abjection," in Peter J. Burgard (ed.), *Nietzsche and the Feminine* (Charlottesville, VA: University Press of Virginia, 1994), 53–67, at pp. 60–63.
12. Nietzsche, *Human, All Too Human*, 45.
13. Friedrich Nietzsche, "Ecce Homo," in Ridley and Norman (eds.), *The Anti-Christ, Ecce Homo, Twilight of the Idols and Other Writings*, 69–151, at p. 79.
14. Nietzsche, *Human, All Too Human*, 150–151.
15. Nietzsche, "Ecce Homo," 105.
16. Nietzsche, *Thus Spoke Zarathustra*, 90.
17. Ibid., 217.
18. Ibid., 41.
19. Ibid,, 83.
20. Ibid., 82.
21. Ibid., 83.
22. Nietzsche, "Twilight of the Idols," 157.
23. Fuss and Shapiro, *Nietzsche: A Self-Portrait from His Letters*, 51.
24. Ibid., 114.
25. Nietzsche, *Thus Spoke Zarathustra*, 231.
26. Friedrich Nietzsche, *The Gay Science* (Cambridge: Cambridge University Press, 2001), 41.

4

Existentialism, Nihilism, and the Meaning of Life for Doctor Strange

Paul DiGeorgio

At least on the surface, *Doctor Strange* is a movie about a gifted physician who horrifically injures himself and, in trying to restore his health, acquires magical powers and helps to defend humanity from an evil, otherworldly entity. Beneath the surface, though, and perhaps even more significantly, the movie is about a profound shift in personal philosophical perspective. Throughout the course of the movie, we see Stephen Strange experience a magnificent existential conversion, a change of heart and mind in the way that he views the meaning of life and what it means to exist. Strange starts out thinking that life does not have much meaning at all beyond its scientific utility, but by the end of the film he realizes that his choices and decisions are what give life both meaning and value.

A Strange Beginning

Early in the film, Strange holds a philosophical perspective that has three primary features: it is empirical, practical, and scientific. His scientific, observation-based worldview is useful because, at least in theory, it can explain a vast array of phenomena, which lets Strange excel as a brilliant physician.

While a general perspective like this can explain a good deal, it is also restricted by its scientific empiricism. It assumes that the only "real" things are those capable of being observed, which a scientist

Doctor Strange and Philosophy: The Other Book of Forbidden Knowledge,
First Edition. Edited by Mark D. White.

or philosopher might refer to as "material" or "physical." With a perspective like this, Strange is forced to deny the existence of things that science can't observe, like spirits or souls. Strange also can't coherently discuss the worth or meaning of things, even physical things, outside science.

This "physicalist" perspective is one that serves Strange well in his career as an illustrious and talented surgeon, but it also contributes to his intense egotism and intellectual vanity. "The work I'm doing is gonna save thousands for years to come," he tells Doctor Christine Palmer. "In the ER you get to save one drunk idiot with a gun?"[1] Early on, Strange is so confident about the new work that he's doing, and the exclusively empirical worldview on which it is based, that he looks down upon his fellow physicians and their work. It doesn't make much sense to him to spend his time saving individual lives in the emergency room when he can produce cutting-edge medical advances in the lab. Strange thinks that he's one of a privileged few who realize this, and he looks down on everyone who doesn't share his view.

Indeed, in the first part of the movie, Strange has a prominent superiority complex. We see it on display when he recklessly pilots his exotic sports car on the way to a speaking engagement, weaving between other cars as he consults with another medical professional on the phone. He dismisses case after case as not sufficiently complex or difficult to warrant his time or attention. Here Strange is quite intentionally electing *not* to help or even save the lives of people. Life does not seem to have value, nor does it mean very much to him at this point in the movie—which is ironic, considering that his chosen profession has its very basis in saving and enhancing life.

At the end of this sequence, we see Strange's spectacular crash, leaving his hands and his highbrow bravado devastatingly injured. After another physician refuses to perform an experimental procedure for him, Strange finally experiences the frustration that he so often inflicted on others with his elitist, self-important attitude. For the first time, Strange realizes that he may no longer be able to perform his work, work that in large part defined him and accounted for his superiority complex. "Life without my work…" he begins to tell Palmer, which she completes with "…is still life. This isn't the end. There are other things that can give your life meaning." He asks, bluntly, "Like what? Like *you*?" Here it is obvious that Strange does not care about anyone other than himself. His character is in tension, drawn between his commitment to medical science, on the one hand, and his commitment to himself, on the other.

Strange is pushed toward realizing his cognitive dissonance when others show him how it feels to be treated as unimportant. Jonathan Pangborn, who had recovered the ability to walk after a devastating spinal injury, is ready to turn Strange away after he recalls that Strange had refused to see him as a patient in the past, but then later decides to help him by pointing him towards Kathmandu, where he can try to seek out the Ancient One. Foreshadowing Strange's future, Pangborn shows us that radical change can occur after healing. Before Strange can undergo his healing, which will be mostly philosophical, he has to acknowledge—and then transcend—his inauthentic scientific façade.

Bad Faith and a Paradox

How can Strange be so self-centered, or think so much about himself, if he is truly committed to the idea that, outside of science, life doesn't have any real significance? In other words, how is his self-importance consistent with his scientific principles that deny any importance to that which cannot be observed?

While it's obvious that, as a member of the scientific community, Strange is helping to further the progress of a scientific agenda, he goes so far with his ideas that he looks to be living what an existentialist philosopher would call an "inauthentic" life: he isn't actually invested in the values he says he holds. It seems at first glance that Strange, judging by his behavior, either cannot really believe what he professes he believes, or, he behaves in a way that makes him look hypocritical.

The problem is that Strange often seems only to be "playing the part" of brilliant physician, while behind this role he's fundamentally defined by his egomania. His inauthenticity grows more apparent after his fight with Palmer when he departs on his quest to fix himself. At this point it becomes even more obvious that he's living in "bad faith," as the existentialist philosopher Jean-Paul Sartre (1905–1980) would say. For Sartre, bad faith comes down to taking on false values, thereby betraying one's freedom to choose truly for oneself.[2] Sartre thought that in bad faith, people prevented themselves from possible change by simply going along with things. This is precisely what Strange is doing. It's because he's not meaningfully and personally invested in his worldview that he can be an impetuous egotist while at the same time denying the significance and value of life.

Strange's "bad faith" is unmistakable, particularly after he reaches Kamar-Taj. He initially scorns the Ancient One as he stubbornly clings to his overly scientific conception of reality, the mastery of which has brought him the professional renown he treasures. Even after Mordo advises him to "forget everything" that he thinks he knows, Strange continues to take for granted that *he* is the one who is right about the nature of the world. He insists that he is correct when he says that physical things are the only things that exist, despite the fact that science tells him that there is no possible cure for the injury he has sustained. The Ancient One realizes that Strange is severely cornered by his own perspective:

> You're a man looking at the world through a keyhole. You've spent your whole life trying widen that keyhole—to see more, to know more. And now, on hearing that it can be widened, in ways you can't imagine, you reject the possibility.

Strange replies that he doesn't believe in "fairy tales about chakras or energy or the power of belief." He asserts his worldview plainly when he argues, "There is no such thing as spirit! We are made of matter and nothing more. You're just another tiny, momentary speck within an indifferent universe." Strange's assertion perfectly illustrates the Ancient One's keyhole metaphor, the shape of which corresponds to the scientific theories that dictate his entire notion of reality.

In his bad faith, Strange lives like an egotist, but his worldview is one that holds that human life—including his own—is insignificant. Because he isn't really committed on a personal level to a scientific system of values, but instead only wants fame and wealth, he discards alternative views (or keyholes) of reality that don't promise these things. Strange is merely "acting like a doctor" without really being committed to his profession deep down. As the Ancient One tells Strange, when faced with a new way of explaining something, he "rejects the possibility." These words are similar to how Sartre described the person in bad faith, who stubbornly carries on a life based on a lie. In Strange's case, he is caught in a paradox, suspended between science and egotism.

Scientific Nihilism and Existential Anxiety

Strange's scientific perspective holds that there's no hard evidence of things like the spiritual, supernatural, or metaphysical—those things that lie beyond the physical, observable world. There's nothing obviously inadequate about this empirical worldview, as it is one that enables Strange to live his accomplished life as a surgical virtuoso. However, this worldview also leads Strange to nihilism, the belief that nothing in the world has meaning. He realizes that if science is all he accepts, then his life has no meaning—but he *wants* it to have meaning. Faced with a worthless world, he clings with pride to his erudition and to a strong sense of ego.

But this isn't really Strange, either. The Ancient One realizes that Strange's egotism is inauthentic and false, telling him, "You think too little of yourself," even though the movie up to this point has shown the opposite. Despite Strange's apparent self-importance, however, the Ancient One believes that he doesn't really value his own perspective and is dealing with radical anxiety. The philosopher Martin Heidegger (1889–1976) described this existential anxiety as resulting from our realization that we're caught in a world that itself has no real meaning.[3] A person like Strange feels terrible anguish over this, but must realize that the only way out of it is to focus on making one's own meaning.

Of course, it's true that a scientific perspective can explain the mechanics of countless physical processes, but it cannot account for human—that is, existential—meaning or value. The intense, nihilistic version of the same perspective goes even further to charge that nothing really has meaning at all, aside from whatever humans have simply "made up." While we should differentiate between a general scientific worldview and a more nihilistic interpretation of science, some philosophers have linked the two together. Friedrich Nietzsche (1844–1900), for example, argued that an excessively scientific outlook would inevitably lead to nihilism. He argued that the sciences had a tendency to remove "spirit" from knowledge, and that therefore these sciences could not offer people true education, but instead, only enslavement to lack of real meaning.[4]

In Stephen Strange, we can clearly see the negative side-effects of overly strict scientific ideals. According to his early thinking, even existence itself ultimately means nothing in the final analysis. When it comes to the question of the "meaning of life," then, Strange would be forced to conclude that, in terms of philosophical or existential value, life has no meaning at all. Strange is anguished, struggling with the deep implications of his nihilistic worldview ... but not for long.

The First Existential Step Is the Hardest

In one of the film's most psychedelic sequences, the Ancient One forces Strange to consider the existence of metaphysical reality by exposing him to observable evidence of it. His resulting shift in perspective is gradual, taking him from an overly reductive scientific conception of reality, which is ultimately scientific nihilism, to one that is capable of accommodating and even manipulating the mysterious and the inexplicable.

Strange starts to realize that there might be meaning and value to existence, but that these things can only be found outside of scientific nihilism. In order to have this realization, though, he first has to overcome his paradoxical commitment to his ego. The Ancient One tells Strange that not everything makes sense, and that not everything *has* to make sense. "Your intellect has taken you far in life, but it will take you no further," she tells him. "Silence your ego and your power will rise." These words seem to contrast with what she told him earlier, when she said that he thought too little of himself. The point of this paradox is that Strange thinks too much of himself in one way—his egotism—and too little of himself in another—his nihilism.

The way out for Strange will come from shifting to an existentialist perspective. He learns that not everything has to make sense on scientific terms as he learns to master not only his body, but the infinite, unseen world of possibility and wonder that lies beyond everything he previously knew. More existentially, after his experience of anxiety, Strange learns that meaning is something that we make for ourselves. The Ancient One tells Strange to let go of his ego and realize how insignificant he is in the grand scheme of things—not because she herself is a nihilist, but because it's only by turning away from the ego that Strange can break out of his obedience to his scientific nihilism. He has to realize that it is his choices that give his life meaning, not anything he will find in a scientific textbook.

The fact that Strange is learning spells, by which he crafts weapons and portals out of thin air, is no insignificant detail—it highlights a parallel between existential creativity and magical activity. When he performs these spells, he is literally "making things up," which is a reinforcement of the philosophical shift that he is slowly experiencing. Strange would not have bothered to learn these acts of magic if he had not begun to turn himself away from scientific nihilism. As far as science is concerned, after all, there is no such thing as magic or sorcery. In stepping outside of this worldview, Strange is able to identify meaning and value in a manner that previously had been impossible for him.

Strange versus Kaecilius

It is no coincidence that as Strange's abilities grow more refined, he learns of the metaphysical struggle of the forces of good against evil. Scientifically speaking, this division between good and evil would have been out of bounds for Dr. Strange and his old scientific views. At the same time, he starts to appreciate, as a budding existentialist, that his choices and decisions are what define him and give his life meaning—especially when he compares himself to Kaecilius, one of the representations of evil in the film.

In one of the movie's more striking exchanges, Strange learns of Kaecilius' perspective on this metaphysical struggle between good and evil. What is interesting is that Kaecilius speaks in a way that reminds us of the mindset that Strange used to have not so long ago: "All things age. All things die. In the end our sun dies out, our universe grows cold and perishes." To him, life really doesn't mean much at all, but there is an important qualification to make: Kaecilius ultimately thinks that life has no meaning because it doesn't last forever, making him a nihilist of a different sort than Strange was.

There's another glaringly obvious difference between the two: Kaecilius is willing to kill innocent people. "Time kills everything," he tells Strange. "What about the people you killed?" Strange asks in reply, to which Kaecilius responds, "Tiny. Momentary specks within an indifferent universe." Strange looks to the side, realizing that he has uttered these words in the past, and realizes that, in some way, he used to resemble Kaecilius.

Despite some of their differences, though, Kaecilius and Strange are not complete opposites. In a way, Kaecilius is an existentialist of a different sort: he tries to manipulate reality in order to avoid nihilism, but only toward the objective of eternal life. Kaecilius has not fully moved beyond a nihilistic way of thinking, despite the fact that he resembles an existentialist in certain respects, such as focusing on choices and personal freedom. As we will see, desire for eternal life ultimately makes Kaecilius a bad existentialist. For now, the problem is that Kaecilius has an existentialist perspective focused on the importance of freedom and choice, but his particular choices are bad ones, significantly twisted by a nihilistic conception of meaning and value.

Strange's Hesitation

After facing off with Kaecilius, Strange finds himself in a dilemma once he achieves prowess as a powerful sorcerer and uses his abilities to help defend the New York Sanctum. He can either walk away, having learned to master his injured body once more, or he can be a hero and try to save the world.

After the early battle, Strange meets again with the Ancient One, who is surprised by the rapid development of his abilities. Strange played an instrumental role in the defense of the Sanctum against the invading forces of Kaecilius. It seems that no one had really expected him to be so involved, but now everybody realizes the important role he played.

Strange hesitates, though. He tells the Ancient One that he wants to abandon the fight because he had to kill someone in order to defend the base, and he says that he cannot do this again. He explains that he became a doctor to save people, not kill them. In this, we see that he has begun to value his choices much more than he did before. Nonetheless, the Ancient One points out that Strange has not fully moved beyond his old ways of thinking. She corrects him and says that in fact he became a doctor to save one person: himself. This is reinforced when Mordo tells Strange that he lacks spine and thinks of himself as a hero although he really only saved himself.

Strange is faced with an existential choice, one that has deep implications for the meaning of his life. If he chooses to leave the company of his fellow sorcerers and magicians, he would be choosing himself over humanity. The meaning of his life would, in that case, be the preservation of himself, as well as the continued elevation of himself and his ego in terms of professional fame and recognition. On the other hand, if Strange chooses to stay and help his friends defend the world and humanity against Dormammu, then he's committing himself to the idea that meaning and value cannot be found in simple, egotistical self-preservation, but only in fidelity to, and confidence in, his choices and his decisions, especially those made in service to others.

Strange's conversation with the Ancient One on her deathbed helps him resolve his existential dilemma. She tells Strange that time is relative, and that she cannot see any alternative futures; everything leads to the present moment when she will perish. Regarding Strange's future, she could only see his future's possibilities, again reinforcing his new, existentialist outlook. "You have such a capacity for goodness," she tells him, adding that his fear of failure is what makes him excel. Strange adds that this fear is what made him a great doctor, but the Ancient One says that it is "precisely what kept you from greatness. Arrogance and fear still keep you from learning the simplest and most significant lesson of all." She does not finish the thought, so Strange asks, "…which is?" "It's not *about* you," she replies.

Notice how different this remark is from what she told Strange upon their first meeting: that he "thinks too little of himself." Why the change? As was the case when she instructed him to "silence his ego," the idea here is that Strange has to fully rid himself of his egotism in order to find real meaning. While it is sometimes said that existentialism is concerned with self-importance, this is inaccurate. The central idea for most existentialists is authenticity: choosing freely for oneself. The problem for Strange was that he was living a radically inauthentic life, caught in the paradox of saying life had no meaning while also believing that his own life had more meaning than anything else.

The Final Turning Point

Although Strange started with a perspective that was mostly nihilistic about the meaning of life, by the end of the film, he has discovered his freedom to make authentic choices and decisions which are ultimately more powerful and effective than his old ones. Thus, the journey Strange takes is one that starts by stating that existence means nothing, and ends by concluding that existence—and the actions and choices that define it, should one be true to oneself—mean everything.

The specific way in which Strange chooses to outsmart Dormammu bears strong existential significance. By using the Eye of Agamotto, Strange forces Dormammu to repeat with him the same sequence of time, over and over. This part of the movie is evocative of an idea scattered throughout the works of Nietzsche, who discusses a thought experiment that is often referred to as "eternal recurrence." In one version of this thought experiment, he writes:

> What if, some day or night a demon were to steal after you into your loneliest loneliness and say to you: "This life as you now live it and have lived it, you will have to live once more and innumerable times more" … Would you not throw yourself down and gnash your teeth and curse the demon who spoke thus? Or have you once experienced a tremendous moment when you would have answered him: "You are a god and never have I heard anything more divine."[5]

Here Nietzsche contemplates how we might radically reframe our decision-making if we knew that we would repeat every decision over and over again for eternity. Specifically, we might make more meaningful choices if we knew that we would be subject to this endless repetition. We might take more time to think about whether we really want to do something, instead of treating our freedom and possibilities as trivial.

The fact that Strange uses endless repetition to force Dormammu to surrender is a testament to the full completion of his existential conversion. During this scene, Strange tells Dormammu that he is prepared to repeat his faceoff eternally if his foe won't back down. Obviously, this requires a profound amount of courage, but it also requires complete and total commitment—in the sense of existential authenticity—to the choice that is being made.

Strange's decision to remain and fight with his friends in the final showdown against Dormammu to save all of humanity is also evocative of Sartre's idea of the *universal decree*. Sartre wrote that when a person like Strange chooses for himself, he in effect also chooses for everyone, and therefore sets forth a universal decree.[6] Before making a decision, Sartre says that we should experience that classical existentialist feeling of anxiety over what we should choose. He says that we should make sure that we only commit ourselves to choosing something authentically, which would be the choice that we would want anyone else to make, were this person in our shoes.

Late in the movie we see Strange in precisely this sort of existential situation. He experiences anguish when he considers leaving the battle. By deciding to stay and defend humanity, Strange chooses not just for himself but for all of humanity, because he hopes that anyone else would make the same decision in his situation. Unlike his earlier worldview where he worried only about himself, in the final scene we see Strange completely transcend this old way of thinking when he focuses upon himself in a different, productive way: narrowing in on his freedom and his responsibility. By doing this, Strange not only looks inward but also looks outward, finding meaning and value in the powerful choice that he makes to stand up and fight Dormammu.

The Existential Redefinition of Doctor Strange

By the end of the movie, Strange has escaped the throes of nihilism as he comes to view his life, and the world, in existentialist terms. His change evokes a central existentialist idea, popularized by Sartre, that "existence precedes essence."[7] Existence, and its choices and possibilities, are what define a person and give life meaning and value. Sartre argued that what you do with your life is more important than how you define yourself with essentialist qualities, like "brilliantly gifted surgeon." Far more important than your title as surgeon is what you *choose to do* as surgeon.

Earlier in the movie, Strange was devoted to scientific explanations of reality, which gestured at truths concerning the essences of various things, from the hydrogen atom, to humanity, and to the universe. As we have seen, Strange's preference for the essentialist way of thinking is what led him down the road of nihilism. But by the final scene, Strange is no longer concerned with his old scientific accounts of the essence of things. Instead, he has reoriented himself toward his very existence, which is no longer insignificant or tiny, even if it is, in the sense of an existentialist, something that is indeed momentary. By acknowledging this momentary nature of his existence in a productive way, Strange is able to transcend his old egotism and make more powerful and meaningful choices. In so doing, the Sorcerer Supreme radically redefines himself, becoming the Existentialist Supreme as well.

Notes

1. All quoted dialogue is from the 2016 film *Doctor Strange*.
2. Jean-Paul Sartre, *Being and Nothingness*, trans. Hazel Barnes (New York: Washington Square Press, 1984), 93.
3. Martin Heidegger, *Being and Time*, trans. John Macquarrie and Edward Robinson (New York: Harper & Row, 1962), 230–231.
4. Friedrich Nietzsche, *The Anti-Christ, Ecce Homo, Twilight of the Idols, and Other Writings*, ed. Aaron Ridley and Judith Norman (Cambridge: Cambridge University Press, 2005), 188.
5. Friedrich Nietzsche, *The Gay Science*, ed. Bernard Williams and trans. Josefine Nauckhoff (Cambridge: Cambridge University Press, 2001), 194.
6. Jean-Paul Sartre, "Existentialism Is a Humanism," in *Existentialism: From Dostoevsky to Sartre*, ed. and trans. Walter Kaufman (New York: Meridian, 1975), 292.
7. Ibid., 289. This idea had featured in the work of other philosophers such as Kierkegaard and Heidegger, but Sartre framed the idea using this specific language.

Part II
"FORGET EVERYTHING THAT YOU THINK YOU KNOW"

5

"Through an Orb Darkly"

Doctor Strange and the Journey to Knowledge

Armond Boudreaux

In an early story, a villain called the Silver Dagger breaks into the Sanctum Sanctorum in order to kill Doctor Strange and kidnap Clea, Strange's protégé and lover. Bent on eradicating all the magicians in the world, he penetrates Strange's protective spells using occult powers and stabs the Sorcerer Supreme in the back with his signature weapon, a silver dagger. (Insane sorcerer hunters aren't very original when thinking about names for themselves!) Thinking that he has killed Strange, Dagger takes the Eye of Agamotto and kidnaps Clea so that he can "save her" from Strange's occult influence.

Strange tries to use the Orb of Agamotto, a scrying crystal ball, to find out where the Silver Dagger has taken Clea, but when he sees Dagger's face in the Orb, it turns into a skull, and tentacles reach out to drag Strange into the Orb. Strange lands on the surface of the Realm of Agamotto only to be greeted by a huge caterpillar smoking a hookah. The caterpillar tells him, "I'm *not* a hallucination. ... I'm *real*!" At the same time, the caterpillar says that Strange has entered a world of "unreality." The caterpillar's words raise fascinating questions about the nature of knowledge and reality, which are repeated in one form or another throughout Doctor Strange's adventures. To answer these questions, we turn to epistemology, the area of philosophy that explores what we can know, why we think we know it, and how we know it. The answers will help us to make sense of the strange world of Stephen Strange.

Doctor Strange and Philosophy: The Other Book of Forbidden Knowledge, First Edition. Edited by Mark D. White.
© 2018 John Wiley & Sons Ltd. Published 2018 by John Wiley & Sons Ltd.

How Do *You* Know?

One of the primary goals of epistemology is to determine the most reliable source of knowledge of the world so we can trust that what we believe is actually true. For example, think about Stephen Strange's knowledge of medicine and human anatomy. Strange can easily distinguish between the parts of the brain stem like the *pons* and the *medulla oblongata*, and long before he becomes the Sorcerer Supreme, his detailed knowledge of the human nervous system allowed him to save many people's lives (all the while being an arrogant jerk, of course—but nobody's perfect). Doctor Strange's patients place trust in his knowledge and skill because they've heard about his reputation and can verify his credentials, but an epistemologist might ask exactly *how* Strange knows the things that he claims to know about human anatomy.

Some philosophers who focus on epistemology, such as David Hume (1711–1776) and John Locke (1632–1704), are *empiricists*, believing that our knowledge comes primarily through sense experience. For example, Strange's medical knowledge comes primarily through his senses. Before he could become a neurosurgeon, Strange had to go to medical school, where he studied books that gave him detailed information about anatomy and biology, learned from his professors and from other students, and dissected cadavers, all to develop his skills as a surgeon in different ways. In all of these cases, Strange gained knowledge through sense experience, whether visually (through books), aurally (through lectures), or tactilely (through surgical practice).

Empiricists would argue, however, that it isn't just his medical knowledge that Strange learned through sense experience. From a purely empiricist point of view, *all* our knowledge comes to us ultimately through the senses. When we're born, we're *tabula rasa* or a "blank slate" (to use John Locke's term) on which sense experience "writes" knowledge. As we grow older, more and more new experiences write more and more knowledge on the "surface" of our minds. Long before he ever became a doctor, then, Stephen Strange began to learn everything that he would ever know using his senses, a process that continues into his present day as Sorcerer Supreme.

Most people would probably consider themselves empiricists—as the cliché goes, "seeing is believing"—and modern society is based largely on the belief that we should trust our senses. Courts of law rely on physical evidence and visual reports to convict people of crimes; students in every discipline read textbooks, listen to lectures, and get hands-on experience, just like Strange did. Indeed, the scientific method depends on testing hypotheses that scientists observe with their senses. But empiricism as a theory of knowledge is not perfect—in fact, if we take empiricism to its logical conclusion, we might end up not being able to know anything at all!

Imagine you're a pure empiricist, and then try to prove that you can trust your senses. You're holding a book (a pretty good one, if I do say so myself) right now in your hand. How do you know that it's there? "Because I can feel it and see it," you say. Okay, but try to prove to me that you can trust what your eyes and fingers tell you—it's very difficult without simply asserting that you see it or feel it. Maybe you ask a friend whether or not she sees the book that you're holding, and she says, "Yes, of course I see it." But how do you know that your friend sees it—just because she just told you? And how do you even know that she told you? You know because you heard her. For that matter, how do you know that *she's* even there?

Seeing Is *Not* Believing

Empiricism makes sense of a lot of things. It allows Dr. Stephen Strange, master surgeon, to repair severed nerves, and it allows his "Awesome Facial Hair Bro" Tony Stark to build a suit of armor. It allows us to build hospitals, cars, and computers, to cure diseases, and to solve crimes. It can provide evidence for all sorts of claims, but there's one claim it can't support: that we can actually trust our senses. And if you're an empiricist who can't trust your senses, then you might find yourself wondering if you can sincerely claim to know anything at all.

Doctor Strange seems to recognize the difficulty with pure empiricism when he travels through the Orb of Agamotto in search of a way to escape it. Following the caterpillar's advice, Strange doesn't trust his own senses inside this world. He does, however, decide to trust the caterpillar himself and follow his advice to go to the center of the Orb to find his way out, and as he travels through the weird dimension, Strange finds himself confronted with one epistemological conundrum after another. For instance, what can he know about what he sees in this place? The strangeness of the world inside the Orb puts into question just about everything he thinks he knows.

Things get even more complicated when Strange meets people from the real world while inside the Orb. First, he runs into the Silver Surfer, who doesn't recognize him but sympathizes with his plight. The Surfer directs him to the castle of the "White Queen," where Strange meets more of his friends who should know him but don't, including Hawkeye, Beast, the Hulk, Spider-Man, Namor, Nick Fury, and Valkyrie. Even though he knows that these doppelgängers feasting in the castle aren't actually his friends from the real world, Strange can't help marveling at how much they look and act like their counterparts: "Incredible—simply incredible! If I weren't so painfully aware of being within the Orb, I would swear these are men I've known!"[1] Again, Strange runs the risk of being deceived by his senses because of how convincingly real these copies of his friends are. But instead of falling for the deceit, he recognizes that he can't trust his eyes and ears, and politely tells the counterfeit heroes that he cannot stay and feast with them, and continues on his journey.

Such a scene would be enough to make many pure empiricists despair of ever knowing the truth about reality. Indeed, if the senses can be as thoroughly deceived as Strange's are inside the Orb, how can he ever truly trust his senses at all? It appears that we need something more than just sense experience in order to be able to know things inside the Orb.

Enter the Rationalists

An epistemological alternative to empiricism is *rationalism*. To be clear, the term "rationalist" does not mean that certain philosophers are more reasonable or sensible in their thinking than others. Instead, rationalism gets its name from its emphasis on the role of reason in the act of knowing: where an empiricist would argue that our knowledge begins with sense experience, a rationalist would say that all of our knowledge begins with our reason.

For example, if you're a rationalist, like the philosophers Gottfried Wilhelm Leibniz (1646–1716) and Baruch Spinoza (1632–1677), you might say that you know mathematical truths not by empirical methods, but instead because numbers are *innate ideas*—that is, ideas that were built into your head from birth. Because of these innate ideas, once you understand the meaning of the words "two," "four," and "plus," you have to acknowledge that "two plus two" is the same as "four." There is no need for you to go out and find real-world examples of pairs and start putting them together to verify this belief; as a rationalist, you believe that you can know mathematical facts without any sensory experience.

Mathematical principles are one of the most common examples of innate ideas claimed by rationalism, but there are others as well. For example, imagine that the Silver Surfer arrives at the Sanctum Sanctorum in order to warn Doctor Strange that Thanos has assembled all of the Infinity Gems and plans to eradicate all life in the universe. Nova then bursts into the room and says that Doctor Doom actually has the Infinity Gems, and he plans to use them to expand his rule from Latveria to the entire universe. Experience has taught Strange that he can trust both the Surfer and Nova, but he will naturally conclude that one of these statements is false. Even though he trusts both his fellow heroes, he can't believe both stories because they're logically inconsistent. Philosophers have a fancy name for this: the Law of Non-Contradiction, which says that a statement cannot be both true and false at the same time and in the same way. In other words, the statements "Thanos has the Infinity Gems" and "Doctor Doom has the Infinity Gems" cannot be true at the same time because they are mutually exclusive, with each contradicting the other. This concept is so obvious that a rationalist might say that it's an example of an innate idea, one of the ideas that come pre-programmed in our minds to help deal with logical puzzles in everyday life.

But while rationalism might offer us a possible alternative to empiricism, so far none of this really solves Doctor Strange's dilemma inside the Orb. Like a good rationalist, Strange clearly doesn't depend upon his senses for all of his knowledge, and he doesn't take what he sees at face value. (To be fair, most empiricists know not to take their sense experience at face value, either.) And even though the concept of innate ideas might offer us a possible solution to the problems with taking empiricism to its extreme, Strange needs something more than just mathematics and the Law of Non-Contradiction to help him navigate the world inside the Orb of Agamotto.

Descartes to the Rescue

To help explain how Strange can have true and reliable knowledge inside the Orb, we need to turn to René Descartes (1596–1650). Descartes was dissatisfied with the epistemology of the classical and medieval philosophers who had come before him, which relied heavily on divine revelation in addition to reason and sense experience, and he doubted its ability to support the new sciences that were rapidly developing in the early seventeenth century. In his *Meditations on First Philosophy*, he set out to discover a solid foundation for all knowledge.[2] (Not ambitious at all!)

Descartes begins his search for this foundation by first adopting an attitude of radical skepticism and systematically trying to doubt everything that he believes. He concludes that he can reasonably doubt everything that he knows through sense experience because our senses can be deceived, as are Doctor Strange's inside the Orb. He questions the findings of modern science, which depend almost entirely on empirical evidence, resulting in reasons to have "doubt about all things, especially material things, so long as we have no foundations for the sciences other than those which we have had up till now."[3] He even casts doubt on his own sense experiences, since he could very well be dreaming in his bed instead of sitting by the fireplace in his room. After all, in his dreams he's believed many things that weren't true, and if he can be convinced in a dream that what's happening is real, then how can he ever prove that he's not dreaming now?

Furthermore, Descartes realized that he could be awake but living in a false world (not unlike the world inside the Orb of Agamotto). Or worse, he could be living inside an illusion created by an evil demon (which Doctor Strange would call "Tuesday"). Theoretically, that demon could make the deception so convincing that *everything* Descartes believed would be false. By the time he finishes the first of the six *Meditations*, then, he has all but demolished everything that people might believe that they know.

Descartes goes through this exercise not because he's actually a philosophical skeptic, but because he believes it's the best way to clear his mind of all knowledge that isn't absolutely certain: "Its greatest benefit lies in freeing us from all our preconceived opinions, and providing the easiest route by which the mind may be led away from the senses."[4] Once he eliminates all "preconceived" ideas and beliefs that he cannot truly know with certainty, Descartes hopes to find those beliefs that he cannot reasonably doubt, and thereby discover the foundation of knowledge.

Cogito, Ergo Strange

In stark contrast to the epistemologists who came before him, Descartes finds that foundation by looking inward. Once he has convinced himself that he can doubt the existence of the Earth, the sky, his own body, and everything else in the world, he runs into one truth that he cannot doubt: his own existence (or, more precisely, the existence of his mind). For Descartes to doubt anything, Descartes himself has to exist:

> I have convinced myself that there is absolutely nothing in the world … Does it not follow that I too do not exist? No: if I convinced myself of something then I certainly existed … So after considering everything thoroughly, I must finally conclude that this proposition, *I am, I exist*, is necessarily true whenever it is put forward by me or conceived in my mind.[5]

Descartes can say to himself, "I cannot know with certainty that the world exists," but as soon as he does so, he implicitly proves the existence of his own mind. After all, for there to be thoughts, there has to be a thinker. This seems to be true about all intellectual claims, but Descartes believes that it is especially true about the claim, "I exist." He sums up the idea with one of the most famous phrases in all of philosophy: *cogito, ergo sum*, or "I think, therefore I am." In short, Descartes can doubt everything in the universe, but it's impossible for him to doubt his own existence.

The "I" in "I think, therefore I am" is not Descartes the seventeenth-century Frenchman who is of a certain height, weight, and appearance, but rather Descartes' mind alone. He doesn't take for granted that his body exists because he knows his body only through his sense experience, and he's just gone to great lengths to show that we can reasonably doubt what our sense experience tells us. This leaves only the existence of his mind that he can reasonably believe and trust.

One consequence of Descartes' exercise in skepticism is *mind-body dualism*, the belief that humans are made up of two distinct but intimately related substances: mind and body. For a dualist like Descartes, the mind is an immaterial substance, a "thinking thing," the non-physical part of our selves, while our bodies (including our brains) are the material parts of our selves. While most philosophers are skeptical of dualism, wondering how a purely non-physical substance like the mind could interact with a purely physical substance like the body, Doctor Strange himself *has* to be a dualist. After all, when he projects his astral form from his body, he is temporarily separating his mind from his body, and this would be possible only if mind-body dualism were true.

As he journeys through the Orb, Doctor Strange goes on an intellectual trek that is in many ways similar to the one that Descartes takes in the *Meditations*. He begins with the doubt cast by the hookah-smoking caterpillar and then reasons from there into doubting everything else that exists inside the Orb, so that when he encounters friends like the Silver Surfer and the Hulk, he understands that they're only very convincing illusions. After he battles the counterfeit heroes who aren't happy that he refused to feast with them, Strange is understandably disturbed that duplicates of his friends declared their plans to kill him. As he casts a spell to stop them, he also reasons his way to his own *cogito, ergo sum*, as the narration reads: "'Kill him?' Can the mage have heard aright? Disbelieving, he gestures them back—but their gestures make emphatic reply! Nothing merits belief here—except oneself!"[6] Strange seems to have arrived at the same place as Descartes in his own skeptical journey. He can doubt everything around him, but even if it's all an illusion, he can't doubt that he himself is experiencing the illusion, and therefore he must exist in this world.

Defeating Descartes' Evil Demon

But while this recognition keeps Strange from utter despair, it isn't enough to help him know what he can and cannot trust inside the Orb. Luckily, Descartes offers a possible solution to that problem, too. At the end of the second *Meditation*, when he has effectively demolished nearly everything that he previously believed and reduced all his certainty down to the existence of his own mind, it might seem that his epistemological experiment has failed. After all, his main goal in the book is to provide a solid foundation for all knowledge, not destroy it! How can he reason from his own existence to the trustworthiness of the human senses and the existence of everything he's just cast doubt upon? It's a daunting problem, and if he fails, then Descartes is now a *solipsist*: someone who believes that he can't know anything except for his own mind. But like Doctor Strange using sorcery to get himself out of a tight spot, Descartes proposes an ingenious way to escape solipsism. To understand that escape, we'll have to return to the rationalist notion of innate ideas.

Like many other rationalists, Descartes believes in innate ideas. He also believes that innate ideas can't be fictitious or imaginary, but must correspond to formal realities, like mathematical principles and the Law of Non-Contradiction. Even though we can know that our own minds exist and that mathematical facts are true, however, that doesn't get us to the point where we can trust our senses. After all, the world we inhabit might be no different than the world inside the Orb of Agamotto.

All is not lost, though, because Descartes discovers a reason that we should be able to trust our senses. In addition to ideas like mathematical principles, we have other innate ideas in our minds, and one of them is the idea of God, an infinite, perfect, benevolent being. Because Descartes believes that all innate ideas must correspond to something real, he concludes that God must exist, and he uses the existence of God to prove that we have to be able to trust our senses.

Wait ... couldn't what Descartes calls "God" simply be the evil demon that he imagines in the first *Meditation*, not a benevolent being at all but a malevolent force like Dormammu or Mephisto? Isn't it possible that Descartes' "God" is actually a deceiver? No, Descartes replies: God is by definition an infinite, benevolent, and perfect being, and since deception is an imperfection, God cannot be a deceiver. Therefore, we have to be able to trust our senses.

Many philosophers have criticized Descartes' reasoning here. For example, some have countered that the idea of God is not innate as Descartes believes, or that even if a belief in a perfect God is innate, it doesn't imply that a perfect God exists. Whether Descartes is right about God's existence or what it implies about sense knowledge, the interesting thing here is the way in which Doctor Strange's journey through the Orb resembles Descartes' intellectual journey in the *Meditations*. And just as Strange's trip through the world of "unreality" mirrors Descartes' first two *Meditations*, there is another parallel between the sorcerer's journey and the philosopher as well, including a divine figure inside the Orb who is the key to what Strange can know.

By the Eye of Agamotto!

Descartes depends upon God to prove that we can know things with certainty. While many people doubt or deny the existence of God in the real world, there can be absolutely no doubt about the existence of a divine force in the Marvel Universe, a creator deity called "God" or the "One-Above-All."[7]

The One-Above-All probably won't be much help in solving Strange's epistemological problems inside the Orb, but there are other divine figures in the Marvel Universe, as well. One of those figures is Agamotto, who is a member of the trinity-like Vishanti and the source of many of Doctor Strange's powers and magical objects. One of Agamotto's epithets is "The All-Seeing," and he is the creator of the Eye of Agamotto, an amulet that among other things can dispel illusions and reveal things that have been hidden.[8] And true to his epithet, Agamotto is the ultimate source of knowledge for Strange while he is inside the Orb.

Agamotto's appearance inside the Orb might be easy to miss for those who have not read later Doctor Strange stories. As gradually becomes apparent, he's the very first being that Strange meets inside the Orb: the hookah-smoking caterpillar. The last three panels of the first installment of this story offer the first real clue to the caterpillar's true identity: as he disappears, he tells Strange, "I'll keep my eyes on you!", and as he fades away, the last thing we see is a single glowing spot, much like an eye.[9]

This caterpillar seems more like something out of *Alice in Wonderland* than the Christian God that Descartes believes in (or the Marvel Universe's One-Above-All), but he has many of the same divine attributes, such as being the creator of his world inside the Orb. Unlike the infinitely perfect being of Descartes, however, Agamotto certainly isn't always nice.[10] All the same, when Strange meets him at the beginning of his journey through the Orb, Agamotto is the only source of truth about this world. Moreover, Agamotto's guidance is the only way that Strange is able to escape the Orb. After all, Strange naturally believes at first that the way out is the same way that he came in, and it is only from Agamotto that he learns that he must travel further *inside* the orb in order to reach the outside.

Even though he speaks in cryptic and half-ironic ways, Agamotto is no deceiver. In fact, he is like Descartes' God in that he helps Strange to understand which knowledge he can trust and which he cannot. Because of that help, Strange is able to escape the world of the Orb and return to the real world, where knowledge and truth are (hopefully) a little more certain.

Out of the Orb

Questions about what we know, how we know it, and why we trust what we know, are some of the most difficult in philosophy. We've been wrestling with them since the beginning of philosophy, and many thinkers have taken their shot at giving us theories that show what we can know with certainty. Some philosophers have concluded that we can't know anything, which has led others to resort to kicking a rock, as Samuel Johnson (1709–1784) did to refute George Berkeley's theory that matter does not exist. Although there are many theories of knowledge, none of them is likely to satisfy everyone's questions about knowledge any time soon, which gives Doctor Strange—and us—the opportunity to explore many different possibilities in comics and movies for years to come.

Notes

1. *Doctor Strange*, vol. 2, #2 (August 1974), collected in *Doctor Strange Epic Collection: A Separate Reality* (2016).
2. René Descartes, *Meditations on First Philosophy*, ed. John Cottingham (Cambridge: Cambridge University Press, 1641/1996).
3. Ibid., 9.
4. Ibid.
5. Ibid., 16.
6. *Doctor Strange*, vol. 2, #2.
7. For more on the divine within the Marvel Universe, see Adam Barkman, "'No Other Gods Before Me': God, Ontology, and Ethics in the Avengers' Universe," in Mark D. White (ed.), *The Avengers and Philosophy: Earth's Mightiest Thinkers* (Hoboken, NJ: John Wiley & Sons, 2012), 183–193.
8. *Strange Tales*, vol. 1, #115 (December 1963), "The Origin of Dr. Strange," collected in *Doctor Strange Epic Collection: A Separate Reality*.
9. Dr. Strange, vol. 1, #1 (June 1974), collected in *Doctor Strange Epic Collection: A Separate Reality*. Agamotto appears as a caterpillar again, such as in *Doctor Strange, Sorcerer Supreme* #43 (July 1992), collected in *Doctor Strange, Sorcerer Supreme Omnibus Volume 2* (2018).
10. More recently, Agamotto, wanting to take back his Eye from Strange, disguises himself as the Ancient One and falsely accuses Strange of having stolen the amulet (*New Avengers*, vol. 2, #1–6, August 2010–January 2011, collected in *New Avengers by Brian Michael Bendis: The Complete Collection, Volume 6*, 2017).

6

Forbidden Knowledge and Strange Virtues
It's Not What You Know, It's How You Know It

Tuomas W. Manninen

Is there really some knowledge that ought to be off-limits? In the 2016 film *Doctor Strange*, the Book of Cagliostro is a repository of forbidden knowledge of dark magic. Kaecilius uses the spells in this book in his attempt to bring an end to death by opening a portal to the Dark Dimension where there is no death—with the unfortunate side effect of destroying the entire world. According to Mordo, the Book of Cagliostro contains spells that violate the laws of nature—the very ones that the sorcerers have vowed to protect, no matter the cost. For Mordo, using knowledge of the spells is beyond the pale, even when this is done with the best intentions. At the same time, it's thanks to the very spells in the Book of Cagliostro that the Ancient One has become ancient, using its knowledge to draw from the Dark Dimension to allow her to live way past her natural life expectancy and to thwart many threats to human existence. It is also this knowledge that allows Doctor Strange to fight off the threat of Dormammu.

But what is knowledge and what might make it forbidden? This question takes us into the strange realm of *epistemology*, the branch of philosophy dedicated to the study of knowledge. This chapter will use epistemology to look at the four sorcerers who were once students of the Ancient One: Jonathan Pangborn, Kaecilius, Mordo, and (of course) Stephen Strange. But instead of trying to determine exactly *what* each of them knew of the mystical arts, we will focus on *how*

Doctor Strange and Philosophy: The Other Book of Forbidden Knowledge,
First Edition. Edited by Mark D. White.
© 2018 John Wiley & Sons Ltd. Published 2018 by John Wiley & Sons Ltd.

they knew it. In the process, we will see why Master Wong was correct when he said: "No knowledge in Kamar-Taj is forbidden, only certain practices."[1]

"This Doesn't Make Any Sense ..."

The notion of "forbidden knowledge" is deeply ingrained in the collective consciousness. In the Bible, Adam and Eve—and thereby the entire human race—were expelled from Paradise because they were tricked into defying God's decree and ate the apple from the Tree of Knowledge. According to Greek mythology, Prometheus stole fire from the gods and gave it to humans; as a punishment, he ended up being eternally tormented. But this doesn't tell us which knowledge is declared as forbidden—or by whom. As it turns out, defining what items of knowledge are (or, ought to be) forbidden is not as straightforward as making a titan suffer for eternity. In his book *Forbidden Knowledge*, literary scholar Roger Shattuck admits as much: "My subject is too extensive and elusive to submit readily to a system and theory."[2]

As it turns out, philosophers have some trouble answering this question as well. On the one hand, it appears that partial knowledge of the Book of Cagliostro can be used to bring about disasters (like summoning Dormammu). So it seems the book and the knowledge it contains would best remain forbidden. On the other hand, partial knowledge of the spells in this tome can help to avert a disaster, as was done both by Doctor Strange and the Ancient One. So perhaps it would be imprudent to forbid such knowledge. Perhaps, if a certain piece of knowledge is used to bring about beneficial results, then people should be allowed to know about it and form beliefs about it. This is the approach of traditional epistemology, with its focus on questions of the justification and evaluation of beliefs, where beliefs are the primary objects of analysis, evaluation, and justification.

The film *Doctor Strange* illustrates these issues in a number of ways. The Ancient One has amassed a vast amount of knowledge over her years, and some of the knowledge is recorded in her private collection of tomes in the library at Kamar-Taj. As Wong, the current Guardian of the Library at Kamar-Taj, explains to Stephen Strange, "Those books are far too advanced for anyone other than the Sorcerer Supreme." Yet the Ancient One has dispensed some of this knowledge over the years to those who have studied with her; the roster of students includes Kaecilius, Mordo, Joseph Pangborn—and Dr. Stephen Strange.

Strange Epistemological Virtues?

According to the saying, it's not what you know, it's *who* you know. In light of *virtue epistemology* we need to revise this statement slightly: It's not just *what* you know, it's *how* you know it. Virtue epistemology shifts the focus to the person who has the beliefs, and considers the way the person forms belief—by way of intellectual virtues and vices—to be more important than the traditional questions about beliefs themselves.

Virtue epistemology is largely based on the ideas underlying Aristotle's (384–322 BCE) ethics. According to Aristotle, for an action to count as virtuous, it is not enough that we reach the desired results; the action must also produce the desired result in the correct manner and for the right reasons.[3] Specifically, a virtuous person acts on the basis of his or her virtues, character traits that reflect moral excellence and produce good results. Virtues represent the "golden mean" between two extremes. (For example, the virtue of courage lies between the extremes of cowardice and foolhardiness.) When we take this approach to ethics and translate it into epistemology, we get virtue epistemology, which focuses on the intellectual virtues that lead to the effective acquisition of knowledge and formation of beliefs.

There are two competing approaches in virtue epistemology: *reliabilism* and *responsibilism*.[4] When it comes to epistemic virtues in the *reliabilist* sense, we talk about having traits like keen eyesight or acute hearing; a reliable epistemic ability tends to provide accurate (and reliable) knowledge to inform true beliefs. During his training at Kamar-Taj, Strange boasts about how he was able to become a world-renowned neurosurgeon partially due to his highly reliable photographic memory. In contrast, possessing epistemic virtues in the *responsibilist* sense means using those traits in a responsible manner.[5] After all, a supervillain could have amazing powers of observation and perception that lead to reliable information and beliefs, but then use them to do evil rather than use them responsibly (or ethically). Even if we grant that some of the other neophytes at Kamar-Taj had very reliable cognitive abilities, we see very quickly in *Doctor Strange* how these abilities can be used to serve one's own interests (in the case of Pangborn) or a misguided ideology (in the case of Kaecilius).

By contrast to the practicality of reliabilism, responsibilism emphasizes the ethical aspect of the acquisition of knowledge, demanding not only that it be acquired well but virtuously (aside from how it is ultimately used). According to contemporary philosopher James Montmarquet, there are three character traits that are conducive to being epistemically virtuous in this sense: impartiality, courage, and the ability to unite these two in proper ways.[6] Impartiality is "an openness to the ideas of others, the willingness to exchange ideas and learn from them, the lack of jealousy and personal bias directed at their ideas and the lively sense of one's own fallibility."[7] This is pretty much the opposite of what Strange exhibited when he first met the Ancient One and refused to even consider a world beyond what he knew. (Never mind that he had no sense of his own fallibility at that point!)

Courage—or, specifically, *intellectual* courage—is

> the willingness to conceive and examine alternatives to popularly held beliefs, perseverance in the face of opposition from others (until one is convinced that one is mistaken), and the … willingness to examine, and even actively seek out, evidence that would refute one's own hypotheses.[8]

Again, Strange initially gets low marks here, judging from his response to the Ancient One: "I spent my last dollar getting here … and you are talking to me about healing through belief?" The third virtue is achieved through uniting the first two, which is important because "they concern opposite, but it seems equally important, sides of the balanced intellectual personality."[9] Through his training at Kamar-Taj, Strange needs to learn to be open to new ideas and thoughts while remaining confident in those he has, integrating knowledge both old and new in a responsible manner.

"Finally, I Found My Teacher"

Over the course of the film, we follow the paths of four individuals—Kaecilius, Mordo, Joseph Pangborn, and Stephen Strange—each of whom arrived at Kamar-Taj as broken individuals in search of knowledge that could help them overcome their uniquely dire situations. Although all of them were trained by the Ancient One, each of them took that training in different directions.

Let's start with Jonathan Pangborn, who suffered a spinal injury that paralyzed him from the chest down. After his time with the Ancient One, he recovered from his injuries rather miraculously. When Strange first meets him in person, Pangborn tells him about his attempt to elevate his mind at Kamar-Taj, which subsequently allowed his physical body to heal. It is not until later that the Ancient One reveals that Pangborn achieved his recovery through channeling dimensional energy directly into his body—or, more bluntly, that he used magic to walk. Pangborn's epistemically virtuous abilities seem to have been restricted to the reliable kind. Ultimately his education in Kamar-Taj merely served to advance his self-interest.

Next, we have Kaecilius. Like the others, he suffered a personal tragedy: he came to Kamar-Taj to find solace after the loss of his family. Unfortunately, however, Kaecilius seems to have been motivated by the idea that "this world does not have to die." Though Kaecilius displays intellectual courage in his thinking, he fails when it comes to impartiality. When Strange asks him, "What about the people you've killed?" Kaecilius retorts that they were mere "tiny, momentary specks within an indifferent universe," not worthy of his consideration while seeking his ultimate goal.

This brings us to Mordo, who has become a Master at Kamar-Taj, suggesting that he possesses the intellectual virtues. However, there are two telling exchanges that illustrate certain excesses in his thinking that violate the ideal of virtue as the "golden mean" between extremes. Mordo dismisses Strange's persistent questions about the Ancient One's background, telling him to "trust your teacher … and don't lose your way," which displays his own epistemic rigidity. When Mordo discusses Kaecilius' personality, saying that "he was proud, headstrong, and he questioned the Ancient One, rejecting her teachings," he highlights his own blind reliance on authority figures. Impatient with Strange, Mordo shows a lack of impartiality, telling him "No more questions."

Mordo fails to display ideal epistemic virtues later in the film as well. He's aghast when he learns that the Ancient One has been using spells from the Book of Cagliostro to draw power from the Dark Dimension. Even in the midst of a life-or-death fight against Kaecilius and his zealots, it takes time for Mordo to acknowledge this: "It's true. She does draw power from the Dark Dimension." Later, after Mordo reluctantly agrees to help Strange fight to save the Sanctum in Hong Kong, he decides that he has had enough with sorcery: "Yes … We did it… but by also violating the natural law … We broke our rules, just like [the Ancient One]. The bill comes due. Always." Mordo may have displayed intellectual courage in some ways, such as persevering in his beliefs, but he did so in excess. He also seems to have closed his mind against considering alternatives, nearly as much as Kaecilius did.

Is Strange Epistemically Virtuous?

We turn now to Dr. Stephen Strange. In his previous life, he was a world-renowned neurosurgeon who, despite his faults, exemplified multiple intellectual virtues. Notably, it was his highly reliable memory that enabled him to earn his Ph.D. and his M.D. at the same time. After witnessing Strange cast spells from the Book of Cagliostro, though, Mordo pointed out that "what you just did takes more than just a good memory." It obviously takes more than mere recollection for Strange to deduce, as he did earlier in the film, that an ostensibly brain-dead patient was merely suffering from lead poisoning from an uncoated bullet lodged in his brain. As the film clearly establishes, Strange exemplifies many epistemic virtues of the reliabilist variety—simply put, he is exceptionally brilliant.

As Strange learns in his first encounter with the Ancient One, however, his perspective is quite limited. During his period as a novice at Kamar-Taj, Strange is able to extend his perspective, to the surprise of Wong and the Ancient One alike, and during the battle with Kaecilius and his zealots, he hold his ground. But after being scolded by Mordo and Wong for accessing some of the spells in the Book of Cagliostro and being told about the dangers residing within its spells, Strange seems to want to get out of all of it: "OK, I'm out ... I came to heal my hands, not to fight in some mystical war."

While Strange perseveres through many more battles that test his newfound knowledge of the mystic arts, it isn't until he encounters the Ancient One as she is dying that he learns the most important truth. Despite the fact that Strange used to be a brilliant neurosurgeon, and has quickly picked up the skills of a sorcerer, the Ancient One tells him of things that are still holding him back:

ANCIENT ONE: You have such a capacity for goodness. You always excelled, but not because you craved success. But because of your fear of failure.
STRANGE: That's what made me a great doctor.
ANCIENT ONE: That's precisely what kept you from greatness. Arrogance and fear will keep you from learning the simplest and the most significant lesson of all.
STRANGE: Which is...?
ANCIENT ONE: It's not about you.

The Ancient One explains to Strange that he could have followed the path of Jonathan Pangborn, and *merely* used the mystical arts to heal himself and return to his past life—but also that "the world would be lesser for it." The fact that he didn't do this suggests that he is more epistemically virtuous than Pangborn, especially in a sense of realizing greater responsibility for how he acquires and uses the gift of knowledge.

In the final exchange between Strange and the Ancient One, she offers a justification for her use of the so-called forbidden knowledge in the Book of Cagliostro: while she knew the risks, she saw that the power could be used for the greater good. Moving away from the ethics of the issue, and back to the epistemological questions, we see that not only does Strange acquire a new piece of information, but his transformation is now complete: "It's not 'Mister Strange' or 'Master Strange'—it's 'Doctor Strange.'" The Ancient One lauds Doctor Strange's flexibility while she warns that he will also need Mordo's strength to defeat Dormammu, emphasizing the point that both intellectual virtues need to come together for him to be truly virtuous.

A Strange Ending

Though none of the Ancient One's students display perfect intellectual virtue, Doctor Strange ultimately comes the closest to the virtues of impartiality and intellectual courage in their proper balance. But many questions still remain. Most pointedly, even if Strange managed to display these virtues in this particular instance, what will this mean for the future? As was pointed out by Aristotle (around the time when the Ancient One might just have been called the One), it is not enough that one performs virtuous action *just* once. A truly virtuous character will show itself through consistency. Virtue is not an accomplishment or achievement but a way of life. Only time—and sequels—will tell if Strange has learned this most important lesson of all.

Notes

1. All movie dialogue in this chapter is from the 2016 film *Doctor Strange*.
2. Roger Shattuck, *Forbidden Knowledge: From Prometheus to Pornography* (New York: St. Martin's Press, 1996), 327.
3. Aristotle, *Nicomachean Ethics* (350 BCE), available at http://classics.mit.edu/Aristotle/nicomachaen.html

4. For more, see Heather Battaly, "Virtue Epistemology," *Philosophy Compass* 3/4(2008): 639–663, and John Greco and John Turri, "Virtue Epistemology," in the *Stanford Encyclopedia of Philosophy*, available at https://plato.stanford.edu/archives/win2016/entries/epistemology-virtue/
5. As a famous web-crawling virtue epistemologist knows, "with great power comes great responsibility."
6. James A. Montmarquet, "Epistemic Virtue," *Mind* 96(1987): 482–497.
7. Ibid., 484.
8. Ibid.
9. Ibid.

7
Doctor Strange, Socratic Hero?

Chad William Timm

A bite from a radioactive spider, exposure to radioactivity, or a super-soldier serum are not enough to make someone a hero. Sure, adamantium claws, repulsor-powered armor, and concussive eye-beams make it easier for our favorite superheroes to do what they do, but true heroism requires something more—the choice to live the kind of life that helps separate the good from the bad in the Marvel Universe.

Stephen Strange, the Master of the Mystic Arts, not only chose to live the life of a hero, but did so in such a way that links him to one of the most important philosopher-heroes of all time. In making the choice to pursue the Mystic Arts and dedicating himself to living a life devoted to seeking wisdom, acting rightly, and improving society, Doctor Strange set out on a trail blazed more than 2000 years ago by the original philosopher and hero, Socrates (469–399 BCE). What does making the choice to be a hero have to do with Socrates, and is the life of a philosopher even heroic? Is there such a thing as a Socratic Hero?

Intellectual Humility—Who Has It?

For Socrates, the philosopher's life involves admitting what you don't know, examining your life, seeking wisdom, living rightly, and being courageous enough to challenge your neighbors to live similarly. Well, Socrates lived this life in Athens back in the day, and made many enemies who accused him of corrupting the minds of the youth and

Doctor Strange and Philosophy: The Other Book of Forbidden Knowledge,
First Edition. Edited by Mark D. White.
© 2018 John Wiley & Sons Ltd. Published 2018 by John Wiley & Sons Ltd.

believing in false gods. They tried and convicted him, and eventually put him to death.[1]

The foundation of Socratic heroism is *intellectual humility*, the willingness to recognize the limits of our knowledge and admit our mistakes. Socrates went even further—he actually claimed he had no wisdom. When the Oracle at Delphi told his good friend Chaerephon that Socrates was the wisest person in all of Athens, Socrates responded by disagreeing with the Oracle: "For I'm too aware that I've no claim to being wise in anything either great or small."[2] The foundation of Socrates' wisdom and his philosophy rested on a belief in wondering, questioning, and seeking answers to important philosophical questions, like what it means to be wise, virtuous, and beautiful? The key for Socrates, and therefore Socratic Heroism, is approaching these questions with the humility to admit that which we don't know.[3]

Does the word "humility" apply to Doctor Strange? Before becoming the Master of the Mystic Arts, Stephen Strange the neurosurgeon was hardly humble. In fact, he would be better described as egotistical and arrogant. Before the accident that ended his medical career, Strange was self-centered and materialistic, as fellow physician Christine Palmer pointed out in the film when she told him, "Stephen, everything is about you!"[4] Strange only performed procedures that either made him money or fame; as he told a colleague, "I might agree to help your research project—for a slightly reduced fee—if you agreed to name any cures we discover after me!"[5] Instead of recognizing the limits of his own knowledge and accepting responsibility for his mistakes, Strange proclaims: "I must be the best ... the greatest!!! Or else ... nothing!"[6] There's no way *this* Stephen Strange is a Socratic Hero—it's not until his life-changing accident that he is forced to confront the limits of his knowledge.

Wisdom and the Wizard

Socrates displayed intellectual humility when, as a result of the Oracle's proclamation, he set out on a journey to discover wisdom. Instead of accepting the Oracle's statement at face value, Socrates set out to doubt all assumptions, accepting only those truths that could be supported through logic, reason, and evidence. While recognizing he did not know everything, Socrates set out to question those who claimed to be wise. By the time Socrates faced the charges of corrupting the youth and believing in false gods, he had developed quite the reputation for embarrassing some of the most influential men of Athens.

Because Socrates believed in using reason and logic to understand the world around him, he approached those individuals who claimed to be wise and questioned them in a systematic way that we now call the Socratic Method. After first asking someone to define wisdom and to explain why they believed they were wise, Socrates would ask follow-up questions and point out errors in the person's logic. According to Socrates, "Where wisdom is concerned, those who had the best reputations were practically the most deficient, whereas men who were thought to be their inferiors were much better off."[7] Socrates concluded that those who claimed to be wise really weren't wise at all, just as the Ancient One quickly sized up Strange when he arrived in Kamar-Taj.

After questioning a self-proclaimed wise man, Socrates concluded that

> I'm wiser than that person. For it's likely that neither of us knows anything fine and good, but he thinks he knows something he doesn't know, whereas I, since I don't in fact know, don't think that I do either.[8]

For Socrates, the first step to acquiring wisdom was recognizing how little he knew. Once a person does this, they can seek out those who claim to be knowledgeable in certain areas in the hopes of learning from their wisdom, as Stephen Strange finally did when he decided to seek out the Ancient One in Kamar-Taj. Strange's debilitating hand injuries forced him to confront the limits of his own knowledge, but he didn't do so easily or gracefully. Even in his vulnerable state, he continued to be arrogant, as exemplified by his challenge to his physical therapist: "Answer me this, bachelor's degree, have you known anyone with nerve damage this severe do this and actually recover?" It isn't until he travels to Kamar-Taj and meets the Ancient One that Strange discovers how little he really knows, and it is at this point that his journey in search of wisdom truly begins.

Socrates recognized the limits of human knowledge, and as a result devoted his life to the search for wisdom. Stephen Strange's arrogance caused him to take wisdom for granted, since he believed he already knew everything he needed to know, and certainly more than anyone else. Just as Socrates questioned the Athenians who claimed to be wise, the Ancient One questioned Stephen Strange. The Ancient One told him that his intellectual arrogance prevented him from recognizing the limits of his own knowledge when she said, "You're a man who's looking at the world through a keyhole," and that he "could see in part, but not the whole." Likewise, Mordo told him to "forget everything you think you know." This theme is found in the comics, as well, where the Ancient One told Strange, "There are more ways to see than with your eyes, man of the western world!"[9]

The Ancient One's demonstration of the Mystic Arts allows him to see the importance of saving the world from unforeseen inter-dimensional foes. On one occasion in the comics, Eternity—the living embodiment of the universe—told Strange that "you already possess the means to defeat your foes! Power is not the only answer! Events have occurred which require a key... and wisdom is that key!"[10] As a result of this training and advice, Strange finally realized that "I have truly gained the greatest power of all... that which is the fountainhead of all other power... I have gained the gift of knowledge!"[11] Through his initial encounter with the Ancient One, Doctor Strange began to resemble a Socratic Hero in that he recognized the limits of his own knowledge and committed his life to the search for wisdom.

Doctor, Examine Thyself!

Intellectual humility requires, and depends on, a constant process of self-examination in which you take a hard look at yourself, your society, and its traditions, question your assumptions and perspectives, and act only on those conclusions that are reasonable and logical. In order to widen the keyhole, you first must realize that you're looking through a keyhole. Socrates believed that everyone except philosophers assumed what they experienced with their senses was true and real, whereas he believed the actual truth existed only in the heavens.[12] In order to learn the truth of wisdom, virtue, and beauty, Socratic Heroes must step outside themselves and engage in deep self-examination.

The Ancient One reflected this Socratic Heroism when telling Strange on one occasion, "The mind, my son, is the truest realm of all! He who controls it ... controls the very soul of its owner!"[13] Strange initially resisted this notion, preferring to rely on his scientific knowledge of the natural world, and confusingly asked himself: "Am I a man of science—or a helpless prey to superstition?"[14] Strange first recognized the limits of his own knowledge in the film when the Ancient One explained that "we're just another tiny momentary speck within an indifferent universe" and pushed Strange's astral form out of his physical form, "a place where the soul exists apart from the body." After Strange experienced being in his astral form and returned to his body, he asked the Ancient One why she did this. She replied, "To show you just how much you don't know." Thanks to the Ancient

One, Strange literally left his body and was able to look at it from an entirely new perspective, examining himself through a keyhole he never could have imagined existed.

This, according to Socrates, is the essence of the examined life. As a matter of fact, Socrates argued that living without this kind of self-examination wasn't living at all and asserted that

> It's the greatest good for a man to discuss virtue every day, and the other things you've heard me discussing and examining myself and others about, on the grounds that the unexamined life isn't worth living for a human being.[15]

Following his encounter with the Ancient One, Strange chose to devote his life to study and self-examination, as detailed in his 1963 origin story:

> And so it began! The days turned to weeks, to months, to years, as Dr. Strange studied the long-dead mystic arts! Slowly he changed … Slowly his life took on a new deeper meaning … Slowly he prepared himself for the epic battles ahead, the battles which could only be won by Dr. Strange, Master of Black Magic![16]

With his newfound intellectual humility and passion for learning, Doctor Strange set down the path of Socratic Heroism.

A Sorcerer Supreme Stands Up for Others

While intellectual humility and the examined life shine the spotlight directly on the "wannabe" philosopher, Socratic Heroism also includes a social component that looks outward. Socrates believed that seeking wisdom and living virtuously mattered in and of itself, but he also felt that living a life of self-examination leads one to help others. After all, Socrates claimed: "The most important thing isn't living, but living well … and living well and living rightly are the same thing."[17]

Part of living well and rightly is seeking to improve society. Socrates loved his home city of Athens and the people who lived there. In fact, he loved his fellow Athenians so much that he risked his life to challenge them to examine their own lives. When he was tried for corrupting the youth and preaching about false gods, Socrates could have apologized, brought his family before the jury, and begged for forgiveness. Instead he used the Socratic Method and systematically refuted the charges against him, embarrassing his accusers in the process. Why? Because it was the correct thing to do for someone who challenged his neighbors to live rightly and examine themselves in order to save Athenian society from moral decay.

A dedication to saving society from the unseen forces of interdimensional evil served as an important factor in Doctor Strange's transformation from intellectual arrogance to humility, from his tunnel vision of selfish ambition to his literal self-examination upon leaving his physical form. Once enlightened by the wisdom of the Ancient One, Strange dedicated himself to saving the Earth, proclaiming, "Mine is the mastery of the mystic arts! And I shall use it for good—as long as I live!"[18] In the film, Kaecilius sought to use the Dark Dimension to grant himself immortality, at the expense of anyone who stood in his path. By contrast, Strange chose to use the mystic arts to preserve the natural order and save human life.

Both this commitment to justice and his aversion to causing harm exemplify Socratic Heroism. After being unjustly convicted and sentenced to death, Socrates could have escaped with the help of his followers to live another day. Instead, he argued that leaving Athens without convincing the jury of his innocence would break the law, thus purposefully harming those who made the law: "So one shouldn't do injustice in return for injustice, as the majority of people think—seeing that one should *never* do injustice."[19] Doctor Strange regularly seeks to protect others from injustice, going so far as to exclaim, "No fellow man in need of help is a stranger."[20]

To Dare Danger

Doctor Strange sees himself as the sole defense against unimaginably dangerous threats to civilization. Of course, it's overwhelming at times. As he says,

Why has this dread mantle—the weight of a world besieged—fallen upon my shoulders? Why must it be I who suffers—who must stand almost alone against the powers of ancient evil? I am but a mortal ... a mere man![21]

Despite the incredible challenge of saving the entire world, Strange forges on because, as he notes, "My oath provides that I must aid any and all humans—I dare make no exceptions!"[22] Similarly, for Socrates, living the life of a philosopher took immense courage, a key feature of a hero.

The life of a Socratic Hero can be dangerous, and there's a chance that living this life could result in severe physical harm—especially when the hero tries to improve and protect society by confronting threats to its existence. Playing the gadfly and pointing out the faults of your neighbors won't make you the most popular person in town, but is nonetheless essential, as Socrates recognized during his trial:

> It's as just such a gadfly, it seems to me, that the god has attached me to the city—one that awakens, persuades, and reproaches each and every one of you and never stops alighting, everywhere on you the whole day.[23]

While Socrates sought to protect Athens from the threat of moral decay, Doctor Strange devoted himself to protecting the world from dark and evil inter-dimensional forces. In both of these cases, the Socratic Hero must possess great courage to act on what they believe to be right and wrong, despite great pressure to do otherwise. (Who would have thought that the life of a philosopher could be so dangerous?)

Socratic Heroism requires that you maintain your principles in the face of great pressure to do otherwise. The examined life of the philosopher in Socrates' day was counter-cultural, and even his students tried to pressure him to escape punishment. While Socrates was sitting in jail awaiting his execution, Crito, one of his best students, revealed a plan in the works to help Socrates escape to another city. If Socrates didn't escape, according to Crito, "Many people, who don't know you or me well, will think that I didn't care about you, since I could have saved you if I'd been willing to spend the money."[24] True to his philosophy, Socrates challenged Crito with a series of questions about whether the opinion of the many matter more than the opinion of the few experts, concluding that "We should not give so much thought to what the majority of people will say about us, but think instead of what the person who understands just and unjust things will say—the one man and the truth itself."[25]

Before his accident, the arrogant and self-centered Stephen Strange lived for what others thought of him, seeking glory, fame, and wealth. After Strange began a life of self-examination and intellectual humility, though, the concerns of the many faded from his mind and he instead—as Socrates advised—sought the opinion of a wise one, looking for truth itself. He professed, "Ancient One, I crave a boon—though I am totally unworthy to receive it! I wish to study at your feet... learn the knowledge of the mystic arts which is yours alone!"[26] Slowly but surely, Strange transformed, not only into a man of humility and a sorcerer supreme, but a true Socratic Hero, by accepting his own limitations and looking for wisdom in the right place.

Socratic Heroes must be willing to sacrifice their own safety for what they believe to be right. Time and time again, Doctor Strange faced death in order to save humanity. When confronting a foe in the comic, he thinks to himself, "I must do something! I can't let my friends perish," then announces, "I'll give up my life trying to hold the Shambler back."[27] Like a true Socratic Hero, Doctor Strange consistently and repeatedly placed his own life at risk in defense of the helpless. Similarly, Socrates told his trial jury:

> You see, men of Athens, this is the truth of the matter: Whenever someone has stationed himself because he thinks it best … he should remain, steadfast in danger, taking no account at all of death or of anything else, in comparison to what's shameful.[28]

Socrates didn't apologize or admit guilt, because that would have been an admission of wrongdoing. Living the life of the philosopher wasn't something he felt he should apologize for, and he willingly faced death instead of renouncing the philosopher's life, whether that meant standing by his principles or preserving the well-being of the Athenian people.

The Sorcerer Socratic

While Stephen Strange began as a successful but flawed man, through his transformation, he gradually became a Socratic Hero. Both Socrates and Doctor Strange admitted the limits of their knowledge, devoted their lives to seeking wisdom, and demonstrated great courage in working to improve society. Strange expressed astonishment at the effects of his self-examination when he said to himself,

> Ironic—because there was a time when I would have scorned all uncertainty… secure that I was master of my own fate! How very little I knew then—and how self-confident I was, in those days that seem so long ago.[29]

Also, like Socrates, Strange learned to distrust the material world and instead rely on that which can't be seen, in his case, the magic he learned at Kamar-Taj. Demonstrating a commitment to bettering society, Strange devoted his life to challenging the mystic foes that threaten our world, seeking to enlighten and open the eyes of those too blind to see the threats to humanity.

Just because you aren't a mage who wakes up in the Sanctum Sanctorum with mystic relics and books around you doesn't mean you can't live the examined life of a Socratic Hero. You don't need to be a genius or a sorcerer to be humble, seek wisdom, live rightly, and improve those around you by challenging their assumptions. But keep in mind that this work never ends. As Doctor Strange recognized: "There is still more that I must know. For knowledge is the mightiest power of all. And the wisest of all is him whom I now summon."[30] What might you find once you begin your own process of self-examination?[31]

Notes

1. Socrates' trial is recounted in six dialogues; see *The Trials of Socrates: Six Classic Texts*, ed. C.D.C. Reeve (Indianapolis: Hackett Publishing, 2002).
2. Ibid., 33.
3. See I.F. Stone, *The Trial of Socrates* (New York: Doubleday, 1988). (This is a modern book about the trials, distinct from the classic texts collected by Reeve as listed in note 1.)
4. All quoted dialogue (for which citations to comics are not given) is from the 2016 film *Doctor Strange*.
5. *Doctor Strange*, vol. 1, #169 (June 1968), collected in *Marvel Masterworks: Doctor Strange, Volume 3* (2007).
6. *Strange Tales*, vol. 1, #115 (December 1963), "The Origin of Dr. Strange," collected in *Marvel Masterworks: Doctor Strange, Volume 1* (2003).
7. Reeve, *Trials of Socrates*, 33–34.
8. Ibid., 33.
9. *Doctor Strange*, vol. 1, #169.
10. *Strange Tales*, vol. 1, #138 (November 1965), "If Eternity Should Fail!," collected in *Marvel Masterworks: Doctor Strange, Volume 1*.
11. *Strange Tales*, vol. 1, #133 (June 1965), "A Nameless Land, a Nameless Time!," collected in *Marvel Masterworks: Doctor Strange, Volume 1*.
12. Socrates goes to great lengths to describe the immortality of the soul and universal truths in the dialogue *Phaedrus*, where he makes the point that when one witnesses beauty, or experiences that which is truly good, that beauty and goodness are reflections of the universal forms of beauty and goodness that the soul experienced in the heavens (*Phaedrus*, trans. Alexander Nehamas and Paul Woodruff, Indianapolis: Hackett Publishing, 1995).

13. *Doctor Strange*, vol. 1, #169.
14. Ibid.
15. Reeve, *Trials of Socrates*, 55.
16. *Strange Tales*, vol. 1, #115, "The Origin of Dr. Strange."
17. Reeve, *Trials of Socrates*, 69.
18. *Marvel Premiere* #3 (July 1972), collected in *Doctor Strange Epic Collection: A Separate Reality* (2016).
19. Reeve, *Trials of Socrates*, 70.
20. *Marvel Premiere* #4 (September 1972), collected in *Doctor Strange Epic Collection: A Separate Reality*.
21. *Marvel Premiere* #5 (November 1972), collected in *Doctor Strange Epic Collection: A Separate Reality*.
22. *Strange Tales*, vol. 1, #119 (April 1964), "Beyond the Purple Veil!," collected in *Marvel Masterworks: Doctor Strange, Volume 1*.
23. Reeve, *Trials of Socrates*, 46.
24. Ibid., 64.
25. Ibid., 69.
26. *Doctor Strange*, vol. 1, #169.
27. *Marvel Premiere* #6 (January 1973), collected in *Doctor Strange Epic Collection: A Separate Reality*.
28. Reeve, *The Trials of Socrates*, 43.
29. *Doctor Strange*, vol. 1, #169.
30. *Marvel Premiere* #3.
31. I'm indebted to my colleague Professor Steve Snyder for teaching me about what it means to be a Socratic Hero. For all things heroic, check out his blog at http://myfallsemester.blogspot.com/

Are We All "Looking at the World Through a Keyhole"?
Knowledge, Ignorance, and Bias

Carina Pape

Neurosurgeon Stephen Strange believes only in science and himself—until he crashes both his Lamborghini Huracán and his "magic" hands. Since no modern medical treatment can restore his medical abilities, he takes a chance and heads for Kathmandu to find a cure there. The Ancient One gets to the heart of Strange's problem with the metaphor of "looking at the world through a keyhole."[1] Before Strange can begin to heal, he needs to acknowledge his limited perspective, to see his blind spots and admit his biases. The claim that you can see your blind spots or know your own ignorance sounds like a Zen Buddhist's *kōan*, a paradox such as "the sound of one hand clapping," and philosophers of all types love a good paradox. Is it possible to acknowledge our own ignorance? How can we know what we know at all?

Believing in One's Knowledge and Knowing One's Ignorance

Philosopher Francis Bacon (1561–1626) was pretty confident of scientific knowledge and skeptical toward magic. Not only did he reject the belief in magic, he judged its adherents as dangerous, especially "writers on natural magic or alchemy, and men of that sort; who are a kind of suitors and lovers of fables."[2] (Too bad he didn't live to read *Doctor Strange* comics!) Bacon advocated the scientific method, based on making observations, forming hypotheses, and testing them though

Doctor Strange and Philosophy: The Other Book of Forbidden Knowledge, First Edition. Edited by Mark D. White.
© 2018 John Wiley & Sons Ltd. Published 2018 by John Wiley & Sons Ltd.

experimentation. His slogan was: "Human knowledge and human power meet in one." This certainly sounds like the early Stephen Strange: both have a firm belief in science and knowledge (especially their *own* knowledge). When Strange argues with the Ancient One, because he doesn't believe in "healing through believing," he says, "I do not believe in fairytales about chakras, or energy, or the power of belief. There is no such thing as spirit! We are made of matter, and nothing more."

Bacon was forced to take a stand against superstition among the people, the church, and the scholastic tradition. The irony is that Bacon's belief in the power of science to generate knowledge was just as much a belief. This belief led to a tremendous increase in human knowledge, progress, and well-being, but that simply makes the belief in the scientific method a useful belief. As a belief, it can be biased, just like Strange's disbelief in the power of belief.

If Bacon can be considered a "master of the philosophical arts," then Socrates (470/469–399 BCE) is likely philosophy's Ancient One who gave us the paradox in which he claimed an awareness of his own ignorance. As the common paraphrasing goes: "I know one thing: that I know nothing."[3] In other words, Socrates was aware of his own blind spots. This is actually less paradoxical than it seems: To *be aware of* your blind spots is not the same as *seeing* your blind spots. You can be aware that there's something missing without being able to describe it. To acknowledge one's lack of knowledge at all, though, is wisdom worthy of an Ancient One.

Somehow, Socrates was as critical toward human knowledge as Bacon was toward believing and magic. Does such a self-critical approach save us from bias, though? Just before the Ancient One dies, she and Doctor Strange watch lightning in slow motion in their astral body forms. She tells him, "I spent so many years, peering through time, looking at this exact moment. But I can't see past it." If the Ancient One in *Doctor Strange* has a blind spot, what about philosophy's Ancient One?

"We're Not Savages"

In *Doctor Strange*, the partiality of knowledge and understanding resulting from bias is a running gag. Consider what happens when Strange introduces himself to his enemy Kaecilius:

KAECILIUS: How long have you been at Kamar-Taj, Mister...
STRANGE: "Doctor."

KAECILIUS: Mister Doctor.
STRANGE: It's "Strange."
KAECILIUS: Maybe. Who am I to judge?

The joke is on Strange, though, who's taking his medical title too seriously, even after losing the ability to perform surgery. While Kaecilius
is blind to the meaning of this title, Strange is blind to the fact that in
the realm of sorcerers, he is indeed just a "Mister"—and that it isn't
the end of the world.

Strange and Kaecilius demonstrate that such ignorance is possible
even when you speak the same language, because they lack a common
cultural background. Bias also becomes evident when there are dis-
parities rooted in gender and race. For example, the white colonialists
who conquered North America weren't able to understand the native
people, missing their words and their meaning (and probably didn't
worry about it too much). Throughout their history, both comic books
and philosophy have missed the perspectives of both women and people of color. Although in recent years there has been an encouraging
increase in the number of women visible and successful in the comics
scene, it is still largely a male realm—just like philosophy. Most of the
people recognized as influential in both comics and philosophy since
their beginnings have also been white. Those white men naturally saw
the world through a certain, and limited, perspective.

While science has issues with gender and race, it has a specific bias
regarding its own objectivity. Objectivity and impartiality might be
fine intentions, but science is practiced by human beings who usually
don't have all-seeing eyes or supernatural powers that enable them to
"peer through time." Scientists are people with goals, ambitions, and
flaws like the rest of us, who aspire to noble ends but cannot do so
perfectly, in part because of their inherent biases and blind spots. Even
a genius with a photographic memory like Stephen Strange doesn't
see the big picture, but only parts of it. Many feminist philosophers
argue that the ideal of impartiality itself is biased or characterized by
partiality.[4] Ironically, the longing for objectivity, universality, and
impartiality leads to a partial and biased perspective—if we ignore the
wise words of Socrates and the Ancient One to "be aware of your
ignorance."

As a man of medicine, Doctor Strange has a scientific mindset and
holds a partial perspective in many ways, concerning not only his
own lack of knowledge but also other people (his girlfriend,
colleagues, and the sorcerers) and other cultures. For example, when

he's brought to his chamber at the Kamar-Taj, Mordo gives him a small paper with the word "Shamballa" on it. Strange asks, "And what's this, my mantra?" Mordo answers with a knowing smile: "The wifi password. We're not savages." This exchange succinctly shows the biased attitude of western people toward others, which grounds cultural, ethnic, or racial prejudices. By reproducing these prejudices, Strange reveals himself to be the opposite of the self-critical Socratic. He represents unknowing instead, because he doesn't know what he doesn't know, and doesn't acknowledge his own lack of knowledge.

Looking at the World Through a Keyhole... or a Colored Glass

But... aren't we all biased? Aren't we all looking at the world through a keyhole? Of course! Scientist and explorer Georg Forster (1754–1794) claimed that we all are looking through a "colored glass"—green glasses were a popular fashion accessory in his time—shaped by our cultural background. Looking through a colored glass is another metaphor for being biased. Whether you look through a keyhole or green glasses, in both cases you're not able to see the true big picture, but only a truncated or filtered version. Forster emphasized that we can't simply take off our filters, which are our individual cultural backgrounds.

On the bright (green) side, limitations—or, more precisely, the frustration linked to them—can motivate us to overcome them, like infants learning to crawl or walk. Once we realize that we don't see the big picture, we often start trying to figure out how to see more, leading us to overcome our biases and filters. Also, scientific progress wouldn't be possible without some degree of bias. For example, to specialize in one problem or area of scientific inquiry requires us to put on metaphorical blinders, to focus on one thing and to block out others. Acknowledging one's own biases, and having the desire and will to overcome them, are already big steps. In this sense, maybe Forster's self-critical attitude enabled him to describe the people of Polynesia with empathy instead of western bias.

One popular example of this bias was the romanticized idea of the "noble savage." Though it's a so-called "positive prejudice" to say that "all savages are noble," it's more of a backhanded compliment—"savage" is still an insult. Strange stumbles on exactly that prejudice when he misinterprets the wifi password as a mantra. In this way, the movie *Doctor Strange* goes one step further and *addresses* this prejudice by mocking its source. The partiality of perspectives is seen in many instances throughout the movie, but the main one is the clash of the modern and scientific with the ancient and mystical, as well as their equation with "Western" and "Eastern" resulting from cultural biases. As with the wifi example, we can ask: Does *Doctor Strange* perpetuate these biases or help to expose them? To answer that, we'll step outside the story and consider an example of bias with the film itself.

Whitewashing the Ancient One

The term *whitewashing* refers to the tendency of Hollywood moviemakers to cast white actors to play characters originally written or portrayed as people of color, for financial, political, or prejudicial reasons. For example, producers of the 2010 videogame adaption *Prince of Persia* chose to cast Jake Gyllenhaal rather than a Persian actor, and producers of the 2017 live-action remake of the classic 1995 Japanese anime film *Ghost in the Shell* chose to cast Scarlett Johansson (also known as Black Widow from the Marvel movies) rather than an Asian actress.[5] The 2016 film *Gods of Egypt* featured an almost exclusively white cast, and in M. Night Shyamalan's *The Last Airbender* (2010), a live-action adaptation of the beloved animated series *Avatar*, whitewashing was taken even further: "not only the ethnicity of the individual characters, but the message of acceptance and cultural diversity that the original series advocated" was distorted.[6]

In *Doctor Strange*, the character of the Ancient One, who in the comics is old, male, and Asian, was played in the film by Tilda Swinton, a marvelous and enigmatic performer who is young, female, and white. This decision, as with the others mentioned, was criticized as yet another example of Hollywood whitewashing. But there's another complication due to the fact that the character of the Ancient One as originally portrayed in the comics is controversial as well. One of the movie's screenwriters, C. Robert Cargill, compared the task of casting the Ancient One to the Kobayashi Maru, the no-win scenario from *Star Trek*: Casting a non-Asian actor would be seen as whitewashing, but casting an Asian actor could have reproduced the racist stereotype inherent in the original character.[7] Cargill mentioned that they wanted at least to avoid a stereotypical Asian villain, especially given the questionable actions the Ancient One takes in the film, such as lying to her disciples, defying natural law, and drawing magic from the Dark Dimension to prolong her life. In addition, the Ancient One, as introduced in Doctor Strange's first appearance in *Strange Tales* #110 (July 1963), looked less like the kindly, wise Tibetan monk we now think of, and more like a typical Fu Manchu-type character from the days of the "Yellow Peril," a time of irrational and hateful fear of the East.

According to Cargill, there is "no other character in Marvel history that is such a cultural landmine; that is absolutely unwinnable." But that's not true, and this is not the first time that Marvel Studios had to face this issue. Although the Ancient One may be a racist stereotype, he's definitely no villain, unlike Iron Man's arch-foe, the Mandarin. Not only is the Mandarin an obvious descendant of the Fu Manchu stereotype, but the character himself claims to be a descendant of Genghis Khan, one of the real-world sources of the stereotype itself.

Stereotypes, Supervillains, and Fortune Cookies

The best thing to do with such a stereotype may be to sidestep it and transform it into something completely different. For example, all that remained from the Mandarin in the first two *Iron Man* movies is the terrorist group named "The Ten Rings" after the otherworldly jewelry that gives the Mandarin his power. However, avoiding offensive stereotypes is not the only reasons that filmmakers change characters and settings. Sometimes, as with *Ghost in the Shell* or *Prince of Persia*, economics is the main reason: the producers felt that Scarlett Johansson and Jake Gyllenhaal would simply be larger box-office draws, despite the backlash around whitewashing.

Another practical consideration is to ensure the widest audience possible, for which filmmakers often change controversial characters that have some relation to politics in a major international market to avoid the movie being banned by local authorities. Cargill cited the fear that *Doctor Strange* would not be shown in China, "one of the biggest film-watching countries in the world," as one of the reasons they changed the location of Kamar-Taj from Tibet to Nepal. Other times, settings are changed simply to reflect the times. The location of Tony Stark's capture and development of his original armor with Ho Yinsen was changed from the Vietnam War of the comics to Afghanistan in 2008's *Iron Man*. As director Jon Favreau explained, they did this to "maintain an emotional reflection of the fear of our times."[8]

In this context, it seemed risky to have the Mandarin be the leader of the Ten Rings in 2013's *Iron Man 3*, because his name bears a strong association with Chinese ethnicity. Furthermore, he was portrayed by Ben Kingsley, best known for his portrayal of the title character in the 1982 film, *Gandhi*. Kingsley was born Krishna Pandit Bhanji; his mother was a white actress and model from London, and his father was a medical doctor born of Indian descent. This actually quite parallels the Mandarin's own heritage in the comics: his father was a wealthy Chinese of Mongolian descent and his mother was a British noblewoman.

Despite the apparent similarity between Kingsley and the Mandarin, the filmmakers subverted the Fu Manchu stereotype in another way. In the film we learn that "the Mandarin" is just a character portrayed by the British actor Trevor Slattery (played by Kingsley), used to leverage Western biases and prejudices to make the Ten Rings more frightening. The real villain is Aldrich Killian, a white American and scientific genius, who was rejected and humiliated by Tony Stark years earlier. When detailing his evil plans to Stark, he explains that he invented the Mandarin because people need a "target," comparing him to Osama bin Laden and Saddam Hussein.

In this way, the filmmakers transform the Mandarin into a critical comment on both racial biases and whitewashing. A white man, Killian, constructs a crude amalgam of stereotypes in the Mandarin: the name's Chinese association, props associated with the East in his fake propaganda videos, and the Middle Eastern aspects tied to the Afghan terrorist group. And the *pièce de résistance* is that he picks a British actor to portray this absurdly manipulative character (which refers back to the casting of the British, white actor Christopher Lee to play Fu Manchu in the 1960s films). As the Mandarin puts it in the film, "A true story about fortune cookies: they look Chinese, they sound Chinese, but they're actually an American invention, which is why they're hollow, full of lies, and leave a bad taste in the mouth."

Strange Transformations

While the Mandarin was transformed into a kind of jester who holds a mirror up to the tradition of Hollywood's adoption of racist stereotypes, the character of the Ancient One is transformed even more while not becoming a parody of itself. The filmmakers behind *Doctor Strange* not only avoided the Fu Manchu stereotype of the original comics portrayal, but went even further by casting a white and female performer in the role. In a Socratic sense, resistance to stereotypes is more powerful when they're referred to. By doing so, filmmakers (and other artists) acknowledge their own inability to simply get rid of biases, and instead shines a light on both this inability and their own biases—sometimes in a humorous way.

As mentioned, prejudices and biases are a running gag throughout the movie, mostly at the expense of Doctor Strange himself. For example, when he first enters Kamar-Taj, Strange addresses an elderly Asian man as the Ancient One without any good reason. The man, who is actually another sorcerer named Master Hamir, doesn't answer, but leaves the room silently, after which the real Ancient One reveals *her*self. In the comics, Hamir the Hermit is the servant of the Ancient One and also the father of Wong, who in turn becomes Doctor Strange's servant. This depiction in itself is not very flattering, rendering most of the Asian characters in the Doctor Strange comics as either servants or villains. (Despite his wisdom and power, even the Ancient One is often cast as a helpless victim or captive in the comics who must be rescued by his favorite student.)

Hamir's upgrade in the movie from servant to master was acknowledged by the critics (although they took exception with his portrayal as the stereotype of the "silent Asian"). The same critics, however, praised the movie for offering "a glimmer of hope when it comes to Asian representation, in the character of Master Wong," shown as "funny, smart, and, supposedly skilled."[9] As the same time that several Asian characters were shown in a better light than usual, the main Caucasian character, Stephen Strange, was knocked down a few pegs. In the comics, he is shown as cool, collected, and amazingly competent, both before and after his life-altering accident. In the movie, his transformation is more drastic. He changes from an astonishingly arrogant man to a humble disciple of the Ancient One.

Casting a woman as the Ancient One also addresses a pervasive bias: equating power with maleness. Instead of having a younger man trained in powerful magic by an older man, the film makes the teacher a woman, subverting yet another stereotype about the transfer of power and knowledge from man to man, with women a secondary consideration. Strange is a confident male in a powerful position in the beginning, but nonetheless with a very limited perspective on knowledge, culture, and gender. Just as he assumes the Ancient One would be a man, he also doubts his colleague and former lover Doctor Christine Palmer's value, responding to her advice that "there are other things that can give your life meaning" with a dismissive, "Like what? Like *you*?" In both cases we see his biases with respect to women, and in both cases those women lead to his personal enlightenment.

We Can All Be Socratics Supreme

Bias can't be completely avoided, and stereotypes and prejudices formed through centuries won't disappear in our lifetimes. Because they survive through mindless reproduction, they must be actively confronted to expose them to our consciousness, expanding our personal keyholes. *Doctor Strange* does both, addressing issues of bias with insight and a dash of humor. It makes us reconsider our biases regarding gender, race, and culture, as well as the ways we try to address these biases in our lives, including the ways we choose to critique bias itself. We don't need the Eye of Agamotto to reflect on our own limited perspectives and ignorance—just a little inspiration from the Socratic Supreme!

Notes

1. Unless stated otherwise, all quoted dialogue is from the 2016 film *Doctor Strange*.
2. Francis Bacon, *Novum Organum* (1858), Book II, Chapter XXIX, available at https://en.wikisource.org/wiki/Novum_Organum/Book_II_(Spedding)
3. In general, see Plato's *Apology*, available at http://classics.mit.edu/Plato/apology.html
4. See, for instance, Miranda Fricker, "Feminism in Epistemology: Pluralism without Postmodernism," in Miranda Fricker and Jennifer Hornsby (eds.), *The Cambridge Companion to Feminism in Philosophy* (Cambridge: Cambridge University Press, 2000), 146–165.
5. For more examples, see Jessica Kiang, "The 20 Worst Examples of Hollywood Whitewashing," *IndieWire*, February 23, 2016, available at http://www.indiewire.com/2016/02/the-20-worst-examples-of-hollywood-whitewashing-268110/. *Ghost in the Shell* is perhaps the best-known recent example, although the issue is more complicated in that case. The director of the original anime, Mamoru Oshii, approved of the casting because the character was a cyborg whose face in the original resembled Johansson's. Also, the question of race or ethnicity is complex when it comes to manga and anime. For example, Usagi

Tsukino, better known as Sailor Moon, has a distinctly "Caucasian" appearance to Westerners. To Japanese readers, however, the light eye and hair color are not related to race or ethnicity, but rather have a metaphorical meaning based on color symbolism: purple hair points to royalty, for example, and blonde hair to childlikeness. My Japanese friends tell me that manga and anime characters basically "have no ethnicity or race at all." Nevertheless, *Ghost in the Shell* has several other questionable aspects: for instance, none of the philosophical conversations from the original survived the adaptation and, as a result, the innovative female role of Major Kusanagi lost a lot of her intellectual appeal. (But that's a topic for another book!)

6. Michael Le of Racebending.com, as quoted in Deepti Hajela, "Critics: 'Airbender,' 'Prince' Were 'Whitewashed,'" *The Washington Times*, May 25, 2010, available at http://www.washingtontimes.com/news/2010/may/25/critics-airbender-prince-persia-whitewashed/

7. This and all subsequent quotes from Cargill are from "Exclusive! Doctor Strange Writer C. Robert Cargill – Double Toasted Interview," April 22, 2016, available at https://www.youtube.com/watch?v=eEpbUf8dGq0

8. Edward Douglas, "Exclusive: An In-Depth Iron Man Talk with Jon Favreau," *SuperHeroHype*, April 29, 2008, available at http://www.superherohype.com/features/96427-exclusive-an-in-depth-iron-man-talk-with-jon-favreau#FZH5ybP75MBE3Heb.99

9. Olivia Truffaut-Wong, "'Doctor Strange' Avoids One Asian Stereotype with the Ancient One But Reinforces Another," *Bustle*, November 4, 2016, available at https://www.bustle.com/articles/192678-doctor-strange-avoids-one-asian-stereotype-with-the-ancient-one-but-reinforces-another. For more on the complexity of Wong, see Chapter 18 by Malloy in this volume.

Stephen Strange vs. Ayn Rand

A Doesn't Always Equal A

Edwardo Pérez

When Doctor Strange strikes a "bargain" with Dormammu—one that forces the extradimensional demon to leave Earth or spend eternity in an endless time loop—it doesn't just save the world. It also represents the culmination of a philosophical debate on natural law throughout the 2016 film *Doctor Strange*, suggesting that sometimes, such as when the world is about to be devoured by an evil dark lord, it might be okay to fudge the rules a bit. Strange and Wong are happy with the results: things return to normal, with people eating dinner, kids bouncing balls, and Kaecilius and the zealots shriveling up and drifting away to oblivion.

Not so much for Mordo, however, who points out to Wong and Strange that, while they won, they did so "by also violating the natural law," just as their teacher, the Ancient One, did when she drew power from the Dark Dimension to extend her life. Mordo asks, "You still think there will be no consequences, Strange? No price to pay? We broke our rules, just like her. The bill comes due. Always! A reckoning. I will follow this path no longer."[1] Mordo isn't just angry, he's disillusioned; his worldview has been shattered, driving him to quit his life as a sorcerer. Strange, on the other hand, doesn't see immutable laws—he sees possibilities. Whether as a surgeon or sorcerer, the only limitation he's bound by is his own imagination. To Strange, natural law isn't as natural or as lawful as Mordo might think.

In this chapter, we'll look at several ways philosophy deals with natural law, especially through the work of Ayn Rand (1905–1982),

Doctor Strange and Philosophy: The Other Book of Forbidden Knowledge, First Edition. Edited by Mark D. White.
© 2018 John Wiley & Sons Ltd. Published 2018 by John Wiley & Sons Ltd.

whose thought was a major influence on one of the creators of Doctor Strange, Steve Ditko. What is natural law and what's wrong with violating it? Does the bill always come due, as Mordo claims—or does Mordo just lack imagination, as Strange claims? And, did Strange really violate natural law? Or did he actually uphold it?

Stop! Tampering with Continuum Probabilities Is Forbidden!

Natural law suggests there are universal laws in the world that are self-evident and binding on us. While philosophers from antiquity to the present have tried to list and explain these laws, offering many elaborate and nuanced positions, they haven't been able to all agree on what these laws are or how exactly they work.

Philosophers like Cicero (106–43 BCE) and St. Thomas Aquinas (1225–1274) view natural law as divinely eternal.[2] We're universally bound to follow the dictates of natural law, which we are able to know intrinsically (or *a priori*) through our reason, which is itself a gift from the divine. Furthermore, because the natural law reflects what is divinely revealed to us by our rational capacity and is not contingent on worldly circumstances, it will never change or differ over time or by place.

There are many other subtle ways we could explore natural law through the lens of philosophy, science, and governmental law (including non-Western perspectives), but there's one version that has particular relevance to Doctor Strange: the view espoused by Ayn Rand. Steve Ditko, who created the character with Marvel Comics guru Stan Lee, was such an avid follower of Rand that he seems to have modeled his life after Howard Roark, the protagonist of her novel *The Fountainhead*, who refuses to compromise his beliefs (and who Rand portrayed as an example of an ideal man).[3] Indeed, there are shades of Howard Roark in Stephen Strange. Most notably, both are supremely self-confident geniuses.

There Is No Other Way

Rand's philosophy, known as *Objectivism*, covers a lot of ground, but for our purposes, we will focus on what she perceives to be its foundation, the three basic axioms of life: existence, consciousness, and identity. For Rand, these axioms are self-evident and unassailable: existence is that which is, consciousness is that which we perceive, and identity is that which has a nature. As contemporary objectivist philosopher (and Rand's designated intellectual heir) Leonard Peikoff explains, the three axioms "must be used and accepted by everyone, including those who attack them and those who attack the concept of the self-evident."[4] As such, existence, consciousness, and identity "are at the base of knowledge and thus inescapable."[5] Or, as Rand explains, "Reality exists as an objective absolute—facts are facts, independent of man's feelings, wishes, hopes or fears."[6]

Sounds like Mordo, doesn't it? In fact, this type of absolute logic—believing that something is beyond questioning, cannot be compromised, and has no alternative—resembles the logic Mordo used with Strange. Consider the argument he makes after Kaecilius first attacked the New York Sanctum:

MORDO: These zealots will snuff us all out and you can't muster the strength to snuff them first?
STRANGE: What do you think I just did?
MORDO: You saved your own life! And then whined about it like a wounded dog.
STRANGE: Oh, you would have done it so easily?
MORDO: You've no idea the things I've done. And the answer is yes. Without hesitation.
STRANGE: Even if there's another way?
MORDO: There is no other way.
STRANGE: You lack imagination.
MORDO: No, Stephen. You lack a spine.

To some extent, Mordo gets this perspective from the Ancient One, who told Strange earlier in the film, "You want to go back to the illusion that you can control anything, even death, which no one can control. Not even the great Doctor Stephen Strange."

Certainly, the Ancient One, for all her ability and knowledge, and all her teachings that reality is shaped by thought, couldn't control her own death in the end. No matter how much power she drew from the Dark Dimension, the best she could do is postpone it, "stretching one moment into a thousand." For Mordo, "there is no other way," just as Rand's objectivism holds there are no alternatives to reality, which is not something "to be rewritten or escaped, but, solemnly and proudly, *faced*."[7] This is precisely what Mordo and the Ancient One do: they not only face reality, they embrace it. The Ancient One may have cheated death for millennia, but no matter how long she tried to stretch it out, she still accepted it when it came.

Do Two Wongs Make a Right?

But what if you *could* control death? What if Rand's axioms that Mordo and the Ancient One believe in *are* refutable? What if Strange is right, and all we need is a little imagination (and some really cool relics)? Consider what happens to Wong at the end of the movie. When Kaecilius attacks the Hong Kong Sanctum, Wong dies. After Strange uses the Eye of Agamotto to roll back time, Wong is alive again. So ... did Wong die or not?

This is a problem for the objectivist axioms. Let's focus on the third axiom, the Law of Identity. As Peikoff explains, "To be is to be something, to have a nature, to possess *identity*. A thing is itself; or, in the traditional formula, A is A."[8] Wong dies, so Wong is Dead. But Wong lives, so Wong is Alive. But Dead is not Alive, so only one statement can be true: but which is the true axiom (which A is A)? If the Law of Identity is self-evident, then which Wong is the self-evident Wong?

An easy solution would be to say that Wong is Wong because Wong is still Wong. After all, he does retain some sense of "Wongness." But this would mean that both Wongs are the same—but are they? Or did he change when Strange manipulated time? Let's see what Rand says:

> The fact that certain characteristics are, at a given time, *unknown* to man, does not indicate that these characteristics are excluded from the entity—*or from the concept*. A is A; existents are what they are, independent of the state of human knowledge; and a concept means the existents which it integrates. Thus, a concept subsumes and includes *all* the characteristics of its referents, known and not-yet-known.[9]

Rand immediately points out that characteristics must be discovered through "scientific study, observation and validation" because, as she maintains, our knowledge is open-ended.[10] We simply don't know everything (even if our astral self is able to read books while our body is sleeping) and when we learn something we add to that knowledge.

If Rand is correct, then Wong is the same Wong in both realities because his identity doesn't change. We simply gain knowledge about him that we didn't know before. We knew he died, and now we know he's alive: Wong is Wong. But here's the problem: if Wong dies and gets reanimated, is the reanimated existence really the same? He seems to be the same Wong, as if he hadn't died so much as taken a short nap or been knocked unconscious for a bit. Certainly, his personality and demeanor seem to remain the same, as do his knowledge and experience. The only thing that's different is that he knows he died and he knows Strange brought him back. (Strange apologizes for this, but Wong doesn't seem to mind, telling him, "Well, don't stop now.")

In fact, the only people who know what happened, who experienced more than one reality, are the sorcerers: Strange, Wong, Mordo, and Kaecilius and his Zealots. Given that we see the people on the street in Hong Kong return to normal, as if time simply stopped and then started again without missing a beat, we are left to assume that no one else on Earth has any idea what happened. So, is it a dilemma or not? If no one knows things have changed, does what Strange did matter?

Rand's logic suggests that we can account for the change in reality as new knowledge, but this doesn't seem enough. Certainly, Wong and Mordo remain the same people, but they have also changed. They've retained the substance of themselves, their identities, but they're also different. Wong now accepts natural law as being broken, but Mordo doesn't (and changes his life because of it). Strange changes, too, as does everyone else on Earth, even if they don't realize it. What Strange did seems to matter: there's just too much change and difference between realities to claim equivalence any more.

What if I Told You That Reality Is One of Many?

In the film, both realities exist whether people are aware of them or not, even though the second reality negates or replaces the first, and Wong lives and Earth is saved. This worked because Strange created a temporal loop hole—which, by the way, creates a third reality in which time is an infinite loop that allowed Strange to negotiate his bargain with Dormammu. In a sense, Strange's imagination permits three realities to simultaneously exist, and allows him to choose which one would ultimately prevail. (He literally controlled the fate of everyone on Earth, not bad for a Sorcerer Not-Yet-Supreme.)

Rand's objectivism seems inadequate to account for this. Unless she were to observe the three realities in the same manner as Strange did, she would have no idea that they all existed simultaneously; she would have no new knowledge. While the axioms may still be correct in each reality for those who exist in each reality, they don't apply to Strange, Mordo, Wong, Kaecilius and his Zealots, and especially to Dormammu—and this is the problem Rand's objectivism didn't anticipate. What axioms form the foundation of a multiverse? Rand says "existence exists," but which one?[11] Rand claims consciousness is "limited, finite, lawful," but what if it's unlimited, infinite, and unlawful?[12] Rand claims A is A, but what if A is the multiverse? This is why Rand's new knowledge argument doesn't work: it wouldn't be able to be scientifically explored. The multiverse can't be observed or validated except by a sorcerer like Strange. It also couldn't be dismissed on the grounds that our consciousness can't perceive a multiverse because that would be akin to dismissing reality—which we can't do if we believe in her first axiom: *existence exists*.

For Rand, saying that the reality we perceive isn't real (like Morpheus explains to Neo in *The Matrix*) dismisses our human senses. It's saying that our eyes lie to us, but this can't be true for an Objectivist because Objectivism would then collapse. According to Peikoff:

> Objectivists reject the key skeptic claim: that man perceives not reality, but only its effects on his cognitive faculty. Man perceives reality directly, not some kind of effects from it. He perceives reality *by means of* its effects on his organs of perception … Every process of knowledge involves two crucial elements: the object of cognition and the means of cognition—or, *What* do I know? and *How* do I know it? … There can be no conflict between these elements … The "how" cannot be used to negate the "what," or the "what" the "how"—not if one understands that A is A and that consciousness is consciousness.[13]

This, of course, dismisses the wealth of scientific and casual observations that show how our eyes "lie to us" all the time and that what we see is first filtered through our brain, suggesting that we see what we *want* to see or what we *need* to see, not necessarily what's actually there.

What such studies show, and what Strange and Wong acknowledge, is that what we know and how we know it could be in stark conflict. If we concede that reality is the result of our direct experience, as Peikoff and Rand contend, then the Objectivist should at least recognize the possibility that the results of that experience—the reality we perceive—may not be complete, as the Ancient One says, using her keyhole metaphor. In that analogy, Strange is initially Rand, denying the keyhole can be widened because he can't perceive its width. When the Ancient One shows him the multiverse, however, Strange is no longer Rand, but a sorcerer having to acknowledge a different perception of reality.

This doesn't imply that we should deny what our senses tell us or regard reality as an illusion, and it's more than a matter of accounting for the unknown as new knowledge. Rather, it's an acknowledgment that our senses filter reality, not in an imaginary sense, but in a protective one, recognizing that we don't need to know everything about reality in order to exist in it. Indeed, how traumatic would it be if everyone were able to perceive multidimensional space or thrust their astral bodies out of their physical bodies at will? What would happen if anyone could create a mirror dimension or manipulate nature with a relic? To paraphrase Mordo, such a scenario would definitely create "too many sorcerers" who would have trouble navigating normal life, not to mention their newfound abilities.[14]

Sorcerers' Greatest Weapons

As the Ancient One tells Strange before her death, "I've hated drawing power from the Dark Dimension. But as you well know, sometimes one must break the rules in order to serve the greater good."[15] This perspective is precisely what Mordo doesn't understand, and not just because it's antithetical to Rand's overall philosophy. For example, we might say killing is always wrong, but how many circumstances can we imagine that justify ending someone's life? More generally, we might say violating natural law is wrong, but what if we violate it to serve a higher purpose, such as the greater good?

What would Mordo have us do in such a situation? Should we obey natural law and let the world be consumed by Dormammu? Quitting your job rather than compromising your ideals is one thing, and it's what ideal men and women do in Rand's philosophy, but letting humanity perish for the same reason is another. It seems extreme and morally wrong and, as it turns out, it's also unnecessary, especially in light of Rand's conception of consciousness outlined by her second axiom.

As Peikoff explains, "Consciousness is an active process … the object of awareness, reality, simply exists … but it does not do a man's cognitive work for him nor force itself on his mind."[16] In other words, as human beings, we have to think, and for Rand, thinking is an act of choice. "You are not free to escape from your nature, from the fact that *reason* is your means of survival," writes Rand.[17] "So that for *you*, who are a human being, the question 'to be or not to be' is the question 'to think or not to think.'"[18]

Isn't this what Strange does? He arrives in Hong Kong to find the Sanctum destroyed, Wong dead, and Dormammu ready to suck Earth into his Dark Dimension. Mordo claims, "It's too late, nothing can stop him," to which Strange replies, "Not necessarily." Strange, who seems to follow Rand's directions precisely, realizes the only weapon he has is time, and he wields it like a sword, effectively defeating Kaecilius, the Zealots, and Dormammu. In other words, if we follow Rand and Peikoff, reason was Strange's means of survival. Strange didn't violate nature by manipulating time: he upheld nature and protected it by manipulating time. This is what sorcerers are supposed to do. As Wong says, "The Avengers protect the world from physical dangers. We safeguard it against more mystical threats." How do sorcerers do this? It's not just with sling rings, mirror dimensions, and magic, but with the greatest weapons they have: knowledge and reason.

They Really Should Put the Warnings Before the Spell

For an Objectivist like Mordo, knowledge must serve natural law. For Strange, however, knowledge serves the mission: he sees violating natural law as another option, and one that sometimes allows him to uphold it in a broader sense. As Wong says after catching Strange experimenting with the Eye of Agamotto, manipulating time while playing with an apple, "No knowledge in Kamar-Taj is forbidden. Only certain practices." Strange is confused because from his perspective he "was just doing exactly what it said in the book," later adding that "they really should put the warnings before the spell."

It's a nice parallel to the Garden of Eden story: Why put the Tree of Knowledge in the middle of the garden, with nice juicy apples, if you don't want anyone to eat its fruit? For Kamar-Taj, this reveals something Mordo hadn't considered: simply forbidding something doesn't work. Rather, respecting knowledge and knowing when to use it is the better lesson—and one that actually fits into Rand's objectivism. By violating natural law in the original reality and the time-looped reality, Strange restores natural law in the second reality. It was the only option Strange had to sustain existence and life in *any* reality, and therefore the best time to use that knowledge and make a choice.

Peikoff explains that, in Objectivism, man must "be in control of his own person, his own character and mind, of his inner world. Otherwise he is a helpless puppet, unintelligible to himself, ruled by a mindless destiny."[19] The point is not just that man must be able to choose but that man creates himself through choice (as Strange shapes reality).

> Man is born without innate ideas, and when he reaches the conceptual level, he is the sovereign. It is his choice to exercise his mind or not, to think or not, and that choice which he has to remake at every moment in every issue, that choice affects and controls the conclusions he comes to, the ideas he accepts, the value judgments he forms, and therefore, the actions he takes, and the emotions he feels.[20]

If this is so, then one is free to choose to violate natural law; otherwise, one couldn't be the sovereign of one's being. This means that if Mordo is free to choose not to violate natural law, then Strange must also be free to choose to violate it. Whether natural law is universal, or self-evident, or inviolable, isn't the point—what matters is the choice one makes regarding natural law.

I Control It by Surrendering Control?

In effect, Strange had the spine that Mordo and the Ancient One lacked. Strange was not only willing to defend Earth by using his knowledge and choosing to violate natural law, but in doing so he became the only one able to stand up to Dormammu and defeat him. For all the Ancient One's claims regarding Strange's ego, it may be she and Mordo who are shown to be self-centered—which, to be fair, is also part of Rand's philosophy. Was the Ancient One drawn to the possibility of immortality offered by the Dark Dimension to serve the greater good, as she claims, or for her own selfish reasons? Did Mordo quit to pursue his mission of reducing the sorcerer population because he cared about the greater good and natural law, or because his pride and his ego were hurt?

In contrast, Strange didn't choose to violate natural law for himself. Rather, he chose to sacrifice himself for natural law. Like Prometheus or Sisyphus, Strange was willing to endure a repetitive punishment for the sake of humanity—not for his ego, not because he was enslaved by morality or laws, but because he wanted everyone in the world to live. More important, he did it by exercising his Objectivist right and responsibility to make a choice. In doing so, Strange demonstrated how breaking natural law is sometimes the best way to uphold it. Will this make Rand, Peikoff, Ditko, and Mordo happy? Probably not— but that's their choice.

Notes

1. All quoted dialogue is from the 2016 film *Doctor Strange*.
2. Cicero, *The Republic and The Laws*, trans. Niall Rudd (Oxford: Oxford University Press, 2009); Thomas Aquinas, *Treatise on Law*, trans. Richard J. Regan. (Indianapolis: Hackett Publishing Company, 2000). For more on this conception of natural law, see Chapter 22 by Klofft in this volume.
3. Ayn Rand, *The Fountainhead* (Indianapolis: Bobbs-Merrill Co., 1943).
4. Leonard Peikoff, *Objectivism: The Philosophy of Ayn Rand* (New York: Meridian, 1991), 9.
5. Ibid., 11.
6. Ayn Rand, "Introducing Objectivism," available at https://campus. aynrand.org/works/1962/01/01/introducing-objectivism
7. Ibid.
8. Peikoff, *Objectivism*, 6.
9. Ayn Rand, *Introduction to Objectivist Epistemology*, expanded second edition, ed. Harry Binswanger and Leonard Peikoff (New York: Meridan, 1990), 99.
10. Ibid.
11. Peikoff, *Objectivism*, 4.
12. Ibid., 48.
13. Ibid., 51–52.
14. For more on multiple dimensions and the questions about the nature of reality they raise, see Chapter 14 by Berghofer in this volume.
15. Ibid.
16. Ibid., 55.
17. Ibid.
18. Ibid., 56.
19. Leonard Peikoff, "What Is Man? Philosophy and Human Nature," available at https://campus.aynrand.org/campus-courses/the-philosophy-of-objectivism/what-is-man-philosophy-and-human-nature
20. Ibid.

Part III

"REALITY IS ONE OF MANY"

10
Astral Bodies and Cartesian Souls
Mind-Body Dualism in *Doctor Strange*

Dean A. Kowalski

In the 2016 film *Doctor Strange*, the title character suffers a horrific car accident that damages the nerves in his hands and fingers beyond repair. Strange believes he can heal himself, which would have been quite a sight, and also attests to his hubris as a medical doctor and scientific researcher (or maybe simply his over-inflated ego as a human being). In any case, his reaction to his accident makes us aware of his entrenched belief that all there is to a human being is nerves, muscles, blood, bone, and other sorts of tissue and fluids. If a person can learn all there is to know about the physics, chemistry, and biology of the body—as Strange may come close to doing—then there is nothing left to know. In part, this is why he rages over his injury: if he is as knowledgeable and skilled a surgeon as he thinks he is, then (he believes) he should be able to fix his hands.

Philosophers are one with Strange in his pursuit of knowledge in general, but they are much more concerned with abstract or conceptual questions about how things ultimately are (or ought to be). One of the more intriguing philosophical questions is about the fundamental nature of human beings. Are we simply flesh and bone, as Strange seems to think, or is there more—especially when it comes to the nature of our minds and souls? In this chapter, we'll use the good Doctor Strange to look at how some philosophers attempt to answer this important question. In the process, we'll gain some deeper insights about philosophy itself.

Doctor Strange and Philosophy: The Other Book of Forbidden Knowledge, First Edition. Edited by Mark D. White.
© 2018 John Wiley & Sons Ltd. Published 2018 by John Wiley & Sons Ltd.

"Let's Get Physical," Olivia Newton-John, 1981

Strange's worldview at the beginning of the film is effectively summed up in his brazen rant to the Ancient One: "I do not believe in fairy tales about the power of belief. There is no such thing as spirit! We are made of matter and nothing more. You're just another tiny, momentary speck within an indifferent universe."[1] Whether he knows it or not, Strange is invoking a *metaphysics* debate straight out of the philosophy classroom. Metaphysics seeks answers to fundamental questions about what, why, and how things exist, such as "Are human persons merely physical beings?" Philosophers (and one clever neurosurgeon) who answer this question "yes" maintain a view called *physicalism*, the metaphysical theory that human persons are nothing over and above the sum total of their working physical parts. To a physicalist, any fact about human beings can be explained using facts about the human body, including facts about consciousness. According to this view of the world, our abilities to think, feel, believe, and remember are effectively understood as features and functions of the (physical) human brain.

The fact that Strange accepts physicalism is not surprising, because most physicalists rely largely on science to argue for their position. After all, science has enabled us to explain many features of the physical world. Using science, we know that, despite appearances to the contrary, the sun does not actually set over the horizon and that the Earth rotates on its axis. Physicalists also turn to neuroscience to discover surprising and hidden truths about human beings, such as the nature of mental disorders and how to treat them. Even though there are aspects of consciousness that neuroscience finds difficult to account for, physicalists hold that neuroscience will continue to unearth truths about our mental lives until nothing about us is left unexplained.

When the Ancient One suggests that she can heal his hands as she cured Pangborn's paralysis, she asks Strange, "What if I told you that your own body could be convinced to put itself back together in all sorts of ways?" Strange assumes that she's developed a "bleeding-edge" experimental procedure for cellular regeneration. If he could learn this technique, not only would he be in a better position to heal his hands, but he could also regrow cells so that they effectively self-heal. (Obviously, he would call it the Ancient-Strange technique—or better yet, the Strange-Ancient technique.) This is so cutting-edge that it would also explain why she practices medicine inconspicuously in Kamar-Taj—to avoid the prying eyes of a "governing medical board." Finally, he has found the cure he so desperately sought. This justifies having spent his last dime to journey to Kamar-Taj. In all of this excitement, however, Strange forgot Mordo's advice to "forget everything you think you know." Soon he'll be forced to.

"Soul Man," Sam & Dave, 1967

The Ancient One has a very different view of the world and the human beings in it: we are both body *and* spirit. Contrary to Strange's assumption, her expertise is not in cellular regeneration; instead, she knows "how to reorient the spirit to better heal the body." Once he realizes that she believes spirit is something in addition to the body, Strange becomes dismissive. This explains his quip about fairy tales, and his crass comment that persons are merely tiny physical specks in an unimaginably large (and indifferent) universe.

However, some philosophers agree with the Ancient One that the spirit (or soul) is a thing unto itself and can affect and influence the body, a view called *substance dualism*. Substance dualists contend that there are two radically different features of human existence. Of course, there is the physical, which Strange knows so well and which physicalists believe explains all of human experience. Substance dualists, however, insist that we are more than simply the sum total of our physical facts. Once the physical is accounted for, we still have to account for mental states, like the regret that Strange feels for treating Christine Palmer so badly or the anguish he feels about her not replying to his emails.

These mental states are qualitative in nature, more amenable to description than measurement. They have subjective meaning that can only be experienced by the person having them and cannot be observed directly from outside. Because these feelings are difficult to connect with any physical fact, substance dualists argue that there must be non-physical facts about us, and such facts "reside" with the non-physical spirit or soul. Substance dualists further hold that your non-physical facts, including the soul itself, account for who you "truly" are—your beliefs, choices, desires, and memories—while your body, the non-thinking, fleshy component of you, is the physical aspect of your self. Combined, they comprise the fundamental nature of any human person.

René Descartes (1596–1650) is a well-known substance dualist, and, in fact, substance dualists are often referred to as *Cartesian dualists*. Descartes explains his theory this way:

> Because we have no conception of the body as thinking in any way, we have reason to believe that every kind of thought which exists in us belongs to the soul ... We must [also] know that the soul is really joined to the whole body, and that we cannot, properly speaking, say that it exists in any one of its parts to the exclusion of the others.[2]

When we see the Ancient One dislodging Strange's "astral form" from his "physical form" and forcing it into a "place where the soul exists apart from the body," it serves as a fantastic dramatization of substance dualism and a refutation of physicalism—especially to Stephen Strange.

"Miss You," The Rolling Stones, 1978

Strange's soul embarks on a mystical journey, but his body remains in the temple. During this journey, he experiences various otherworldly sights, sounds, and sensations. When conjoined again with his body, his conviction in physicalism is shaken. Because Strange could not have experienced what he did if physicalism were true, and the Ancient One assures him he was not drugged, he has no choice but to accept that persons are more than tiny physical specks in an indifferent universe. It is here that his mystical training truly begins.

Twice we see Strange using his astral form to his advantage. The first involves Strange's clever strategy to learn as much about the mystic arts as he can. When Strange "borrows" books from the library, we see him reading them, but at the same time we see his body asleep in his bed. Strange's astral form—his soul—is shown sitting upright at the foot of the bed holding one of the books that Wong refused to lend him and turning its pages. This scene presupposes substance dualism in that Strange's soul is not only able to exist apart from the physical body, but it is also capable of reading, thinking, and learning—and turning pages in a physical book—even when not embodied. (The nature of this interaction between the physical and non-physical is an issue we'll return to later.)

The second time Strange uses his astral self is more involved, both thematically and conceptually. After Strange is badly injured by one of Kaecilius' acolytes, he escapes by creating a dimensional gateway to the hospital where Christine Palmer works as an emergency room doctor. She puts him on an operating table and prepares to remove blood and fluid from his pericardium when he loses consciousness. Suddenly, Strange's astral form emerges from his body. He floats to the right side of the table, observes Christine about to plunge a large-bore syringe into his torso, and then makes himself visible and audible so he can "Strangesplain" to her how to perform the procedure correctly. Christine is taken aback—and so is the viewer—as we all see Strange's astral form protruding through some sort of dimensional rift. When Christine asks, "Stephen, what am I seeing?" he replies, "My astral body." Wondering if Strange has become a disembodied ghost, she asks, "Are you dead?" He answers, "No, but I am dying," as if to remind her of her medical task. He places his astral hand inside the chest cavity of his physical form, and illuminates exactly where he wants Christine to insert the syringe.

But alas, their inter-dimensional reunion is cut short. Strange isn't the only one who can separate his astral form from his physical form: Kaecilius' acolyte, whom Strange trapped in the Cloak of Levitation, does the same and follows Strange to the operating room. When Strange sees him, he tells Christine, "I'm gonna have to vanish now. Keep me alive, will you?" As Strange and the acolyte fight, their astral bodies crash into each other and occasionally, especially in their more violent interactions, affect the physical operating room. Their scuffle lands them on the operating table, where Christine is trying to save Strange's physical form, and she seems to sense their presence. As the two sorcerers whisk out of the room, their astral forms plunge through a vending machine, upsetting some of the snacks (from which a doctor serendipitously benefits when he gathers them up).

When they make their way back to the operating room, the acolyte lands a devastating blow that seems to stop Strange's heart in the physical world. Christine recognizes the sound of Strange flatlining and charges the defibrillator paddles. The electrical blast not only restarts his heart in his physical form but also surges through his astral form, incapacitating the acolyte. When Strange reappears to Christine, he tells her to increase the voltage and charge him again, and this time the more intense blast causes the acolyte's astral form to explode—and his physical form to expire. With the immediate threat to Strange's life averted, Christine muses, "After all this time, you show up here flying out of your body?" To which he quietly replies, "I've missed you, too."

"Body and Soul," Billie Holiday, 1957

It is undeniable that what happens to one's body affects one's mental life and vice versa. In the real world, because Benedict Cumberbatch agreed to play the character of Dr. Stephen Strange, he decided to grow a beard and trim it in the iconic style of the Sorcerer Supreme. In the movie, when Strange was pierced in the chest with a mystical weapon that damaged his heart, it caused him a great deal of pain and led to a desire to seek out Christine to save his life.

The odd relationship between the physical and nonphysical worlds is one of the great puzzles facing metaphysics in general and substance dualism in particular. Descartes realized the significance of these interrelationships and their implications for his worldview:

> By means of these sensations of pain, hunger, thirst and so on, nature also teaches me that I am present in my body not merely as a sailor is present in a ship, but that I am most tightly joined and, so to speak, commingled with it, so much so that I and the body constitute one single thing. For if this were not the case, then I, who am only a thinking thing, would not sense pain when the body is injured; rather, I would perceive the wound by means of the pure intellect, just as a sailor perceives by sight whether anything in his ship is broken.[3]

Descartes anticipates the objection that says that the body and soul cannot be radically distinct because our experiences tell us that our physical and mental lives are closely intertwined. His response is that the so-called "commingling" of the body and the soul allows for the two to interact. Indeed, most substance dualists follow Descartes and ascribe to *interactionism*, which is the idea that the soul and body cause changes in each other. Interactionism is the "explanatory glue" holding Cartesian dualism together, and without it, the Cartesian dualist cannot account for our experience of a unified wholeness of our physical and mental lives.

Descartes further argues that, although the soul is "commingled" with the whole body, the interaction takes place in the brain's pineal gland.[4] Descartes believes that the pineal gland is infused with what he called (according to standard translations) "animal spirits," which transfer information from the body to the mind and vice versa. However, as many soon realized, Descartes's "solution" only succeeds in inviting further questions: How do these spirits accomplish information transfer between mind and body? If the spirits are physical, then how do they impact the non-physical mind (to say nothing of why Doctor Strange has never seen them during brain surgery)? If the spirits are non-physical, then how do they come into contact with the physical pineal gland?

Yet these sorts of philosophical concerns are not limited to the pineal gland. The issue is not *where* body and soul interact, but *how* they are able to interact at all. The deeper problem is the nature of interactionism itself. How can one's soul be both radically distinct, and thus separate from one's body, and also causally conjoined to it, and thus able to account for all that human persons accomplish?[5] Contemporary philosopher Garrett Thomson tidily summarizes the conceptual difficulties with interactionism:

> How does the mind control something that is physical, if it is not physical? If the mind has no location in space, then it is wrong to imagine it close to the brain. Why then does it have a direct causal influence only on my brain? ... If non-spatially located acts of will cause changes in my brain, this must be a form of psychokinesis or magic.[6]

Thomson, not so subtly, contends that interactionism is little more than wishful thinking, and describes the problem of substance dualism without offering hope of solving it.

We see these same issues in the scenes described above featuring Doctor Strange's astral self. How is Strange's astral form capable of holding a book and turning its pages? Likewise, how did Strange's struggle with the acolyte in Christine Palmer's emergency room affect the people and objects in the room? These puzzles are similar to the question of how our minds or souls interact with our brains and bodies, just extended to things outside our own physical forms. In fact, the emergency room scene raises even more issues. When Strange first appears to Christine, half of his astral form remains in the astral plane, but the other half appears and speaks to Christine in the earthly physical plane. She can see it and hear it, which means it reflects light and moves air. So there is a very strong interaction with the physical world—especially for an "astral form." And don't even get me started on the link between Christine's defibrillating Strange's physical form and the final effect of killing the acolyte. It would take a very strange form of interactionism indeed to explain what we see in this movie!

"It's Possible," from *Cinderella*, 1957

Despite the obvious duality of physical and non-physical astral forms in *Doctor Strange*, the film can't avoid the numerous problems with interactionism and substance dualism in general. The apparent need for our bodies and minds (or souls) to interact regularly seems to imply a linkage too close to be waved away with talk of "commingling" or magical glands. Indeed, Thomson suggests that maintaining a belief in substance dualism requires believing in telekinesis or magic.

However, the film *Doctor Strange* may suggest a response on behalf of the substance dualist. Why must it be that everything that occurs on our earthly plane necessarily follows the laws of physics? Indeed, the film suggests that pulling energy from other dimensions into this dimension is central to the practice of the mystical arts. As the Ancient One explains to Strange, "We harness energy drawn from other dimensions of the multiverse to cast spells, to conjure shields and weapons, to make magic." In fact, the Ancient One's explanation—an energy transfer from one dimension to another—sounds more like science than magic. Might the idea of energy transfers across dimensions at least begin to explain the strange events in the operating room? And could there be a similar energy transfer from the non-physical soul to the physical body to explain their interactions?

More generally, this suggestion is but an aspect of the Ancient One's overall message to Strange about his narrow view of the world. Perhaps those suspicious of substance dualism are myopically "looking through a keyhole," and when it is suggested that the keyhole "can be widened in unimaginable ways," they simply "reject the possibility." Some might follow the Ancient One more directly, and complain to those who disagree with Descartes, "You think you know how the world works? You think that this material universe is all that there is?" Because there are so many things for each of us to learn, perhaps we should adopt a bit of the humility Strange is forced to learn and not be so quick to judge interactionism.

Those who disagree with substance dualism usually admit that interactionism is not *logically* impossible, like the idea of a married bachelor or a round square. However, philosophers try to arrive at reasonable, likely, and justified beliefs about the way things are, not just ways they could be. Both telekinesis and magic are possible, but we have no reason to believe that either actually occurs, which underscores Thomson's objection to substance dualism. In fact, given other beliefs that we are justified in having, it seems most likely that they do not occur. Moreover, to adopt these more outlandish theories of interactionism demands that we wildly reinterpret or reject what scientific researchers have established about the so-called multiverse, energy transfers within and across dimensions, brain function, and, indeed, much of physics, chemistry, and biology. Until we have better reason to question basically everything we know about the world and how it works, perhaps we should remain dubious of interactionism.[7]

"Strange Magic," Electric Light Orchestra, 1975

Although learning a bit about philosophy can enrich one's interpretation of *Doctor Strange*, it also turns out that thinking about the film can also deepen one's appreciation for the philosophical process. The metaphysical puzzles so brilliantly shown in this movie remind us of various possibilities about how the world works and what things are in it, seen or unseen. Some of these are difficult to imagine or conceive of clearly, and their existence helps explains why philosophers (should) remain humble about what they know or think they know. Philosophers should emulate Stephen Strange in his quest for knowledge, but not in his hubris about obtaining it.

Notes

1. All quoted dialogue is from the 2016 film *Doctor Strange*.
2. René Descartes, *Passions of the Soul* (1649), trans. E. S. Haldane and G. R. T. Ross, quoted in *René Descartes: Philosophical Essays and Correspondence*, ed. Roger Ariew (Indianapolis: Hackett Publishing, 2000), 298 and 307.
3. René Descartes, *Meditations on First Philosophy, Meditation VI* (1641), trans. Donald Cress, quoted in *René Descartes: Philosophical Essays and Correspondence*, ed. Roger Ariew (Indianapolis: Hackett Publishing, 2000), 136.
4. See Descartes, *Passions of the Soul*, Part I, articles 31–34.

5. Princess Elisabeth of Bohemia, who was something of a student of Descartes, elegantly articulates the problem when she asks Descartes,

> Tell me how the human soul can determine the movement of the animal spirits in the body so as to perform voluntary acts … For the determination of movement seems always to come about from the moving body's being propelled—to depend on the kind of impulse it gets from what sets it in motion, or again, on the nature and shape of this latter thing's surface.
>
> (quoted in *Philosophic Classics*, vol. III, ed. Forrest E. Baird and Walter Kaufmann, Upper Saddle River, NJ: Pearson-Prentice Hall, 2008, 53)

6. Garrett Thomson, *On Descartes* (Belmont, CA: Wadsworth, 2000), 75.
7. Note that if you reject substance dualism, you don't have to adopt physicalism, with which there are also many issues and questions (making metaphysics one of the most interesting and frustrating areas of philosophy). For more, see Daniel Stoljar's entry on physicalism in the *Stanford Encyclopedia of Philosophy*, available at https://plato.stanford.edu/entries/physicalism/

Scientists, Metaphysicians, and Sorcerers Supreme

Sarah K. Donovan and Nicholas Richardson

While Doctor Strange's adventures in the comics have always been philosophically rich, the most recent volume of his comic, by writer Jason Aaron and artist Chris Bachalo, reveals a complex character whose interdimensional adventures can shed light on the historically close relationship between philosophy and science. For hundreds of years in western Europe, many philosophers were also scientists, who studied what was called, at the time, "natural philosophy."[1]

In Aaron and Bachalo's work, Doctor Strange exemplifies the characteristics and methods of the natural philosophers in clashes with his mystical enemies, Lord Imperator and the Empirikul. These exciting and thought-provoking adventures can help us see why the lines between science, philosophy, and magic have not always been so neatly drawn.

Don't Judge a Sorcerer Supreme by His Flashy Cape

It's easy to be distracted by Doctor Strange's fancy spells, unique job title, or flashy cape, but we should also recognize that he is a Sorcerer Supreme, who demonstrates both discipline and intellect. Strange must study, not only magic, but also science and metaphysics, if he is to do his job successfully. *Metaphysics* is the branch of philosophy that studies the fundamental nature of existence, especially those questions that are difficult to answer with the tools of science (hence the name "*meta*physics"). To underscore how metaphysicians are

Doctor Strange and Philosophy: The Other Book of Forbidden Knowledge,
First Edition. Edited by Mark D. White.
© 2018 John Wiley & Sons Ltd. Published 2018 by John Wiley & Sons Ltd.

similar to and different from scientists, we can look at how each of them uses inductive and deductive reasoning.

Inductive reasoning begins with observation and then draws a general conclusion from it that is highly likely but can never be 100% certain. For example, on your way home from work or school, you might drive by four different movie theaters that all list *Doctor Strange* on the marquee. Based on these observations, you can reasonably conclude with a high degree of certainty that, barring highly unlikely problems like inaccurate marquees at four separate places, that *Doctor Strange* is currently in a theater near you, and very probably all four.

Deductive reasoning begins with a general conclusion, and then uses logic to construct the conditions or premises necessary to prove that conclusion with 100% certainty. You might begin an argument with the claim that Doctor Strange is mortal, and then find premises that lead to this claim logically (that is, with absolute certainty), such as "all men are mortal" and "Doctor Strange is a man." If these two statements are true, then it follows logically that Doctor Strange is mortal. Whereas inductive reasoning starts with evidence and sees what statements can be made from it, deductive reasoning relies solely on logic to get from more general statements to more specific ones.

While metaphysicians and scientists each use both types of reasoning, the metaphysician employs primarily deductive reasoning and physical scientists use primarily inductive reasoning. Yet, even as metaphysicians and scientists seem to have different gold standards of truth—logic for philosophers and measurement for scientists—the core of both standards is found in the universal languages of logic and math, supporting the historical evidence that philosophy and science were once much closer than they seem now, especially as practiced by the philosopher-scientists of old—and a certain Sorcerer Supreme of today.

The Sorcerer Supreme Doesn't Make the Magic

Like the historical philosopher-scientists, Doctor Strange studies metaphysics and its relationship to the physical world. For example, in the first issue of Aaron and Bachalo's run, Strange is battling a tribe of other-dimensional soul-eaters who have infested a young boy's soul. As he fights the soul-eaters, we can see the dramatic battle, but the boy's parents cannot. When Strange tells them their son is healed, they react by saying, "Just like that? But… all you did was sit there floating in the air for a few minutes."[2]

Of course, the reason Doctor Strange can work wonders by casting spells is that he learned at the feet of his teacher, the Ancient One. But we must be careful to remember that he does not actually *possess* magic, but rather has been trained to find magic existing in the universe and use its power. He is a part of an erudite tradition of the Sorcerer Supreme whose primary source is the Book of Vishanti, which is only powerful to one who knows how to use it. Like a skilled philosopher or scientist, the Ancient One mentored and trained Doctor Strange to understand how to harness the power of the book and apply its ancient spells to new situations.

The interdimensional mind maggots that plague local librarian Zelma Stanton provide a concrete example of Strange utilizing knowledge to harness power.[3] He does not simply possess such power. Not knowing about the mind maggots, Doctor Strange tries to help Stanton and inadvertently releases them from her mind … and into his home. After Stanton and Wong battle the escaped mind maggots, they find Strange by himself reading. Stanton asks, "Hey, doc, we… wait, are you reading? Have you been sitting here reading all this time?" to which Strange replies, "No, I've been floating here reading all this time, and trying to find an answer."[4] Like a metaphysician and scientist, Strange has to research ways to access and use magic to deal with phenomena that he has not yet encountered. Strange deduces from his book that he can use Stanton's lingering connection with them—through their ectoplasmic mucous strands, *eww*—to lure them back to a central location and trap them in his own body where he knows better how to kill them.

Strange uses both inductive and deductive reasoning throughout this story as he notices that the metaphysical ecosystem is out of balance, which leads him to conclude that something very dangerous and destructive is on the horizon. His intellect and skill to harness magic are both put to the test when, like the historical natural philosophers, he discovers that he has to develop new ways of thinking about the world and his role in it. Over the span of the story, Strange learns that the world of magic has profoundly changed, the Book of Vishanti is no longer useful, and that he must write his own book about this new reality.[5]

Beware the Thing in the Cellar

In Aaron and Bachalo's extended tale, Doctor Strange and all things magic are being hunted and systematically eradicated by the self-proclaimed champion of science and technology, Lord Imperator, and his army, the Empirikul. Strange and Imperator both have overarching worldviews—magic and science, respectively—that they use to interpret reality and guide their behavior. Contemporary logician Patrick Hurley underscores how philosophers (including metaphysicians) and scientists share a common approach when confronting and explaining complex experiences.[6] According to Hurley, both seek to develop theories that will offer explanations of complex phenomena. While scientists might ask "How and why does gravity affect objects?" and philosophers might ask "Does a god exist who created gravity?," both seek to reveal an over-arching and hidden structure to reality that will explain why it functions as it does.

Lord Imperator believes that reality is structured quite simply: magic is pure evil and science is the only good. He thinks he is helping the universe when he kills sorcerers because he is "eradicating the great cancer that infects it."[7] His worldview is so strict that he never asks whether *some* magic needs to be destroyed; he only asks how to use their technology to measure the amount of magic present so they can destroy all of it. When the Empirikul arrive at the Sanctum Sanctorum, they say, "The instruments have never measured an infestation so severe." This information is collected only to craft the most effective response: "The probes will attack its magic at a subatomic level. Purity will be restored."[8] With such an iron-clad perspective about the evil of magic and the purity of science, the only decisions to make are how to best destroy magic when it is found.

Alternatively, Doctor Strange is deeply devoted to his worldview that magic is an essential part of the universe, and he risks his life multiple times to ensure the survival of that magic. To defeat Imperator, Strange is even willing to face one of his darkest secrets and deepest sources of anxiety, fear, and shame—the "Thing in the Cellar," which is the ugly by-product of Strange's magic. As the Ancient One explained to him during his training, every spell has a cost, and the bigger the spell, the bigger the cost.[9] Wong transferred the pain that Strange suffered (as a result of using magic) to the cellar of the Sanctum Sanctorum where it became pain and suffering incarnate, growing and festering behind locked doors.

The Empirikul release the Thing in the Cellar as they try to cleanse the Sanctum Sanctorum of magic, but they are no match for it, and must call in Lord Imperator to fight it. The cellar becomes the final battleground between Imperator and Strange. In a twist, Strange needs the Thing in the Cellar to defeat Imperator. As he says to the Thing, "The Imperator will kill you. The same as me. We're both monsters in his eyes. You have to help me now, hate me later. But please..."[10] For the sake of magic, Doctor Strange is willing to save the one magic entity whose destruction would actually be a relief to him.

Strange further demonstrates his firm commitment to his world-view when he understands that he must embark on the arduous task of rewriting the rules and laws of magic. After the Empirikul are defeated, Doctor Strange is talking to Chondu, a head enshrined in a floating glass case who tends bar in the "The Bar with No Doors," when he confesses, "I feel like I am starting over from scratch." Chondu reminds him, "Then it's your job to find out, Doctor Strange. If the old books of magic don't apply anymore... it's time to write some new ones. One spell at a time, if that's what it takes."[11] And this is exactly what Doctor Strange begins to do, as philosophers and scientists have done for millennia.

Teleology, Acorns, and the Slugs of Een'Gawori

One such philosopher-scientist was Aristotle (384–322 BCE). He developed both a physics and a metaphysics, and his view of nature had an enduring influence all the way up to the scientific revolution of the seventeenth century. Aristotle believed that four types of causes explain everything that happens within nature: (1) efficient (the start of a change of state); (2) material (what something is made of); (3) formal (the essence or blueprint of the thing); and (4) final (the end or purpose of a thing).[12]

In general, causality is important because the goal of Aristotle's science is to explain the *why* of nature, and for him the last cause is particularly important. It represents a *teleological* view of nature, which means that everything has an end or purpose, and a thing is good to the extent it achieves that end. For example, an acorn possesses its end or purpose within itself: to become a healthy oak tree. Its end is a blueprint that unfolds under the correct physical conditions. An acorn doesn't have to know how, or even want, to become an oak tree, because its end, or purpose, guides its development.

We see an example of teleology when Doctor Strange wakes up in his astral form under attack by Een'Gawori slugs who feed on magic.[13] Once he successfully fights off the Een'Gawori and returns to his physical body, Strange puts the slugs in a food coma rather than killing them. Why does he do this? Strange knows that the purpose or end of the slugs is not to destroy worlds but simply to consume magic. When Strange and Wong find Fandazar Foo, the home of the slugs, destroyed, Wong asks if the slugs are responsible, but Strange says no, "they're not capable of destruction on this scale."[14] According to a teleological interpretation of Strange's view of the slugs, when the slugs entered our dimension, they didn't intend to hurt anybody. They were merely trying to fulfill their end or purpose, which is to consume magic. In the same way that acorns cannot be pine trees, mystical slugs cannot be multi-dimensional conquerors. Furthermore, because Doctor Strange knows the slugs' purpose, he can reasonably deduce that something else destroyed Een'Gawori.

Aristotle's view of physics had an enduring influence in Western Europe, even as it was reinterpreted by medieval philosophers—but not right away. For centuries, his writing went unread by the intellectuals of western Europe until they were translated from Greek to Latin during the Middle Ages. Influential medieval philosopher and theologian Thomas Aquinas (1225–1274) contributed to the elevation of Aristotle's ideas in a largely Christian environment whose education system revolved around the monastic class of individuals.[15] Aquinas argued that Aristotle's views were compatible with Christianity because Aristotle believed that the Earth was at the center of the universe and that there was one central divine entity called the "unmoved mover."[16] Although primarily a philosopher and theologian, Aquinas nonetheless influenced the dialogue about natural science. As a leader in the Church, he would help determine what was taught and how in the monasteries (the primary site where knowledge was disseminated prior to the printing press).

Justice in the (Alleged) Name of Science

When intellectuals began to challenge Aristotle's teleological worldview, they faced opposition from both the Catholic Church, who found Aristotle's views consistent with scripture, and the scientific community. Nonetheless, several notable philosopher-scientists pushed back against the teleological view of nature and paved the way for a modern *mechanistic* view, one in which events progress according to natural physical laws rather than according to a pre-ordained purpose.

Four of these individuals deserve mention:

1. Nicolaus Copernicus (1473–1543) famously hypothesized that, contrary to Aristotelian physics, the sun, not the Earth, is at the center of the universe.
2. Francis Bacon (1561–1626) criticized Aristotelian logic and, most importantly, Aristotle's focus on the *why* of nature rather than on *how* to manipulate it.
3. Galileo Galilei (1564–1642), a mathematician and astronomer, was an influential critic of Aristotelian physics through experiments about uniform acceleration, and is also known for his observations of the planets using the newly invented telescope.
4. Johannes Kepler (1571–1630) expanded on Copernicus' heliocentric view of the universe to hypothesize that orbits are elliptical (which contradicts Aristotelian doctrine about circular orbits).[17]

Collectively, these thinkers rejected the Aristotelian focus on teleology (as well as other aspects of Aristotle's thought such as essences and cataloguing) and the accepted division between natural science and mathematics. Furthermore, they did so in a climate that could be hostile to the production of new ideas, as evidenced by Galilei's imprisonment for heresy.

Like the protectors of Aristotle's legacy, Lord Imperator tries to control the proliferation of any worldview that disagrees with his own. He claims to be acting in the name of science, yet he is clearly guided by a fanatical worldview and is impervious to any evidence that might challenge his orthodoxy. As he says when his soldiers report to him that Doctor Strange may know that they are hunting and killing Sorcerers Supreme, "The time has come to liberate another world from evil... Our holy inquisition marches on... Praise the Empirikul and death to magic."[18] Whereas Strange finds value in critical thinking and knowledge of the unknown, Lord Imperator views both as threats to his own controlled, pseudo-scientific worldview.

In spite of his avowed devotion to science, Imperator has more in common with religious fanaticism. Just think of all his talk about cleansing, purifying, and sanctifying people who practice magic. As the Empirikul attack Doctor Strange outside of the Sanctum

Sanctorum, one of the soldiers says to him, "Congratulations, man of magic. You've just taken your first steps toward purity... The power of science burns away all lies and abnormalities."[19] Rather than a science conducted in the name of open inquiry, critical thinking, and carefully documented experimentation, Imperator possesses a warped and nefarious brand of science that seeks the destruction of innocent people. His religious grandiosity shines as he says to Strange, "You will burn just like all the rest. Your inquisition begins now, Sorcerer Supreme."[20]

In fact, we learn that Imperator's "science" did not develop out of a devotion to the open-ended pursuit of truth, but rather out of a vendetta against the magical creature that threatened to kill him as an infant. As Imperator tells Strange, "I was never meant to live past infancy. I was promised from birth, as many of my people were to the god they worshipped and revered in all aspects of their lives. To the great beast called Shuma-Gorath," a longtime mystical foe of Doctor Strange.[21] We also learn that, unlike himself, Lord Imperator's parents seemed to be genuinely good people and honest scientists, who seemed to have worked earnestly to show that Shuma-Gorath was not an actual god to be worshipped, but an evil beast who was killing the children of their planet. Before they died, Imperator's mother revealed that their intentions were to save lives, not punish or harm anyone. As she says to her husband, "You're a good man ... but we can't save this world. We never could."[22] Imperator's parents died at the hands of religious fanatics, but he completely misunderstood their sacrifice; rather than persuade those who disagree with him, he simply kills them.

The Two Sides of Technology

As Doctor Strange learns, Lord Imperator's technology is fierce. After one of his books, *The Grimoire of Watoomb*, loses its magic, Strange travels to the Temple of Watoomb to investigate, and is shocked at what he finds: "All the defenses are dead. This place has been drained of magic." While he wonders what magic could be responsible, he discovers, "Not sorcery at all. Machinery."[23] Strange sends out a desperate message through all mystical wavelengths, warning that "Our enemies are not magicians. Their weapons are technological ... This ... is unlike any technology I've ever seen ... A technology with the power to disrupt magic."[24]

Lord Imperator's vendetta against magic shows that, although we might prefer to think of scientific advances as positive, they can also have a negative side. Imperator uses the mechanization of nature to destroy and conquer. Although he believes that it serves the positive goal of purifying the sinners who use magic, the end result is murder and the wholesale destruction of different dimensions. As Strange describes the Empirikul destruction on Fandazar Foo, "It's all gone. All burned away."[25]

Imperator also shows how technology can be as alienating as it is destructive. He used technology to create a world in which he has no human connections. After escaping his home planet and certain death at the hands of Shuma-Gorath, he says,

> I grew up alone in a womb of science. All I ever cared about was find-
> ing the tools of technology that I needed to obliterate magic. That is
> who I am now. That is what it means to be the Imperator.

He also describes himself as other than human when he says, "Super-science made me what I am. Stronger. More powerful than anyone else on my world ever dreamed they could be."[26] And later, when he is battling Strange and the Thing in the Cellar, he says, "I learned to channel the white-hot fire of the supernova. The speed of the comet. The quantum might of the supermassive black hole. I baptized myself in the waters of science so that I might be reborn."[27] Rather than use technology to improve human life, Imperator used it to erode his own humanity and destroy other worlds as he leaves them in his image, sterile and dehumanized. As Strange puts it in reference to Imperator, "Apparently science makes monsters of men as easily as magic."[28]

In contrast to Imperator's destruction, we can see examples of positive advances in science using mechanization during the Scientific Revolution. For example, René Descartes' (1596–1650) mechanistic and mathematical view of nature provides a stark contrast to the teleological views of Aristotle. Descartes viewed the natural world as inert matter that is there for us to control and manipulate. Innovative thinkers like Descartes pushed the boundaries of the scientific conversation to pave the way for the discoveries of visionaries like Sir Isaac Newton (1643–1727), who is famous for his development of the theory of gravity, the three laws of motion, and calculus—discoveries that led to space travel and quantum mechanics.

Furthermore, while Imperator's science requires a disavowal of everything spiritual, in reality, science and spirituality are compatible.

Neither Descartes nor Newton disavowed religion or spirituality in the name of science. Unlike Imperator, they sought to resolve any conflict between devotion to science and devotion to something larger than themselves. For example, even though Descartes' physics is viewed as a key intellectual doctrine that shifted science away from the Aristotelian view of nature (the view supported by the Church), Descartes crafted a metaphysics that argued that God constructed the human mind uniquely to understand the natural world.[29] While Newton did not accept the dominant religious views of the time, he was deeply pious—but he also experimented with alchemy, a precursor to modern chemistry, which was often shrouded in mysticism and magic.[30]

Philosophy, Science, and... Magic?

Historian Peter Dear's book *Revolutionizing the Sciences* helps situate the work of ancient philosophers, like Aristotle, in the context of the history of the scientific revolution.[31] Dear underscores that intellectual history is complex. In particular, he challenges the presumption that we can neatly characterize the time period leading up to the Scientific Revolution as filled with superstition and belief in magic that then flips unconditionally to the triumphant methods of the new science. Actually, he writes, science remains entwined with magic and superstition past the period known as the Scientific Revolution.

Whether you believe in magic or not, we could argue that scientific explanations have, throughout history, eventually explained what was thought to be magical, and this is a pattern that could continue. In contemporary times, we might say that the belief in out-of-body experiences might eventually be explained in terms of neural firings or even with scientific proof of alternate dimensions. We could read Doctor Strange's knowledge base itself as exemplifying how something that appears as magic to the uninitiated can actually have a logical, scientific explanation. According to Strange, the metaphysical realm appears to mirror the physical realm in following basic yet different rules (even if it is only sorcerers who understand them). We can imagine that scientists who are ahead of their time might experience a similar disconnect between how allegedly unexplained phenomena make perfect sense to them, but seem strange and mystical to others who do not understand their causality.

Quantum physics is an excellent example of modern science that can seem, to the uninitiated, to be more like magic. While Newtonian mechanics describes the motion of everyday objects such as planets moving, objects falling, and waves propagating, quantum mechanics describes subatomic particles, which behave very differently. For example, at the Newtonian level, waves are energy being transferred through a medium (think of sound waves or waves in the ocean), and particles are the objects that make up that medium (the air or water)—definitely not the same thing. But at the quantum level, they appear to be the same: light, for instance, is known to be both a particle and a wave at the same time.[32] While scientists now accept the transcendent, or metaphysical, nature of these mechanics, it broke the Newtonian paradigm. To the layperson, this certainly appears magical—as does quantum entanglement, in which two particles can coordinate their action over tremendous distances *instantaneously*.[33] This phenomenon isn't known as "spooky action at a distance" for nothing![34]

We can see this view of magic in the comics as well. Doctor Strange describes the people who are uninitiated in the alternate dimensions he is familiar with as "confused and utterly terrified," having "just been given their first glimpse of the unseen things that live in the shadows, of a whole spectrum of unimaginable existence."[35] But Strange can explain the metaphysical in similar terms when he says, "The human body is a breeding ground for microscopic monsters … Your soul attracts parasites as well, on a mystical level instead of a microscopic one."[36] Strange has books and theories to guide him in understanding the logic and science behind other dimensions, so they make sense to him—they follow a set of identifiable rules. To most everyone else, it's just scary mumbo-jumbo—or magic.

Doctor Strange demystifies what it means to be a Sorcerer Supreme when he says, "Being a magician doesn't mean you create magic from thin air. You only channel the magical energy that's already around you. It's a little like being an electrician."[37] He does exactly this when fighting Lord Imperator: "Spells failing left and right. The mystical world withering all around me … Have to take all there is. Drain the dragon lines. Drain the earth itself of all its magical energy."[38] Strange isn't creating anything out of thin air or channeling an internal source of magic. He simply knows where to look for natural pockets of energy and how to use them for his purposes, following its own set of rules like those that govern Newtonian and quantum physics (as different as they are).

What is common to both of these examples is that Doctor Strange has logical and scientific explanations for what he does, but to the uninitiated, his actions are unfamiliar and mysterious. While we're not saying that everything Strange does or encounters exists in the real world—we don't actually think that interdimensional soul-eaters or mind maggots are real—we are trying to point out that, historically, innovative philosopher-scientists have appeared unintelligible to the public and even to their peers. Nonetheless, unexplained phenomena that once were the source of superstition were eventually explained in terms so mundane that a child can repeat them, such as an apple falling from a tree.

One Thing We Know Is That Life Is Strange

Science, philosophy, and magic have a tangled history that the adventures of Doctor Strange can help us to tease out. While it's hard to find a modern-day example of a person who is scientist, metaphysician, and Sorcerer Supreme—two out of three, at best—we can certainly agree that one person's science is another person's magic, and that there is much in this world that remains unexplained and downright strange. The eminently talented scientist and science fiction writer Arthur C. Clarke (1917–2008) once said that "any sufficiently advanced technology is indistinguishable from magic."[39] Doctor Strange couldn't have put it better himself.

Notes

1. Also, it was not unusual for scientists to develop philosophical theories about the natural world, ethics, and politics.
2. *Doctor Strange*, vol. 4, #1 (October 2015), collected in *Doctor Strange: The Way of the Weird* (2016).
3. Ibid.
4. *Doctor Strange*, vol. 4, #2 (November 2015), collected in *Doctor Strange: The Way of the Weird*.
5. *Doctor Strange*, vol. 4, #11–16 (November 2016–March 2017), collected in *Doctor Strange: Blood in the Aether* (2017).
6. See Patrick Hurley, *A Concise Introduction to Logic*, 11th ed. (Stamford, CT: Cengage Learning, 2014).
7. *Doctor Strange*, vol. 4, #7 (April 2016), collected in *Doctor Strange: The Last Days of Magic* (2016).

8. *Doctor Strange*, vol. 4, #6 (March 2016), collected in *Doctor Strange: The Last Days of Magic*.

9. *Doctor Strange*, vol. 4, #4 (January 2016), collected in *Doctor Strange: The Way of the Weird*.

10. *Doctor Strange*, vol. 4, #10 (October 2016), collected in *Doctor Strange: The Last Days of Magic*.

11. *Doctor Strange*, vol. 4, #11 (November 2016), collected in *Doctor Strange: Blood in the Aether*.

12. See Aristotle's *Physics*, Book II, Part 3, available at http://classics.mit.edu/Aristotle/physics.html

13. *Doctor Strange*, vol. 4, #3 (December 2015), collected in *Doctor Strange: The Way of the Weird*.

14. Ibid.

15. For more on Aquinas and the influence of Aristotle's work on his views, see John O'Callaghan, "Saint Thomas Aquinas," in the *Stanford Encyclopedia of Philosophy*, available at https://plato.stanford.edu/entries/aquinas/

16. We should note that, as a pre-Christian philosopher, Aristotle's unmoved mover did not create the universe which has existed eternally. Aristotle discusses the unmoved mover in his *Metaphysics*; we recommend the many articles related to it in the *Stanford Encyclopedia of Philosophy*.

17. For a detailed explanation of these developments, we recommend Frederick Copleston's *A History of Philosophy*, vol. 2: *Medieval Philosophy from Augustine to Duns Scotus* (New York: Doubleday, 1993). Copleston's nine volumes of *A History of Philosophy* are breathtaking in scope and detail, and are a great resource for individuals interested in understanding the history of western philosophy more broadly.

18. *Doctor Strange*, vol. 4, #3.

19. *Doctor Strange*, vol. 4, #6.

20. Ibid.

21. *Doctor Strange*, vol. 4, #7.

22. Ibid.

23. *Doctor Strange*, vol. 4, #4. Unfortunately, we could not find a proper citation for *The Grimoire of Watoomb*; our emails to Ms. Stanton went unanswered.

24. *Doctor Strange*, vol. 4, #5 (February 2016), collected in *Doctor Strange: The Way of the Weird*.

25. *Doctor Strange*, vol. 4, #7.

26. Ibid.

27. *Doctor Strange*, vol. 4, #10.

28. *Doctor Strange*, vol. 4, #7.

29. René Descartes, *Meditations on First Philosophy*, 3rd ed., trans. Donald A. Cress (Indianapolis: Hackett Publishing, 1993). For a

discussion of Descartes' views on physics and God, and their conflict with Church doctrine, see Tom Sorrell, *Descartes: A Very Short Introduction* (Oxford: Oxford University Press, 1987), 65–70.

30. Rob Iliffe discusses Newton's experiments in alchemy, and Newton's religious views and contention with Christian orthodoxy, in *Newton: A Very Short Introduction* (Oxford: Oxford Oxford University, 2007), 54–82. In the Marvel Universe, Isaac Newton was actually Sorcerer Supreme for a time, and used his power to seek "The Word of God" (*Doctor Strange and the Sorcerers Supreme #5*, April 2017, collected in *Doctor Strange and the Sorcerers Supreme: Out of Time*, 2017).

31. Peter Dear, *Revolutionizing the Sciences: European Knowledge and Its Ambitions, 1500–1700* (Princeton, NJ: Princeton University Press, 2001). This book is an excellent and clear resource for anyone interested in learning more about the history of science.

32. Don't believe us? See "The First Ever Photograph of Light as Both a Particle and a Wave," *Phys.Org*, March 2, 2015, available at https://phys.org/news/2015-03-particle.html

33. See Frank Wilczek, "Entanglement Made Simple," *Quanta Magazine*, April 28, 2016, available at https://www.quantamagazine.org/entanglement-made-simple-20160428/

34. For more on quantum mechanics and the philosophical puzzles it creates, see Chapter 14 by Berghofer in this volume.

35. *Doctor Strange*, vol. 4, #1.

36. Ibid.

37. *Doctor Strange*, vol. 4, #2.

38. *Doctor Strange*, vol. 4, #7.

39. See Arthur C. Clarke, *Profiles of the Future: An Inquiry into the Limits of the Possible* (New York: Harper & Row, 1973), 21.

12

"This Is Time"

Setting Time in *Doctor Strange* by Henri Bergson's Clock

Corey Latta

The way we understand our relationship to time defines the way we live. If we're not careful, we can get caught up in the darting pace of our hurried modern world, considering time only as it relates to clocks and calendars. The result is that we stretch the most ambitious versions of ourselves out into the future without being mindful of how the present shapes us. By contrast, we can learn to live in an increasingly reflective relationship to time, experiencing it as a force in which we live with emotional, even spiritual, vitality.

The way we experience time is a major theme in the film *Doctor Strange*, which traces the spiritual metamorphosis of the title character as he moves from self-centered materialism to selfless spirituality. To make sense of the good Doctor's enlightened relationship to time, we'll consult the revolutionary philosopher Henri Bergson (1859–1941).

It's Bergson Time

Few modern philosophers left an imprint as wide and indelible as Bergson, who was appointed Chair of Ancient Philosophy at the Collège de France and won the 1927 Nobel Prize for Literature. Known to intellectuals and laymen alike, Bergson's lectures filled halls to standing room only capacity. William James (1842–1910), an American psychologist and philosopher, called Bergson's book

Doctor Strange and Philosophy: The Other Book of Forbidden Knowledge,
First Edition. Edited by Mark D. White.
© 2018 John Wiley & Sons Ltd. Published 2018 by John Wiley & Sons Ltd.

Creative Evolution "a true miracle" and the "beginning of a new era."[1] Philosopher Jean Wahl (1888–1974) said, "If one had to name the four great philosophers one could say: Socrates, Plato—taking them together—Descartes, Kant and Bergson."[2] Bergson was greatly appreciated by U.S. President Theodore Roosevelt, influenced writers like T. S. Eliot and Virginia Woolf, and was heavily criticized by the philosopher Bertrand Russell (1872–1970). Most important for us, Bergson's work on time held a weight in philosophy comparable to what Einstein's theory of special relativity carried in science.

Bergson argued that time had suffered from the scientific rationality of the late-nineteenth and early-twentieth centuries, because scientific approaches to time failed to get at time's essence. According to Bergson, the work of thinkers like Einstein subjected time to a cold empiricism, neglecting the lived experience of time: "Time could be enormously and even infinitely accelerated; nothing would be changed for the mathematician, for the physicist or for the astronomer."[3] Despite its slowing down or speeding up, time remains a static object to the scientist, a mere object of experimentation. The scientist's imperceptive understanding of time would fail to see the power of time on human consciousness.

The experience of actually living in time, however, cannot be so easily controlled. Bergson thought that we existed in a relationship with time, and any change in time would be keenly felt by the human mind. As Bergson puts it, if there occurred a change in time, "the difference with regard to consciousness would be profound."[4] As conscious beings, our relationship to time transcends empirical knowledge; it reaches into the core of our humanity, indeed, of our spirituality.

Bergson's views of time inaugurated a "new spiritualism" that marked a "revolt against mechanism."[5] For Bergson, scientifically closed mechanism, which views reality as nothing more than the inner workings of a clock, distorted the truth of time and eliminated the possibility of living meaningfully within it. Only a philosophically open spiritualism could show time for what it is: a living force.

If physics could not make complete sense of time, as Bergson argued, then we must find a more fitting way of understanding it. To distinguish Time from the quantifiable chronological bent of science, Bergson liked to use the term "duration."[6] Duration acts like a force, and we feel this force at work within us; we do not just exist in Time. In Time, we actually *become*. And because science "no more applies to becoming, so far as that [Time] is moving, than the bridges thrown here and there across the stream follow the water that flows under their arches," we must move beyond science. Our experience in Time depends upon liberation from static rationality and clock-tethered thinking about Time.[7]

"Feels So Good," Chuck Mangione, 1977

Stephen Strange begins on the wrong side of the Bergsonian divide. He is a man of science: brilliant, rational, and closed off to any reality beyond the material world. When we first see Strange in the operating room, he is finishing up a procedure, performing brain surgery with the ease of preparing a salad. To amuse himself and demonstrate the range of his knowledge, the doctor plays a game with the surgical techs in which he has to name random songs. It only takes Strange a moment to identify the first song: "'Feels So Good.' Chuck Mangione. 1977."[8] At first it looks like he got the year wrong, but it turns out that "Feels So Good" was indeed released in 1977 even though it wasn't a hit until 1978. We are meant to see Strange as a man obsessed with the clock. He is given to remembering even the most obscure dates, each one representative of calendar time.

As we get to know more about what kind of man Stephen Strange is, we are taken from a medical space to a materialist one, from the operating room to his penthouse. In his downtown Manhattan apartment, Strange surrounds himself with luxury. As one example, we see his watch collection, rows and rows of watches, each more expensive than the last—time literally sprawled out before him. He chooses a watch given to him by Doctor Christine Palmer, Strange's lingering love interest in the film. The inscription on the back of the watch reads: "Time will tell how much I love you."

The watch foreshadows the fact that time will soon connect Strange to a deeper sense of his emotional self than he has ever known, but not before he is torn from his superficiality. In the subsequent scene, in a moment of reckless megalomania, navigating recklessly while looking at a potential surgical case that might bring him even more accolades, Strange drives his egocentric life off a cliff. In an instant, the fast pace at which Strange blew through life toward the future ceases. For the first time, he faces the present.

Strange Multiplicities

Strange's scientific rationality counts for nothing once he finds himself at Kamar-Taj, the end of his quest for healing and the house of the Ancient One. Here the doctor's relationship with time takes a hard Bergsonian turn. Strange's meeting with the Ancient One is not just a contrast in worldviews—it is a contest between two ways of experiencing duration. Strange represents an ambitious abuse of time: Only looking to what the next moment might bring him, he sees time through a scientific keyhole. In contrast, the Ancient One lives in and embodies the present. Living intentionally in opposition to the haste of modern materialism and scientism's closed assumptions about the supernatural, the Ancient One meditatively taps into a mysterious dimensional power continually animating every present moment.

According to Bergson, the purpose of life is to move from Strange's experience of time to the Ancient One's, to go from what Bergson called *quantitative multiplicity* to *qualitative multiplicity*. We can think of multiplicity as a way of expressing the multi-faceted nature of reality. Reality, or the human experience thereof, is not a singular thing, and the idea of multiplicity captures the diversely intermingled essence of lived experience. While multiplicity gets at the many aspects of *what* we experience of reality, the terms quantitative and qualitative get at *how* we experience them. Quantitative multiplicity is a way of knowing something by measuring and counting it, dealing in amounts and numbers, whereas qualitative multiplicity, as we'll see, is more elaborate and nuanced.

According to Bergson, quantitative multiplicity occurs in a uniform or homogeneous space. Bergson mentions counting sheep as an example: counting distinct and fairly identical objects in a well-defined space. When we come to something more abstract, like time, quantitative multiplicity runs into some problems. We find that we cannot measure time the way we count stars in the sky. In this case, quantitative multiplicity tries to enumerate what cannot be enumerated. Strange starts off with this mechanistic way of understanding duration: When the Ancient One asks him, "What mysteries lie beyond the reach of your senses?", Strange can only answer from a place of quantitative multiplicity. Trapped inside his own scientific worldview, he only knows how to add things up.

But as Strange grows in knowledge and skill at the mystic arts— and as he learns to quiet his rather loud ego—he evolves into a spiritually-minded man able to experience time according to qualitative multiplicity. Rather than trying to quantify duration, he develops an intuitive, subjective perception of time. Bergson believed that life and time could not be measured as if they existed on a homogeneous plain. After all, experiencing time is not like counting stars or sheep. Rather, he thought that our lived experiences in time were marked by profound variety or heterogeneity. Furthermore, not only are our conscious experiences in time heterogeneous, there are no distinguishable parts that could be diced up and counted—if there were, then we would find ourselves back in a state of quantitative multiplicity. The complexity of time must be embraced, not resisted or subdued.

Feeling Time

Quantitative multiplicity is a misguided, analytical approach to life in time. It tries to understand time as one would understand space: dividing and measuring its constituent parts. Qualitative multiplicity, by contrast, understands the force of temporal duration and the way we experience life. The conscious mind feels the force of time at work, allowing itself to be formed by the dynamic nature of lived experience. In qualitative multiplicity, "Several conscious states are organized into a whole, permeate one another, and gradually gain a richer content."[9] Durative flow invests the present with the power of life itself. Once the mind comes to know duration intuitively, it is expanded into each complex moment. Strange thus grows into an emotionally multi-dimensional person during his time at Kamar-Taj. As Bergson would say, Strange learns to delve "beneath the numerical multiplicity of conscious states" to find a "qualitative multiplicity."[10]

A good way to understand qualitative multiplicity—and Strange's personal transformation over the span of the film—is to consider emotion through which we relate to others. Take two of Bergson's favorite examples, sympathy and pity. Sympathy brings us out of ourselves and into the pain of another: by definition, a suffering with someone. It would be impossible to remain self-centered while in a sympathetic state, because sympathy empties the ego. As a state of qualitative multiplicity, sympathy takes us out of calculated rationality whereby we try to measure experience, and brings us into a deep intuitive mode of knowing all that life is.

The same applies to pity, in which we see someone in pain and choose to be in pain with them. We feel for them, and in so doing we strip superficiality from ourselves. Through pity, we know both ourselves and the world around us in a deeper way, which helps us shed the pretentions of quantifiable knowledge. As Bergson says, "The essence of pity is thus a need for self-abasement, an aspiration downward."[11] Bergson called this "qualitative progress," and we see it in the trajectory of Strange's spiritual and emotional growth. His greedy materialism begins to reverse as he progresses into a qualitative relationship to duration. From the Ancient One, he learns a newfound contentment with present time and durative force, which enables him to embrace the complexity and multitude of conscious states, changing him into a man of pathos.

Kaecilius Waits for No One

We first meet Kaecilius as he steals the Book of Cagliostro, a study of time, from the Kamar-Taj library. He uses the book to cast a dark spell to summon Dormammu, an evil demonic entity who exists outside time and seeks to engulf the multiverse with his own Dark Dimension.

Motivated by the painful loss of his family, Kaecilius' goal in summoning Dormammu is to stop time. "Time," Kaecilius explains to Strange, "is the true enemy of us all. Time is an insult." As Kaecilius sees it, because it's only in time that "all things age" and "all things die," the end of time would mark the end of human suffering. If Strange's initial relationship to time is one of scientism and the Ancient One's relationship to time is one of spiritualism, then Kaecilius' relationship to time is one of "chronological nihilism." For the embittered sorcerer, to live in time is no way to live at all.

Because Kaecilius has lost the ability to live within duration, he has lost his grasp on life's meaning, which in turn leads him to amorality. Due to his apathetic relationship to timed existence, he has negated any chance of the qualitative progression that Strange goes through. Nothing in time carries moral meaning for Kaecilius, and because everything exists in time, he does not hesitate to destroy anything that bears the mark of time. To Kaecilius, the very purpose of existence is to undo, so far as everything that exists does so in time, existence itself. Kaecilius' rejection of time proves to be an act of utter selfishness and his eventual demise. Instead of growing the self through qualitative multiplicity, Kaecilius ruins himself through an angry and recalcitrant heart.

The gift Kaecilius believes Dormammu has to offer humanity—
eternal life in a place beyond time where everyone can live forever—
is, in Bergson's view, existentially impossible. The very force of life is
found in duration. Time acts according to the nature of life, and life
itself always "progresses and endures in time."[12] Whereas time neither
harms nor helps inanimate objects, "it is a gain ... for a conscious
being."[13] To remove oneself from time, as Kaecilius desires to do, or to
destroy duration itself, as Dormammu would do, is to attempt to exist
in oblivion. Because duration through qualitative multiplicity is the
means by which we experience the transformative power of time,
Kaecilius' campaign to end durative flow leaves him emotionally and
spiritually self-enclosed, a figure frozen in timeless stagnation.

It's Not About You

Kaecilius' rejection of time serves to emphasize Strange's qualitative
progression, which reaches a tipping point at the film's emotional
apex, the Ancient One's moment of death. In her final scene, the
Ancient One peers into a moment that has captivated her for years, a
vivid stormy night sprinkled with a light snowfall. She tells him that
though she has looked down the corridors of time to see infinite
futures, she never saw Strange's, but only the possibilities his future
held. The reason his future had yet to be determined was that he had,
finally, started to live in the dynamism of durative force.

In the context of Strange's unrealized future, the Ancient One points
to his immense capacity for goodness, a qualitative state that would
serve as the vessel for durative multiplicity. Now free to actualize time,
Strange can create his own future, but only if, the Ancient One reminds
him, he overcomes those last vestiges of arrogance and fear that work
against his learning this secret to life in time: "It's not about you." Life,
time, and human existence all transcend the small-minded egocentric-
ity of quantitative thinking. Strange stands on the precipice of a qualitative epiphany: He needs only to move into full sympathy with others,
to lose himself in qualitative progression for the greater good of
humanity, before he can live in the ever-generating durative present.

What the Ancient One, whose life has continually channeled durative force, says to Strange in her last moments rings with a Bergsonian
tenor: "Death is what gives life meaning. To know your days are numbered. Your time is short." To know time as the precious resource it is

encourages us to live most fully in it. The durative life knows the power of the present moment, relishing time's ability to create conscious connection with existence.

"You'd think after all this time," the Ancient One says before dying, "I'd be ready. But look at me. Stretching one moment out into a thousand... just so that I can watch the snow." The Ancient One's final emotional confession echoes Bergson's description of durative feeling, the kind of intuitive connection to time in which, "a violent love, a deep melancholy invades our soul, provoking a thousand diverse elements that melt together, interpenetrate, without definite contours, without the least tendency to separate themselves one from another." Both the Ancient One and Strange occupy a moment that teems with deep qualitative experience where "feeling is a living being, which develops, and is therefore always changing."[14]

Having learned the crux of meaningful human existence, that life transcends any one person's whims and wants by an infinite degree, Strange departs this final lesson with his teacher ready to embody in a profoundly selfless manner qualitative multiplicity for the greater good.

This is Time

In the movie's clearest reflection of Bergsonian thinking, in a climactic confrontation with the timeless Dormammu, Strange sacrifices himself for humanity by repeatedly reliving the present moment—or, we might say, by recreating the present. Because Dormammu lives outside of temporal flow, he is ignorant of the power of time and its effects on human consciousness. To prevent the evil entity from consuming the world in a timeless hell, Strange uses Dormammu's ignorance of time against him. By using a spell in which he can recreate the present, Strange sacrifices himself again and again, causing time to reset, thereby holding Dormammu captive to the same reoccurring present moment. Bewildered by the déjà vu, Dormammu asks, "What is this? An illusion?"

"No, this is real," Strange answers, "just as you gave Kaecilius power from your dimension, I've brought a little power from mine. This is time. Endless, looped time." Dormammu counts the cost Strange must pay to relive this present moment, warning the sorcerer, "you will spend an eternity dying." Accepting a future made possible by the very capacity for goodness that the Ancient One previously identified, Strange replies, "But everyone on Earth will live." As Dormammu presses Strange, assuring him that "you will suffer," Strange replies in full qualitative multiplicity, "pain is an old friend." Finally capable of the kind of qualitative state that enables true compassion, Strange exhibits the kind of life that durative flow can produce in human consciousness. He's now ready to suffer for others, and in suffering, to transcend his once shallow soul.

Present time, highlighted as a theme in the film's climax by its reoccurrence, serves to expand the personal transformation we have witnessed in Strange throughout the movie. Describing the ways time enlarges the human soul, Bergson writes,

> We are seeking only the precise meaning that our consciousness gives to this word "exist" and we find that, for a conscious being, to exist is to change, to change is to mature, to mature is to go on creating oneself endlessly.[15]

As Strange uses the reoccurring present moment to experience pain, he matures, he expands, and he recreates himself. Not only does he become the kind of person the Ancient One hoped he would, he turns into the kind of person that the very force of life—what Bergson famously called the *élan vital* or vital impulse—would make him. In the power of time's influence on his consciousness, Strange can actualize himself in free volition. And by choosing to suffer, he actualizes himself into the qualitatively ideal human.

To the qualitative life, each new moment brings new realization, actualization, and new life itself. "No two moments are identical in a conscious being," Bergson reminds us.[16] Qualitative multiplicity consists of heterogeneity without separation. The exact nature of each moment varies for Strange, yet in heart, mind, and soul, he progresses continuously, becoming increasingly more sacrificial. As Bergson says, "For in the human soul there is hardly anything but progressions."[17]

All in Strange Time

In Strange's face-off with Dormammu, we also find the idea of time as a restorative agent. Living beings find a fulfillment through time that is impossible outside of time. As we see in the way Kaecilius attempted to renounce time, there can be no improvement, no personal progression or social betterment, outside of time's power. Bergson writes,

> Duration in time seems to act as a cause, and the idea of putting things back in their place after a certain period of time is absurd, since this kind of regression in time has never occurred in a living being.[18]

Time advances in one direction, with each present moment marshaling durative flow to create the next present moment.

Bergson believed that the past—and in the case of Strange's battle with Dormammu, the past would mean each previous present moment—pours into the present, creating in each new present an increased intensity. Thus, each present moment becomes a dynamic *now* charged by the energy of the previous dynamic *then*: "the continuous progress of the past which gnaws into the future and which swells as it advances."[19] So we find a sacrificial Strange standing in an endlessly advancing river of time, changing at the level of his consciousness, as in time "everything changes inwardly," and "the same concrete reality never recurs."[20] If the same, exact reality recurred, time itself would lose its agency in forming qualitative souls, and the human consciousness would be robbed of its power to grow.

Completely changed by the gnawing, swelling vital impulse of durative force, and now a master in the mystic arts, Strange is willing and able to assume responsibility for protecting the world against threats like Kaecilius and Dormammu. The film's climactic battle proves to be the ultimate outcome of its Bergsonian philosophy, the capstone moment in a story about how the flow of time and a spiritual mindfulness of the present create a meaningful, and in this case heroic, human experience. Strange puts on the same watch he carried with him throughout his journey, the one Christine engraved with "Time will tell how much I love you." The glass on the watch face has been shattered, much like Strange's former way of experiencing time. The watch serves as a reminder of the way Strange misused, counted, and hurried through time. This way lies broken to Strange, who now knows how to live truly in time, attaching himself to the qualitative meaning found in the inscription on the back of the watch rather than the quantitative construct represented by its hands.

Only Time Will Tell

Hopefully, Stephen Strange's journey can influence our own. In a film overflowing with sage lines, one that most captures Strange's spiritual growth comes early in the Ancient One's teaching, as she tells him, "You cannot beat a river into submission. You have to surrender to its current. Use its power as your own." Time, of course, cannot be mastered or bent to our will. Only lived in, known, and felt. If Bergson is right, our relationship to time—to the very moment you are in as you finish this chapter—could have as much influence over who we become as it did for the good Doctor. But... only time will tell how well we live in time.

Notes

1. Quoted in Richard A. Cohen, "Philo, Spinoza, Bergson: The Rise of an Ecological Age," in John Mullarky (ed.), *The New Bergson* (Manchester: Manchester University Press, 1999), 18–31, at p. 18; and also in Jimena Canales, *The Physicist & The Philosopher: Einstein, Bergson, and the Debate that Changed Our Understanding of Time* (Princeton, NJ: Princeton University Press, 2015), 12.
2. Jean Wahl, "At the Sorbonne," in Thomas Hanna (ed.), *The Bergsonian Heritage* (New York: Columbia University Press, 1962), 150–155, at p. 153.
3. Henri Bergson, *The Creative Mind*, trans. Mabelle L. Andison (New York: The Citadel Press, 1946/1992), 3.
4. Ibid.
5. Robert C. Grogin, *The Bergsonian Controversy in France, 1900–1914* (Calgary: University of Calgary Press, 1988), 39, 56.
6. Bergson elevated time above scientific understanding with his insistence on capitalizing "Time" in the Foreword to the second edition of *Duration and Simultaneity*. Time, with a capital "T," transcends the clock.
7. Henri Bergson, *Creative Evolution*, trans. Arthur Mitchell (New York: Dover, 1911/1998), 169.
8. All quoted dialogue is from the 2016 film *Doctor Strange*.
9. Henri Bergson, *Time and Free Will: An Essay on the Immediate Data of Consciousness*, trans. F.L. Pogson (New York: Macmillan, 1910), 122.
10. Ibid., 128.
11. Quoted in Leonard Lawlor, "Intuition and Duration: An Introduction to Bergson's 'Introduction to Metaphysics,'" in Michael R. Kelly (ed.), *Bergson and Phenomenology* (New York: Palgrave Macmillan, 2010), 25–41, at p. 36.
12. Bergson, *Creative Evolution*, 34.
13. Bergson, *Time and Free Will*, 116.
14. Ibid., 132–133.
15. Bergson, *Creative Evolution*, 13.
16. Ibid., 164.
17. Bergson, *Time and Free Will*, 131.
18. Ibid., 153.
19. Bergson, *Creative Evolution*, 11.
20. Ibid., 31.

Part IV
"A MAN LOOKING AT THE WORLD THROUGH A KEYHOLE"

13

A Strange Case
of a Paradigm Shift

Brendan Shea

In the 2016 film *Doctor Strange*, the title character undergoes a radical transition from successful neurosurgeon to highly skilled sorcerer. Unsurprisingly, he finds this transition difficult, in no small part because he thinks that sorcery seems somehow "unscientific." Nevertheless, he eventually comes to adopt sorcery as wholeheartedly as he had embraced medicine. Some of his reasons for making this transition are personal, such as his desire to fix his injured hands and, later, to help others. Strange also displays the same sorts of motivations that might drive any scientist: his intellectual curiosity drives him to understand how the Ancient One cured a paraplegic, and his desire to make a positive difference leads him to push the boundaries of sorcery.

This chapter will examine what Strange's transition can teach us about the nature of scientific inquiry. More specifically, we'll think about when it might make sense for scientists like Doctor Strange to *change* their approach. This will also allow us to explore what it means to practice science more generally. Some of what we learn might be surprising. For example, while it might seem *obvious* to us (and maybe even to Strange) that sorcery can't count as a science, there are reasons for doubting this quick conclusion, at least in the sort of world that Dr. Strange lives in. Finally, we'll consider what all of this means for science in *our* world, where things differ quite significantly.

Doctor Strange and Philosophy: The Other Book of Forbidden Knowledge, First Edition. Edited by Mark D. White.
© 2018 John Wiley & Sons Ltd. Published 2018 by John Wiley & Sons Ltd.

Back When Strange Was Normal

Our investigation starts with the ideas of the scientist, historian, and philosopher Thomas Kuhn (1922–1996). In his 1962 book, *The Structure of Scientific Revolutions*, Kuhn argued against the widely held view that scientific progress was the result of the application of a universal "scientific method" that assured regular, incremental progress toward the truth.[1] Instead, Kuhn thought that "scientific revolutions" often looked quite a bit like Strange's experience, where scientists refused to change their fundamental ideas about how the world works, or their *paradigms*, until a series of crises forced them to. If and when they finally did change paradigms, they had to undergo their own version of Strange's conversion experience, which required them to relearn exactly what the "world" is.

While Kuhn's examples are chosen from the history of physics, astronomy, and chemistry, his ideas have much broader import. After all, if rival scientific paradigms really are as different as, say, neurosurgery and sorcery, it might seem that the objectivity of science itself is threatened. It's for this reason that the story of Doctor Strange—who has the ability to understand multiple paradigms—is potentially so interesting, even to readers in a world without sorcery.

Kuhn, like Strange, received his initial training in a discipline very different from that which would eventually make him famous. Kuhn earned a doctorate in physics from Harvard University but, in the early years of career, came to feel that many of his best, most original ideas were actually about the history of science. In particular, he thought that many people had wildly inaccurate views of how science had actually worked in the past, which led them to be confused about how it worked in the present.

According to one popular view of science at the time, the *falsificationism* advocated by the philosopher of science Karl Popper (1902–1994), scientific theories (as opposed to, say, political theories) were defined by the fact that certain sorts of observations could show them to be wrong, and scientists were the sort of people who were willing to change their minds on the basis of such evidence.[2] So, for example, Popper would be quite happy with the early picture of Doctor Strange as the heroic, risk-taking neurosurgeon, who was always willing to oppose the received wisdom in an effort to save patients. Most importantly, Popper would note that scientists like Strange are characterized by taking failure seriously and making changes to their theories and methods in response. If a patient dies, Strange would undoubtedly try something different the next time around.

Though Popper's falsificationism remains highly influential, Kuhn argues that it doesn't accurately capture the way "normal science" actually works. By this, Kuhn simply means the ordinary day-to-day activities of the physicists or biologists who are *not* the Newtons, Einsteins, or Darwins of the world. First, Kuhn notes that innovators like Strange are actually pretty rare. The vast majority of practicing scientists spend their lives working on a small, well-defined set of problems—or "puzzles," as Kuhn calls them—that can be answered using the theories and methods they learned through years of rigorous schooling, and which their communities have picked out as worth solving. They rarely propose entirely novel techniques or methods, and certainly don't consider something as outlandish as sorcery, even if they encounter severe problems. Second, absent special circumstances (more on this later), they almost never reject their most fundamental methods, theories, or values, even in the face of numerous, seemingly unsolvable problems (such as the many diseases and conditions that modern medical science hasn't been able to treat or cure). However, in the vast majority of cases, these failures have not caused biological researchers to abandon the basic ways in which they approach problems.

From Science to Sorcery: How Scientific Revolutions Happen

If Kuhn is right, then Doctor Strange's initial suspicion of sorcery is just what we should expect from a practicing scientist. After all, in normal circumstances, science is all about solving certain sorts of puzzles—identifying new pathogens, developing surgical techniques, designing new drugs, and so on—using the skills and knowledge acquired after years of formal education and professional practice. To abandon all of this in favor of some strange new idea, such as manipulating dimensional energy to fight mystical enemies, is almost to abandon science altogether. In fact, Kuhn argues that "mature" sciences like biology and physics weren't even possible until researchers agreed on a shared paradigm that made it possible for them to focus their time and energy on identifying and solving ever more specific sorts of puzzles, as opposed to having to continually make public arguments about which fundamental theories, methods, or values should be adopted.

At certain points in history, however, scientists have changed their paradigms, such as when they adopted the Copernican, sun-centered model of the solar system over the older Ptolemaic, Earth-centered model. In Strange's particular case, this same sort of shift occurs when he abandons his career as a surgeon for one as an aspiring sorcerer. Kuhn spends a great deal of time in *The Structure of Scientific Revolutions* thinking about why and how scientists make such revolutionary changes. He suggests that this process, at least at the level of the individual scientist, is both more mysterious and less prototypically rational, than scientists, historians, and philosophers have often thought.

Kuhn argues that scientific revolutions have their roots in the sorts of "puzzle-solving" activity that Doctor Strange engages in as a scientist, which by its nature involves making ever more precise measurements and predictions. Over time, however, these sorts of measurements will reveal anomalies, or areas where the existing paradigm's predictions fail, no matter how many tweaks are made. So, for example, while the Earth-centered paradigm in ancient astronomy did surprisingly well for over thousands of years, astronomers eventually found themselves needing to make more and more adjustments, such as positing that the planets moved in ever-more-complex epicycles in their orbits of the Earth, just to keep their paradigm in agreement with their increasingly precise observations of the sky.

In the face of such anomalies, scientists are forced to entertain ever more radical ideas, until they reach the very limits of what their current paradigms allow. In Strange's case, this process takes place with extraordinary rapidity, as his quest to heal his injuries leads him first to the frontiers of medicine, then to the miraculously healed Jonathan Pangborn, and finally to the Ancient One and everything she shows him. Until the very end of this process, however, Strange never gives up on the core commitments of his paradigm: that the treatment for his condition will be explicable in terms of human physiology and the biological and physical theories on which this is based.

On Kuhn's view, Strange's reluctance to jump ship is entirely understandable. In fact, Kuhn argues that the mere existence of anomalies—even glaring, important ones—doesn't cause scientists to abandon a paradigm in which they've been trained. Instead, they will abandon such a paradigm only if they are presented with a new paradigm that they can adopt in the old one's place (and they won't always do so then!). Along with offering a solution to the troubling anomalies, this new paradigm needs to make novel predictions and to offer an attractive, elegant picture that leaves plenty of room for future work, in the form of unsolved puzzles. It is only when the Ancient One presents Strange with such an option that he is finally willing to leave his old life behind.

The Dark Dimension? Why Understanding Is Tougher than It Seems

Much of what we've said so far would fit pretty well with how many scientists, historians, and philosophers have often described the scientific method. Doctor Strange encounters a problem that he can't solve, formulates and tests a number of hypotheses aimed at producing a solution, and finally, finds one that works. Sure, sorcery is a bit different than the sort of scientific theories which work in our world, but that doesn't make Strange's approach any less scientific. For Kuhn, however, this misses the most interesting aspect of the story, which involves the transition between paradigms. When we look back at the history of science (or when the Sorcerer Supreme Strange looks back on his life), we might be tempted to think that the paradigm chosen in the moment of crisis was *obviously* closer to the truth than the old one was, and therefore we've made undeniable forward progress. Kuhn, however, argues that the history of science reveals a much messier process. In many cases, there simply are no clear, "objective" criteria that might allow adherents of one paradigm to rationally persuade adherents of another paradigm to convert and join their cause.

In particular, Kuhn argues that paradigm change is far from the sort of slow, incremental process that one might expect if scientists were simply incorporating new evidence piece-by-piece into their existing paradigms. Instead, new paradigms emerge quite suddenly, and the initial evidence in their favor is often relatively minimal, especially when compared to the historical successes of the old paradigm. The first scientists to adopt a new paradigm do so because they believe that working in the new paradigm will allow them to move forward. However, to adherents of the old paradigm, this often appears as little more than blind faith, especially because the new paradigm almost always involves ideas and methods that are alien to the point of incomprehensibility. (Just think of how Strange's medical school teachers might react if he told them he'd become a sorcerer!) In Kuhn's terms, rival paradigms are *incommensurable*: there is simply no general method for translating the concepts taken from one paradigm into those of another. In a very real sense, scientists who adopt different paradigms literally experience different worlds, which contain very different sorts of things.

Kuhn's claim that paradigms are incommensurable is the most controversial and influential part of his book, but it's also a claim that is easily misunderstood. With this in mind, it will help to look more closely at Strange's experience. When Strange first encounters the evidence of sorcery, such as Pangborn's cured paraplegia and his own initial experiences with the Ancient One, he reacts with disbelief. He eventually changes his mind, though, when he becomes convinced that sorcery really is the best explanation for the anomalies he's observed, and then thinks that sorcery will allow him to solve the sorts of problems that interest him (such as his injuries). However, he doesn't commit to becoming a sorcerer until he finally realizes that he can genuinely make a contribution to the field and help to solve problems that even Mordo and the Ancient One struggle with.

It is at this stage that Strange first encounters the problem of incommensurability. He wants to become a sorcerer, and perhaps even explain some of the general ideas, such as the existence of other dimensions, that sorcery is based on. However, as it turns out, adopting a scientific paradigm requires more than memorizing lists of formulas. To truly understand things like the nature of dimensional energy, Strange has to master the methods for manipulating this energy, which requires long, tedious practice with simple spells. As it turns out, novice sorcerers—much like novice physicists—can't really understand their theories just by reading explanations of them in textbooks or listening to wise old physicists or sorcerers talk about them. Instead, they have to learn how these theories are actually applied to standard sorts of problems, which Kuhn calls *exemplars*. The knowledge that Strange gains from this is much more of a "knowledge *how*" rather than a "knowledge *that*"—it is something he learns to do rather than some theory he has memorized.

Kuhn argues that scientists adopting a new paradigm learn to "see" the world in a new way through this process. So, by the conclusion of his training in sorcery, it's not simply that Strange has picked up a few new tricks and memorized some complex chants and arm gestures. Instead, he finds himself in something like a different world, filled with very different sorts of things than his old world. He is in a world which demands that he respond in very different ways. Moreover, this is something that he will likely find hard to explain to colleagues. And if Kuhn is correct, Strange shouldn't be too surprised if it proves difficult to convince his old colleagues of the correctness of his new ideas, even if he manages to get the idea across. After all, the sorcery skeptics might argue that contemporary medicine has solved lots of problems, and it would be foolish to let a few anomalies centered around one strange doctor cause them to give it up.

Somewhat surprisingly, Kuhn would also argue that a figure like Strange would be especially well positioned to make paradigm-shifting advances in his new field of sorcery. Kuhn notes that, historically, most scientific revolutions were driven neither by the oldest, most experienced practitioners in a field, nor amateurs with little or no training. Instead, they were driven largely by people like Strange: newcomers to the field who have received enough training to understand how the paradigm works but who haven't yet become set in their ways. Like Strange, such innovators often come from other scientific disciplines and are often seeking the solutions to problems that the "normal" practitioners of the field had left unexplored.

Puzzles about Paradigms

Kuhn, like Popper before him, fundamentally changed the way that many scholars looked at science. Where they once had seen a slow, orderly march toward ever-greater understanding, it now appeared as if scientific revolutions had more in common with political revolutions, or even with religious conversions, than with the dispassionate application of the "scientific method" taught in schools. While such methods have their place to play in normal science, revolutionary science is much closer to Doctor Strange's initial, baffling encounter with the Ancient One. Adopting a new paradigm requires scientists to radically rethink not just their theories and methods, but also their overarching view of what the world is fundamentally like and what their role in this world is.

What does this mean for science in the real world? Should we conclude that the paradigm of sorcery is just as trustworthy as that of medicine, and that they have equal claims to be counted "scientific," for good or ill? Kuhn's writing is a bit ambiguous on these sorts of questions. When *The Structure of Scientific Revolutions* first came out, many readers took it to be arguing that the revolutionary decision of a scientific community to abandon one paradigm for another was a fundamentally irrational process, driven by very different factors than those relevant to explaining normal science. On this view, the incommensurability between various paradigms prevented any and all comparisons between them that might allow for rational choice. For example, when working as a neurosurgeon, Doctor Strange is perfectly capable of identifying the best surgical techniques to use, and can even explain and defend his choice to interns and colleagues. When he is working as a sorcerer, he can do the same thing when it comes to spells. What he can't do, however, is present a rationally compelling argument to a neurosurgeon that they ought to become a sorcerer, or vice versa.

In later editions of his book, however, Kuhn put a greater emphasis on the existence of more general scientific norms that could be used to judge between paradigms, and on the possibility of "translating" between competing paradigms. In the end, Kuhn thought the scientists themselves were the ones best placed to see how and when it made sense to change paradigms, even if their reasons for doing so couldn't always be made explicit to outsiders. Kuhn even notes the importance of people like Strange—masters of multiple paradigms— to this process, because they can help scientists in rival paradigms understand what exactly their rivals are up to, and what it might mean to adopt their paradigm as one's own. While these translations would always be partial and incomplete—after all, no one but another sorcerer could fully understand Strange's explanation of sorcery—they provide a good starting point, at least to those who come with open minds.

Like most philosophers and historians of science, Kuhn himself offered little advice on how contemporary scientists ought to do their work. However, he did worry that people were too quick to see "paradigms" wherever they looked, and that this caused them to overlook the ways in which mature sciences like physics and chemistry really were different from other human activities. For Kuhn, mastering a paradigm required much more than simply agreeing on a general outlook on life. Instead, a scientific paradigm required detailed agreements both on what sorts of problems mattered and on the precise manner in which they could be solved. It is only because scientists have these agreements that they can get down to the business of puzzle solving, which makes up their normal work life. Mature science, for Kuhn, was genuinely and fundamentally different from almost everything else humans did.

After Kuhn, Things Got Stranger

The Structure of Scientific Revolutions was among the most important and influential books on philosophy of science ever published, and it led to major changes in the way many people—philosophers, sociologists, historians, and even scientists themselves—saw science. However, rather than ending the debate about the nature of science, Kuhn's book started a number of new debates. To close, we'll take a brief look at two philosophers of science who followed Kuhn, and we'll consider what they might have to add to our account of Doctor Strange's transition from surgeon to sorcerer.

Some post-Kuhnian philosophers, such as Paul Feyerabend (1924–1994), embraced and expanded upon the idea that there were no rational, objective criteria by which one might judge competing scientific theories as better or worse, or even for distinguishing "scientific" theories from religious or mystical ones. Feyerabend's *methodological anarchism* held that, when it came to science, the only rule was "anything goes." After all, he reasoned, once we try to set down rules for excluding certain theories from consideration, we will find that we have ruled out obviously legitimate scientific theories.[3]

For example, consider how sorcery must have originally appeared to Doctor Strange. It contradicted basic physics; it was based on "primitive" ideas that most people had given up long ago; and sorcerers didn't behave at all like contemporary scientists. They didn't publish their findings, present them at conferences, run randomized controlled trials, and so on. This might seem like more than enough reason to reject sorcery. However, Feyerabend argues that, if we look closely at the history of science, we'll discover that many scientific theories (such as the sun-centered solar system) started off in much the same way. Because of this, we ought to be very wary of claiming that certain theories just "can't" work, or that we can simply ignore them as possibilities.

If Feyerabend is right, then real-life neurosurgeons and researchers might benefit from some Strange-like openness to ideas from outside of mainstream science. In particular, Feyerabend argues that if science is to continue to progress, scientists must continually be open to the possibility that some very different ideas might be the source of the next medical or scientific advance, no matter how bizarre they might seem now. Moreover, the mere fact that these ideas seem superstitious or mystical is not itself a good enough reason to reject them.

Even if the vast majority of these theories are flawed in one way or another, the attempt to grapple with them will help us better understand why and how the theories we do adopt actually work. Feyerabend's ideas have remained quite controversial among both philosophers and scientists. After all, it's one thing to claim that sorcery could be a science in an alternate world like the one Doctor Strange lives in. It's quite another to claim that scientists in the actual world should have to consider sorcery as a serious rival for government funding, or as a possible subject to be included in high school science classes.

In contrast to Kuhn's emphasis on the agreement of the scientific community and Feyerabend's call for methodological anarchism, Imre Lakatos (1922–1974) argued that there were clear, objective criteria for distinguishing between *progressive* and *degenerating* scientific research programs. Interestingly, Lakatos argued that the distinction had to do with how the scientists dealt with failure. Like Kuhn, Lakatos argued that scientists almost never abandon the "hard core" of ideas that makes up the heart of their approach to the world. So, the Ancient One doesn't abandon sorcery after one failed spell, and Doctor Christine Palmer doesn't abandon medicine after the death of a patient. Instead, scientists make modifications to the *protective belt* of ideas around their hard core: the Ancient One might try a new pronunciation for a word and Palmer can change the dose of a drug. Lakatos held that research programs were progressive when these modifications to the protective belt led to new predictions and discoveries. By contrast, a program is degenerating when the modifications to the protective belt are merely defensive maneuvers intended to prevent falsification. That is, in a progressive program, the changes made by the Ancient One and Palmer really should lead to better results, as opposed to simply serving as "excuses" for their failures.

Lakatos emphasized that there was no foolproof way in which philosophers or scientists could determine whether a particular, contemporary scientific research program would make progress in the future. After all, the history of science is full of examples of promising programs that ran into unforeseen problems, as well as of old, abandoned theories finding "new life" in the light of experimental results. Lakatos might not have much advice to give to Doctor Strange, other than to remind him of the importance of keeping a careful, honest record of his successes and failures, with respect to both medicine and sorcery. However, Lakatos would insist that when it came time for philosophers and historians to tell the story of how Strange came to abandon medicine for sorcery, they should be able to explain why his choice was a rational one, based on objective criteria. Lakatos thought that both Kuhn and Feyerabend, by playing up the sociological and nonrational aspects of the history of science, failed to do just this.

Of Science, Sorcery, and Philosophy

For Thomas Kuhn and his rivals, the story of a figure like Doctor Strange might have most value when we focus on the contrast between our world and his. Strange provides us with a clear picture of what it would it take for a seemingly outlandish idea like sorcery to become a scientific paradigm. Importantly, Kuhn argues that this would require much, much more than the mere inability of contemporary medical science to solve some problem or other. Instead, we would need to discover, as Strange does, both the existence of significant anomalies within current science and the sorcerous solutions to such anomalies. We would need not only to present a theoretical justification for thinking that spells might work, but also to develop a rigorous education program for young sorcerers on the precise techniques for various spells. Finally, and most importantly, we would need assurance that the paradigm could be extended to new problems through the use of methodical, puzzle-solving techniques, and that we, like Dr. Strange, could eventually find our ways to new dimensions.

More broadly, one might wonder: Why bother with the philosophy of science at all? After all, many scientists seem to get along quite well without considering such matters, and their work doesn't appear to suffer. However, this sort of quick dismissal misses some important benefits. First, as Kuhn emphasizes, the mere fact that scientists *usually* don't need to worry about philosophical issues hardly means that they never do. After all, when scientists like Doctor Strange find themselves in the midst of a scientific revolution, they have no choice but to consider the big, philosophical questions about reality, knowledge, and the relationship between the two. Second, even for those of us who don't aspire to be scientific revolutionaries, philosophy of science can help demystify the "scientific" approach to the world, even when it comes to theories as magical as those adopted by Doctor Strange.

Notes

1. Thomas S. Kuhn, *The Structure of Scientific Revolutions: 50th Anniversary Edition*, ed. Ian Hacking (Chicago: University of Chicago Press, 2012).
2. For a short, very readable introduction to the ideas of Popper, Kuhn, and the other philosophers of science we'll be discussing, see Alan F. Chalmers, *What Is This Thing Called Science?*, 4th ed. (Indianapolis: Hackett Publishing, 2013).
3. Paul Feyerabend, *Against Method* (London: New Left Books, 1975).

14
Doctor Strange, the Multiverse, and the Measurement Problem

Philipp Berghofer

"We harness energy, drawn from other dimensions of the multiverse, to cast spells, to conjure shields and weapons, to make magic." This is how the Ancient One introduces magic into the Marvel Cinematic Universe (MCU) in the 2016 film *Doctor Strange*. So far, the MCU has offered a narrowly scientific universe in which the powers of its heroes are more (Iron Man) or less (Thor) scientifically explained. By contrast, magic is a rather tricky subject, and some fans feared that Doctor Strange, who is all about the magic, might not fit well into this universe. Based on the film, though, we see that the way magic was incorporated is not only scientifically sophisticated but also touches on the arguably most important problem in philosophy of physics: the measurement problem. The nature of the multiverse itself raises further philosophical questions about interpreting quantum mechanics that Doctor Strange can help us answer.

A Strange Cat

In the MCU, according to the Ancient One, magic is created by drawing energy from the other dimensions of the multiverse, which may sound like a concept from science fiction, but the idea that we are living in a vast multiverse is very possibly science fact. In current scientific debates, there are many different concepts of the multiverse, one of them based on ideas from quantum physics.

Doctor Strange and Philosophy: The Other Book of Forbidden Knowledge, First Edition. Edited by Mark D. White.

Physicist and astronomer Adam Frank, who served as the scientific consultant for *Doctor Strange*, provides some insights about what they had in mind when introducing the multiverse:

> [One] idea for a multiverse is the many-worlds interpretation of quantum mechanics, where every time a quantum event happens, the universe splits off into a parallel version of itself, and each one goes on evolving and splitting and evolving and splitting. This idea of extra, other dimensions, what you can think of as other universes—we talked a lot about that idea. And they draw on that pretty heavily [in the movie].[1]

In the *many-worlds interpretation*, the multiverse is like a tree in which every possible outcome at the quantum level forms its own branch of reality. For example, consider the famous thought experiment of "Schrödinger's cat": a cat is in a box containing an unstable atom that may decay and kill the cat. Quantum physics seems to imply that the cat is not alive or dead, but both alive *and* dead, until someone opens the box and observes the cat, thus collapsing it into one state or the other. In the many-worlds version of the multiverse, when we open the box, one branch of reality forms in which the cat is alive, and another forms in which it's dead, both existing in parallel universes of the multiverse.

As outlandish as it may sound, in terms of experimental confirmation and explanatory success, quantum mechanics is our most successful scientific theory. At the heart of quantum mechanics, however, there is a deep philosophical puzzle. The formalism of quantum mechanics seems to imply that even macroscopic objects like cats can be in two contradictory states—alive and dead—at the same time. But we never observe things like this, much less measure them. Does this mean, then, that quantum mechanics is wrong? Or does it mean that our everyday experiences are mere illusions? Different interpretations of quantum mechanics aim at different answers to these questions, and show that interpreting a physical theory is a genuinely philosophical endeavor that, strictly speaking, goes beyond the task of science.

Philosophy and Physics—Not Such a Strange Combination

A recurring and especially important theme in *Doctor Strange* is the role that we human beings are supposed to play in the universe. Are we just tiny, momentary specks within an indifferent universe? More precisely, are we just tiny, momentary specks within an indifferent *multi*verse? The concept of the multiverse is well established in the Marvel comics and has now officially been introduced into the MCU, and the way it's introduced touches on central issues in the philosophy of physics.

Since the very beginning of both disciplines, philosophy and physics have been intimately related. Thales of Miletus (c. 624–c. 546 BCE) is not only widely considered the first Western philosopher and the first Greek mathematician, but also gained considerable fame for predicting the solar eclipse of May 28, 585 BCE. Furthermore, he's credited with introducing a new way of explaining nature that doesn't appeal to mythological explanations, but instead uses observations, hypotheses, and theories—that is, a scientific methodology. For example, you observe an apple falling on the ground, and you form a hypothesis that masses attract each other. It is crucial for a hypothesis to be testable, or make predictions that can be verified or falsified in the process of experimentation. The successful testing of hypotheses can lead to a scientific theory like Newton's theory of gravity. However well verified, though, scientific theories can turn out to be inconsistent with new observations and be replaced by new theories, just like Newton's theory of gravity was superseded by Einstein's theory of general relativity.

Due to the success of the natural sciences, many scientists (and many philosophers too) started to believe that science can answer all meaningful questions. If the empirical method is the only legitimate method of gaining knowledge, then all of philosophy could be reduced to natural science. This is precisely the attitude exemplified by Doctor Strange at the beginning of the movie. But many questions in philosophy cannot be answered through observation and experimentation, such as: What is the difference between right and wrong? What does happiness feel like? How do we know what we know? Many of these questions are *metaphysical* in nature, going beyond the physical world, and by definition are resistant to scientific answers.

Philosophy and physics fit well together because they share many of the same interests, such as the nature of change, time, space, and matter.[2] It shouldn't come as a surprise, then, that some of the most notable philosophers, such as René Descartes (1596–1650), have made crucial contributions to mathematics and physics, and that some physicists, such as Albert Einstein (1879–1955), have made important contributions to philosophy and even have used philosophical methods such as thought experiments to gain crucial physical insights.[3]

The two fields come together in the philosophy of physics, which is concerned with interpreting the theories delivered by physics.[4] Physical theories are often mathematical models capable of predicting natural phenomena. But what do these mathematical models tell us about reality, about the real world? Here quantum mechanics is of special significance. As we know, quantum mechanics is one of the most successful theories ever delivered by physicists. But what does the mathematics of quantum mechanics tell us about the reality we see around us? Physicists—at least, those who care—and philosophers are undecided on this. But the multiverse gives us an opportunity to explore one such interpretation.

Leveling Up

One of the fascinating and beautiful things that physics tells us about physical reality is how the smallest things are connected to the biggest. The shining of the stars and the mass of planets, for instance, can only be explained by invoking particle physics. According to the many-worlds interpretation, the theory of the smallest—quantum mechanics—implies that we are living in a vast and constantly branching multiverse.

While the Ancient One tells Doctor Strange that "this universe is only one of an infinite number," the earliest known scientific reference to a multiverse comes from Nobel laureate Erwin Schrödinger (1887–1961), who declared in a lecture in Dublin in 1952 that the different possible realities predicted by his theories are not alternative possibilities "but all really happen simultaneously."[5] Often, the conception of a multiverse is called a scientific theory. However, it might be more appropriate to call it the *prediction* of certain scientific theories.[6] For instance, there is empirical evidence that space might be infinite. However, if this is so, and if space is not mostly empty space but filled with uniformly distributed matter, then it follows that there are an infinite number of regions in the universe the same size as our observable universe. And within these infinite number of parallel universes there are an infinite number of universes that are identical to ours... Infinity really is at war with our intuitions!

One might say that, in such a picture, our whole universe is "just another tiny, momentary speck within an indifferent [multi]verse." In the terms of contemporary cosmologist Max Tegmark, we just described a Level I multiverse. If the MCU is a Level I multiverse, there exists an infinite number of Doctors Strange—just very far from each other. A Level II multiverse is one made up of Level I multiverses existing parallel to each other, and is actually predicted by some current versions of cosmic inflation. Whereas universes in a Level I multiverse obey the same laws of physics, universes in a Level II multiverse can differ more widely, including their physical constants such as the speed of light.

Wait, it gets even better—even more counterintuitive than the Level I and Level II multiverses is the Level III multiverse, which goes back to physicist Hugh Everett III (1930–1982), who introduced the many-worlds interpretation. Recall that this theory implies that the universe is constantly branching with each and every quantum event. As a result, an infinite number of copies of you and me exist in the multiverse.[7]

This kind of multiverse has important differences from Level I and Level II versions that also make it resemble the multiverse introduced in *Doctor Strange*. In a Level I or Level II multiverse, a person has no influence on the structure of reality or on the other parallel universes, but in a Level III multiverse, you can make reality branch and create whole universes by conducting quantum experiments. Also, some argue that a Level III multiverse is what allows for quantum computation, so success in that area suggest that we really do live in such a multiverse.[8] As Tegmark writes, quantum computers "are most easily explained as, in essence, exploiting the parallelism of the Level III multiverse for parallel computation."[9]

All of this sounds similar to what sorcerers do in the MCU. As the Ancient One explains to Doctor Strange:

> The language of the mystic arts is as old as civilization. The sorcerers of antiquity called the use of this language "spells." But if that word offends your modern sensibilities, you can call it a program. The source code that shapes reality. We harness energy, drawn from other dimensions of the multiverse, to cast spells, to conjure shields and weapons, to make magic.[10]

Strange was initially skeptical about magic; similarly, some contemporary scientists have their doubts about the multiverse, in part, because many of its predictions cannot be tested. While many scientists don't take the idea seriously at all, others have argued that "quantum theory leaves no room for any doubt that multiple universes exist"[11] and that "by this time, the only astonishing thing is that that's still controversial."[12]

The Marvel Multiverse and the MCU

Importantly, the MCU is only one universe within the vast multiverse within Marvel Comics. In the Marvel Multiverse, parallel universes are called Earths. Earth-616 is the universe where most of the comics take place. One of this universe's heroes is Doctor Strange, who is also one of the most powerful beings of this realm. However, the Doctor Strange of Earth-616 is not the only one in the Marvel Multiverse, not by a long shot. For example, there is a Doctor Strange on Earth-199999, which happens to be the MCU. Curiously enough, the MCU (or Earth-199999) is itself a multiverse, which means it is a separate multiverse within the larger Marvel Multiverse.

Compared to Earth-616, science plays a much larger role in the MCU. Over the course of the movies and television series, Marvel has tried to establish a scientifically consistent picture of the MCU in which phenomena that are called "magic" in the comics receive some kind of scientific explanation in the movies. This is not only true for *Doctor Strange* but also for earlier movies such as *Thor*. This can be seen in subtle ways, like Jane Foster originally being a nurse on Earth-616, while in the MCU she is a leading astrophysicist—and more obvious ways, like the Rainbow Bridge (Bifrost) being explained as an Einstein-Rosen bridge (a special kind of wormhole).

As the Collector explains in the 2014 film *Guardians of the Galaxy*, the MCU formed when six singularities collapsed and caused a big bang. In the process, the singularities condensed and formed the six Infinity Stones. One of these Stones is the Time Stone, found within the Eye of Agamotto and used by Doctor Strange at the end of the movie to save Earth by trapping Dormammu in a time loop. Thousands of years ago, the first Sorcerer Supreme, Agamotto, discovered the existence of other dimensions and learned how to draw energy from these parallel universes—and became aware of threats lurking there. Agamotto built three sanctuaries to protect Earth from the greatest extradimensional threat: the dread Dormammu, ruler of the Dark Dimension. Besides the Dark Dimension, other parallel dimensions within the MCU include the Astral Dimension and the Mirror Dimension (seen in *Doctor Strange*), the Quantum Realm (seen in *Ant-Man* as well as *Doctor Strange*), Hell and the Darkforce Dimension (seen in *Agents of S.H.I.E.L.D.*), and K'un-Lun (seen in *Iron Fist*).

Concerning the classification of different types of multiverses in the previous section, we can ask: What kind of multiverse is the MCU? When introducing the multiverse in *Doctor Strange*, the filmmakers heavily drew on concepts and ideas which appear in the famous many-worlds interpretation of quantum mechanics. Unfortunately, though, this question of what kind of multiverse we see in the MCU is very difficult to answer, not only because the movie doesn't give us enough information, but also because of the most important problem in philosophy of physics: the measurement problem.

Can Doctor Strange Both Be and Not Be Sorcerer Supreme?

Quantum mechanics is hands-down one of the greatest accomplishments of science. In terms of explanatory power and accuracy of predictions, it is physics' most successful theory and, together with general relativity, can be considered the foundation of all physics. Its applications range from laser technology, magnetic resonance imaging (MRI), and the electron microscope, to electronic devices we use every day such as our computers and mobile phones. In some sense, however, quantum mechanics is also "the great scandal of physics."[13] Although quantum mechanics is astonishingly successful in telling us the likelihood of events that we can measure—that is, predicting the results of measurements and occurrences of macroscopic phenomena—it fails to provide a firm conceptual framework that can explain its own success. Simply put: What is a measurement? Why is there such a fundamental difference between the quantum realm and the macroscopic one we see?

At the heart of quantum mechanics there is a principle of *quantum superposition* that seems to be in conflict with our everyday observations. After all, we never observe cats in a state of superposition such as being dead and alive at the same time. So we have a dilemma: Either quantum mechanics is wrong, or we are profoundly mistaken with respect to our everyday observations.

One of the most fascinating aspects of quantum mechanics can be seen through the double-slit experiment, which highlights the fact that an object like a photon can be a particle and a wave at the same time—until we try to observe or measure it. While we might expect a photon to act like a particle and pass through either slit 1 or slit 2 in a board, it can also act like a wave and pass through slit 1 *and* slit 2 (in a state of superposition). We see this with the double-slit experiment. Things get really strange, though, when we modify the experiment by placing detectors at the slits; then we find that photons do not pass through both slits but instead only one or the other. When the photons are detected at the slits, they no longer show wave-like behavior, so it seems that observation or measurement *itself* leads to a collapse of the wave function.

Furthermore, the Schrödinger equation implies that "superpositions can 'spread' through interactions" and "be amplified up to the macroscopic level."[14] In other words, it isn't just quantum objects like photons that can be in states of superposition, but even macroscopic objects such as cats, stones, and Sorcerers Supreme. But why don't we ever observe such macroscopic superpositions? Is quantum mechanics wrong? One popular line of thinking is that the wave function collapses upon observation, which brings each of us into the big picture in a fascinating way.

A Cat and an Unstable Atom Walk into a Bar...

Understanding the apparent collapse of the wave function upon observation is the core of the measurement problem. There are different ways of explaining this, which are called "interpretations" of quantum mechanics. Once we get to these interpretations, we are doing philosophy. Physics provides the formalism of quantum mechanics, delivers the equations, and makes testable predictions. But what this formalism tells us about reality—whether, for instance, wave functions are real physical objects or merely mathematical tools—are questions that go beyond physics in the strict sense. The same holds for providing an interpretation of quantum mechanics that explains the apparent collapse of the wave function. The most influential of these, called the Copenhagen interpretation, goes back to Niels Bohr (1885–1962). The Copenhagen interpretation comes in different flavors, but according to the version that is most faithful to Bohr's original ideas, we can know *that* the wave function collapses upon measurement, but we can't know *why* this happens. According to this pragmatic understanding, quantum mechanics and science in general are only supposed to give us a way to make precise and accurate predictions of what we can observe. They're not supposed to explain what the world really is or why.

Many researchers have pointed out that this seems like a cop-out. In general, we don't expect science only to let us make predictions about the world but also we want it to explain how it works. Consider Einstein's general relativity, which, together with quantum mechanics forms the foundation of all current physics. When general relativity told us that spacetime is curved and can be bent by mass and energy, we didn't merely accept that this would let us make useful predictions. Rather, we want to believe that spacetime actually is curved and can be bent. There seems no reason why we should have different standards for quantum mechanics—and this is a philosophical judgment, not a purely scientific one.

Another version of the Copenhagen interpretation, first proposed by John von Neumann (1903–1957) and later picked up by Eugene Wigner (1902–1995), credits the observer's *mind* with the collapse of the wave function upon observation. We see this reflected in the MCU when the Ancient One tells us that "thoughts shape reality." If true, the von Neumann-Wigner interpretation has tremendous philosophical implications regarding the entanglement of mind and matter. For example, it would challenge *dualism*, the metaphysical position that the mental and physical worlds are distinct, and would give a different perspective on *materialism*, which holds that all mental phenomena can be reduced to physical states.

The famous "Schrödinger's cat" thought experiment was meant to demonstrate that the Copenhagen interpretation was untenable, but can be used to argue against the von Neumann-Wigner interpretation more specifically. As summarized above, a cat and an unstable atom are in a box. Within an hour, there's a 50/50 chance the atom will decay or not, and if it does, the cat dies. The unstable atom is in a state of superposition: decayed and not decayed. If superpositions can spread through interactions, then is the cat also in a superposition of dead and alive? The von Neumann-Wigner interpretation implies that only when the box is opened and observation takes place does the state of the cat collapse into either being dead or alive—beforehand, it is literally both at the same time, which seems absurd. But the many-worlds interpretation of quantum mechanics, and the resulting multiverse, can help make sense of it all.

So Many Cats, So Many Doctors Strange

Although the many-worlds interpretation was hardly taken seriously at first, now it is one of the main approaches to the measurement problem and is championed by many notable physicists. According to its proponents, there is no collapse of the wave function. Instead, whenever a quantum event takes place, reality splits and branches into all the possible outcomes. When we open the box and see that the cat is alive, this means that in our branch of reality the atom has not decayed, but in another it has (and there, the cat is dead).

However, the cat, all of us, and our whole universe still exist in states of superposition. In each branch of reality we only observe one outcome of a quantum event—the cat is either alive or dead—but the whole multiverse itself is in a state of superposition, because the cat is both alive and dead in its different incarnations in different universes. The state of the multiverse is itself described by a wave function: the universal wave function. Since quantum events take place all the time, the many-worlds interpretation implies that our universe is constantly splitting and branching, creating infinitely many actual worlds and infinitely many copies of ourselves at different branches within the multiverse. (This also means that in the multiverse there are indeed dark and terrible universes, even universes in which *Doctor Strange*—and this book—have never been released!)

Despite its wider acceptance among scientists, there remain objections to the many-worlds interpretation. One is that it is simply counterintuitive. Intuitions play an important role in philosophical reasoning; as contemporary philosopher Alvin Goldman wrote, "One thing that distinguishes philosophical methodology from the methodology of the sciences is its extensive and avowed reliance on intuition."[15] We simply "know" that a statement can't be both true and false at the same time, that a valid argument is better than an invalid one, or that murder is morally wrong.

However, many of our intuitions about the structure of the physical world have turned out to be wrong. Intuitively, it seems absurd that Earth is not flat but a sphere in space, or that the Earth circles around the sun incredibly quickly. It is even more counterintuitive that space and time are curved and can be bent by mass and energy, although it has been proven by numerous experiments. Our intuitions about the physical world have been shaped, at least in part, by thousands of years of evolution, and the truths about the shape of spacetime or the nature of the multiverse are not necessary to survive and reproduce. Intuitions might be a trustworthy source of knowledge in many areas, but not with respect to the structure of the universe. Mordo's advice to Doctor Strange to "forget everything you think you know" isn't relevant only for budding sorcerers, but also for regular folks like you and me trying to appreciate the fundamental laws of the universe.

The many-worlds interpretation also seems to fall to Ockham's razor, also known as the principle of parsimony, which says "the simpler, the better." If there are two scientific theories that can explain the same phenomena, other things being equal, this principle says to choose the simpler one.[16] On the face of it, this is a plausible claim (and very intuitive). For example, the motion of the planets could be explained by having the sun at the center with all the planets revolving around it, or by having the Earth at the center, with the sun revolving around it and all the other planets revolving around the sun. The difference may be simply a matter of perspective—you can put our moon at the center if you want—but it's definitely simpler to put the sun at the center with Earth as one of the planets circling it. It simply works better in terms of prediction and understanding.

Given that the many-worlds interpretation points to the existence of an infinite number of parallel universes, Ockham's razor seems to be a real threat. Because it's the only interpretation of quantum mechanics that requires the existence of more than one world, it hardly seems to be the simplest theory out there. However, it is much simpler in other important ways, elegantly solving the problems of measurement and superposition without having to resort to alternative explanations such as "hidden variables," to resort to more complicated dynamics, or to implicate the mind of the observer as the all-powerful Collapser of Wave Functions. In this sense, Ockham's razor may pick out the many-worlds interpretation as the simplest theory we have.

We've Run Out of Time... or *Have* We?

The many-worlds interpretation allows human beings to play an amazingly active role in shaping reality. We can make reality split and create whole new universes by conducting quantum experiments, and we can exploit the structure of the multiverse for quantum computation. It has even been argued that the many-worlds interpretation allows solving the "grandfather paradox" of time travel. This means that a person could travel back in time and kill their own grandfather without creating the unfortunate situation of never having been born, because you would just create a different universe (or timeline).[17] The many-worlds interpretation definitely gives us a different way to think of Doctor Strange when he traps Dormammu in a time loop. This is yet another way he manipulates the nature of his multiverse in addition to using it as a source of magic. In a way, Doctor Strange's sorcery can be regarded "simply" as a quantum experiment—like pulling a cat out of a box.

Notes

1. Sarah Lewin, "'Doctor Strange' Physicist Talks Mind-Bending Marvel Science," *Space.com*, November 3, 2016, available at http://www.space.com/34604-mind-bending-science-doctor-strange.html
2. It should be pointed out, however, that many physicists do not share the opinion that philosophy can contribute anything useful to physics; as a famous quote reads, "philosophy of science is about as useful to scientists as ornithology is to birds."
3. Besides Einstein, Galileo Galilei (1564–1642) is most often considered to have conducted thought experiments to gain insights in how nature works. See James Brown, *The Laboratory of the Mind: Thought Experiments in the Natural Sciences* (London: Routledge, 1991).
4. For more, see Dean Rickles, *The Philosophy of Physics* (Cambridge: Polity Press, 2016).
5. David Deutsch, *The Beginning of Infinity* (New York: Penguin, 2011), 310.
6. See Max Tegmark, "Many Worlds in Context," in Simon Saunders, Jonathan Barrett, Adrian Kent, and David Wallace (eds.), *Many Worlds?* (Oxford: Oxford University Press, 2012), 553–581.
7. I should mention that there is one more type of multiverse in Tegmark's classification: the Level IV multiverse. This is where things get really crazy because in this multiverse, everything that is mathematically possible actually exists. Parallel universes can radically differ in their fundamental physical equations, which makes them much stranger than anything you (or the special effects wizards behind *Doctor Strange*) can even imagine.
8. See David Deutsch, "Apart from Universes," in Saunders et al, *Many Worlds?*, 542–552, at p. 542; and also Deutsch, *The Fabric of Reality* (New York: Penguin, 1997).
9. Tegmark, "Many Worlds in Context," 578.
10. All quoted dialogue is from the 2016 film *Doctor Strange*.
11. David Deutsch, "Comment on Lockwood," *The British Journal for the Philosophy of Science*, 47(1996): 222–228, at p. 224.
12. Deutsch, "Apart from Universes," 542.
13. David Wallace, "Philosophy of Quantum Mechanics," in Dean Rickles (ed.), *The Ashgate Companion to Contemporary Philosophy of Physics* (Abingdon: Ashgate, 2008), 16–98, at p. 16.
14. Rickles, *Philosophy of Physics*, Section 7.4.
15. Alvin Goldman, "Philosophical Intuitions: Their Target, Their Source, and Their Epistemic Status," *Grazer Philosophische Studien*, 74(2007): 1–26, at p. 1.
16. As Wong told Doctor Sharanya Misra when she tried to rationalize the mystical phenomena she witnessed: "Simpler explanations are generally

better than more complex ones" (Devin Grayson, *Doctor Strange: The Fate of Dreams*, New York: Marvel Worldwide, 2016, 18).

17. See David Deutsch, "Quantum Mechanics near Closed Timelike Lines," *Physical Review D*, 44(1991): 3197–3217; and David Wallace, *The Emergent Multiverse* (Oxford: Oxford University Press, 2012), Section 10.6.

15
The Strange World of Paradox
Science and Belief in Kamar-Taj

Matthew William Brake

"True believers." That's the phrase the legendary Stan Lee always uses when talking about Marvel Comics fans. People have many different beliefs—beliefs about magic, God, the power of love, and so on. Belief can give life its shape and meaning, but in an age of science, belief in things unseen is often scorned. At best, it's considered wishful thinking or a crutch for the weak-minded; at worst, it's a dangerous, perhaps fanatical delusion. How can we say that something exists if it can't be detected in the physical world?

The movie *Doctor Strange* offers a unique opportunity to explore this question. While the tendency in the Marvel Cinematic Universe has been to explain magic scientifically (as in the *Thor* films), director Scott Derrickson, himself a religious person, makes clear that in his film, "We're not explaining magic scientifically. Magic is magic." He goes on to say, "I can't help but view the world mystically. It's how I see it. I'm not a strict materialist. I think there's much more to the world than what we see with our five senses."[1] Even though Derrickson says that he avoided a simplistic debate between religion and atheism in his film, he did want the movie to be "a third thing where we're talking about magic and we're talking about mysticism and we're talking about possibilities and other realities."[2]

To frame Derrickson's point a bit differently, the *Doctor Strange* film provides us with an opportunity to consider the Danish philosopher Søren Kierkegaard (1813–1855). Asking whether it is possible

Doctor Strange and Philosophy: The Other Book of Forbidden Knowledge, First Edition. Edited by Mark D. White.
© 2018 John Wiley & Sons Ltd. Published 2018 by John Wiley & Sons Ltd.

"to discover something that thought itself cannot think," Kierkegaard invites us to enter a strange world of paradox.[3]

At the Door of Kamar-Taj

A man with a scraggly beard stands outside pounding on a seemingly random door on a random street in Kathmandu, Nepal. "No! Open the door! Please! Don't shut me out. I haven't got anywhere else to go."[4] The man is Doctor Stephen Strange, a gifted but arrogant and self-obsessed surgeon. Fans of the character know that this man is destined to become the Sorcerer Supreme of our dimension, its foremost defender against mystical threats, but at the beginning of this story, Doctor Strange is a worldly physician who nonetheless performs medical "miracles" with his steady hands.

Strange's success as a surgeon changed the night the car he was driving went off the road and his hands were mangled in the wreckage of broken glass and twisted metal. Waking up to a view of his hands covered in braces and metal pins, having suffered severe nerve damage, he realized that he had to find a way to restore his hands to their previous functionality or his career and reputation as a leading surgeon would be over. This brings us back to the door in Kathmandu, which is actually the entryway to a sanctuary called Kamar-Taj, where Strange hopes to find a cure for his condition.

Before Kamar-Taj, Strange sought his cure through the only means he could understand: medicine and science. Medicine and science always push the boundaries of what we can know about the human body and the universe, constantly discovering new methods and drugs through research and experimentation. Yet, Strange found himself pushing up against the limits of what medicine knew and what it was able to do. At one point, he advocated for an experimental surgery that, while very risky, was still possible, saying, "All I need is 'possible.'" Strange sought to push the boundaries of what medicine could do for him, but even he couldn't push those boundaries quickly enough to save his hands.

Strange's struggle to find a way to heal his hands helps us understand what Kierkegaard means when he says, "This, then, is the ultimate paradox of thought: to want to discover something that thought itself cannot think," which isn't a bad thing, "for the paradox is the passion of thought."[5] The passion to discover what thought cannot think drives and motivates us to think more, but a thinker who lacks this paradox "is like the lover without passion: a mediocre fellow."[6] Since his accident, Strange has certainly been passionate to discover what thought has been unable to think. This passion drives his quest, but as Kierkegaard would say, Strange has hit a barrier beyond which is "that which thought cannot think itself."

The Unknown, the Frontier, and the Collision

Kierkegaard writes that "it is also the ultimate passion of the under-standing to will the collision" with the unknown.[7] Although Strange seeks this collision in his journey to Kamar-Taj, he is unaware of the personal price he must pay for even a glimpse of the unknown. Mordo, one of the Ancient One's more advanced students, ominously hints that such a price must be paid when he says to Strange, "Can I offer you some advice? Forget everything you think you know."

Even though Strange is desperate to have his hands healed, he is still self-assured in his knowledge and expertise as a surgeon. This leads to a misunderstanding with the Ancient One, who asks Strange, "When you reattach a severed nerve, is it you who heals it back together or the body?" Strange responds, "It's the cells." For a moment, Strange thinks that the Ancient One has discovered an experimental (but unsanctioned) breakthrough with cellular regeneration. Strange is disappointed, however, when she shows him a picture of an acupunc-turist's map of the human body and equates it with an MRI scan, stating that both are accurate mappings of the body from different perspectives. He then realizes that she is not offering a scientific and medical treatment for him, and he is incredulous, saying, "You're talking to me about healing through belief?"

As a physician and a man of science, Strange has a strictly material-ist worldview. Kierkegaard is biting in his criticism of such people, calling them, "those mere butcher-apprentices who think they can explain everything with a knife and with a microscope."[8] Kierkegaard argues that focusing on physical explanations and calculations can be "a way of providing myself with a lot of sly evasions and excuses. I wonder if my gaze is not turned away from the most important thing by letting myself begin with physiology."[9] The materialist may admit that he can't explain everything, but "what does he do then? He skel-etonizes, he dissects, he pierces with knives as far in as he can, in order to show—that he cannot!"[10] Kierkegaard highlights the folly of what he describes as "the self-contradiction inherent in this quantitative, approximating *almost*" of the materialist thinker.[11] Rather, scientific materialists must "acknowledge that there is something they cannot understand, or, more accurately, something that they clearly understand that they cannot understand."[12]

In all of Strange's attempts to heal his hands, he has sought that which his scientific mind could not think of by itself, but now finding it, he bumps up against what Kierkegaard calls "the unknown as frontier."[13] But understanding can't go beyond this frontier, even though that frontier is "passion's torment [and] also its incentive."[14] It's as if the unknown and absolutely different "seems to be at the point of being disclosed, but not so, because the understanding cannot even think the absolutely different."[15] It is this frontier that Strange is unable (and unwilling) to pass beyond.

In response to Strange's obstinacy, the Ancient One strikes Strange, propelling his soul out of his body and into the "astral plane." When his soul rejoins his physical form, Strange is clearly shaken, and asks the Ancient One, "What just happened?" She answers, "For a moment, you entered the astral dimension. A place where the soul exists apart from the body." When he asks why she is doing this to him, she replies, "To show you just how much you don't know." The Ancient One then sends Strange careening on a trippy tour of the multiverse, his mind unable to conceive of what he's seeing. As he travels, the Ancient One speaks to him:

> You think you know how the world works? You think that this material universe is all there is? What is real? What mysteries lie beyond the reach of your senses? At the root of existence, mind and matter meet. Thoughts shape reality. This universe is only one of an infinite number. Worlds without end; some benevolent and life-giving, others filled with malice and hunger. Dark places where powers older than time lie, ravenous and waiting. Who are you in this vast multiverse, Mr. Strange?

Strange is thrown violently back to the floor of Kamar-Taj, ending up on his knees. He has paid the price that a collision with the unknown demands: his self-knowledge and assurance have been disturbed. Looking up to the Ancient One, he pleads, "Teach me." But she responds, "No," and Strange is thrown out of Kamar-Taj, having caught a glimpse of the unknown but again finding himself with a barrier or frontier between him and what thought cannot think.

Socrates and "the God" as Teacher

Kierkegaard begins his *Philosophical Fragments* with this question: "Can the truth be learned?"[16] Yes, he answers, but one learns it from a teacher. Strange's journey to Kamar-Taj was inspired by a conversation with a man named Jonathan Pangborn. During Strange's recovery, his physical therapist told him about a man who had recovered from paralysis caused by a severe spinal injury. While initially skeptical of this anecdote, Strange eventually finds Pangborn on a basketball court, clearly mobile and active. Pangborn is initially hostile toward him and begins to walk away. Strange shouts after him, "You were untreatable. You came back from a place there's no way back from. I'm trying to find my own way back." Pangborn relents and tells Strange about his own journey to Kamar-Taj, where "I found my teacher. And my mind was elevated," and as a result, he was healed.

Kierkegaard describes two different kinds of teachers in the *Fragments*. The first is the Socratic teacher: According to Kierkegaard, the ancient Greek philosopher, Socrates (469–399 BCE) held that in order to learn the truth, truth must be sought. However, this presents a problem, because

a person cannot possibly seek what he knows, and, just as impossibly, he cannot seek what he does not know, for what he knows he cannot seek, since he knows it, and what he does not know he cannot seek, because, after all, he does not even know what he is supposed to seek.[17]

It's a fair point: how can someone seek the unknown if they don't even know the unknown exists? How would anyone know to even begin seeking it?

The Socratic teacher's reply is that the knowledge of the unknown is already inside of a person—they have just forgotten and need help remembering.[18] Socrates described his own role as teacher in terms of a midwife who helps others give birth to the truth, calling this role "the highest relation a human being can have to another."[19] The teacher is not in a place of authority over the learner but merely serves as a catalyst for the learner to discover that "his self-knowledge is God-knowledge."[20] Every human being is sufficient in themselves, and the teacher is helping to realize this about each person "with equal humility and equal pride"—pride because the teacher is sufficient for himself, and humility in willing to be an occasion "even for the most stupid person" to realize the truth inside of them.[21]

There is a second kind of teacher that Kierkegaard describes: the god as teacher.[22] Kierkegaard discusses what type of teacher is needed if in fact human beings don't have the truth within themselves. What if, in fact, human beings are not only "outside the truth" but are themselves "untruth?"[23] If that's the case, then "what would be the use of reminding him of what he has not known and consequently cannot call to mind?"[24] Rather than being an occasion for the learner to recollect the truth he already has inside of him, the god as teacher is an occasion for the learner to remember that he is untruth and "excluded from the truth, even more than when he was ignorant of being untruth."[25]

When describing this occasion, Kierkegaard seems to describe the Ancient One when she threw Strange out of Kamar-Taj:

> Consequently, in this way, precisely by reminding him, the teacher thrusts the learner away, except that by being turned in upon himself in this manner the learner does not discover that he previously knew the truth but discovers his untruth. To this act of consciousness, the Socratic principle applies: the teacher is only an occasion, whoever he may be, even if he is a god, because I can discover my own untruth only by myself, because only when *I* discover is it discovered, not before, even though the whole world knew it.[26]

All of Strange's medical colleagues knew his weakness, namely, that he thought he knew everything. His ex-girlfriend Dr. Christine Palmer knew it, as did his physical therapist. Mordo knew it even before he invited him into Kamar-Taj. But it was only when Strange encountered something beyond his knowledge and was thrown out into the street that he himself understood his actual condition: that he was outside of the truth, that he was untruth. The only hope for the learner now is that the god will give him not only the truth, but also the very condition for being able to receive the truth.

The Ancient One seems to be a combination of the Socratic teacher and the god as teacher. She admits to Strange that she did not heal Pangborn. He healed himself, and she merely convinced him that he could. This indicates that the knowledge he needed was already inside of him; he needed only to remember or recollect. In her interactions with Strange, however, she revealed his condition as untruth, as the god-teacher would. It was only by the Ancient One's touch that he was able to recognize himself as untruth. He was outside of the truth because of his own arrogance, or as Kierkegaard puts it, "he is untruth and is that through his own fault."[27] Ultimately, it was only through the Ancient One that he was given the condition to receive the truth and embrace the unknown—that which thought cannot think.

Offense and the Paradox

Kierkegaard writes, "If the paradox and the understanding meet in the mutual understanding of their difference, then the encounter is a happy one."[28] As we know, however, Strange's initial encounter with the Ancient One was far from happy. Returning to Strange's incredulous reaction to the Ancient One's description of the acupuncture map of the human body alongside the MRI:

STRANGE: I spent my last dollar getting here, one-way ticket... and you're telling me about healing through belief?

ANCIENT ONE: You're a man looking at the world through a keyhole. You've spent your whole life trying to widen that keyhole. To see more. To know more. And now, on hearing that it can be widened, in ways you can't imagine, you reject the possibility.

STRANGE: No, I reject it because I do not believe in fairy tales about chakras or energy or the power of belief. There is no such thing as spirit! We are made of matter and nothing more. We're just another tiny, momentary speck in an indifferent universe.

ANCIENT ONE: You think too little of yourself.

STRANGE: Oh, you think you see through me, do you? Well, you don't. But I see through you!

To put this exchange into context, let's look at how Kierkegaard describes offense as suffering, which can come in more than one form:

> However it chooses to express itself, even when it gloatingly celebrates the triumph of spiritlessness, it is always suffering. No matter if the offended one is sitting crushed and staring almost like a beggar at the paradox, petrifying in his suffering, or even if he arms himself with mockery and aims the arrows of his wit as if from a distance—he is nevertheless suffering and is not at a distance.[29]

Strange may have tried to act like he was superior to the Ancient One through his verbal attack, but despite this act of distancing himself from her claims, the intensity of his passion reveals "the extent to which [his] offense is indebted to the paradox."[30]

Strange's offense came "into existence with the paradox," stemming from the very encounter with the unknown.[31] Offense misunderstands the paradox; Kierkegaard calls it "the erroneous accounting" of the paradox and "the conclusion of untruth."[32] Offense says that "the paradox is foolishness," but the paradox renders "the understanding [into] the absurd," so "what the understanding regards as very important" is no longer important.[33] The understanding and the offense no longer understand themselves, but are "understood by the paradox."[34] Likewise, Strange didn't understand the offense of his understanding as he bumped up against the paradox of the unknown, but the Ancient One did, as the one who could provide the condition for Strange overcoming his offense and embracing the unknown.

Surrendering to the Unknown

Five hours have passed since the Ancient One evicted him from Kamar-Taj, and Strange has become morose, leaning against the door. Suddenly, there is the sound of a buzzer from inside; the door opens, and Strange falls backward through the doorway, offering a sorry sounding, "Thank you."

The new student, humbled by the recognition that he is untruth, begins his training. He starts by learning to use a sling ring, a device that allows one to create a portal to anywhere one can picture in one's mind. Strange attempts, albeit unsuccessfully, to create a portal; he blames his hands, but the Ancient One demonstrates through one of the other masters, who is missing a hand yet still wields the sling ring expertly, that the problem is not with Strange's physical injury, but rather with Strange's understanding:

ANCIENT ONE: You cannot beat a river into submission. You have to surrender to its current and use its power as your own.
STRANGE: I control it by surrendering control? That doesn't make any sense.
ANCIENT ONE: Not everything does. Not everything has to. Your intellect has taken you far in life, but it will take you no further. Surrender, Stephen.

If one wants to discover what thought cannot think, then one must give up the control one assumes over it through one's understanding. Here again, the possibility of offense is present, and the question becomes "will you or will you not obey... or will you take offense?"[35]

One cannot grasp the unknown as though it were an object controlled by one's ability to comprehend it. What is the solution then? For Strange, the solution came as he heeded the words of the Ancient One, such that as "the understanding surrendered itself ... the paradox gave itself."[36]

A life surrendered to the unknown is a life of faith or trust, operating according to principles beyond what the mind can comprehend. As Kierkegaard writes,

> To have faith is simply to achieve buoyancy by taking upon oneself a considerable gravity; to become objective is achieving buoyancy by tossing cargo overboard. To believe is like flying, but one flies with the aid of a counteracting gravity.[37]

Faith is like flying higher and higher the heavier gravity gets—or like controlling magic by surrendering to it. It means letting go of one's vanity, "the vanity of not willing to obey as a child but of wanting to be an adult who can comprehend and who then will not obey what he cannot comprehend."[38] When it comes to the unknown, we must submit to its tutelage and "defend [ourselves] against the vain thought of wanting to comprehend and against the vain imagination of being able to comprehend."[39] If one wants to discover the unknown, however, one must travel down a road "where all human road signs point: back, back, back."[40]

Knock and the Door Will Be Opened... Eventually

Kierkegaard writes in his journals, "It is eternally true that if one knocks, the door will be opened. But suppose that the difficulty for us human beings is simply that we are afraid to go—and knock."[41] Returning to the image of Doctor Strange desperately knocking on the door to Kamar-Taj, the quest to find "that which thought cannot think" can feel like pounding on a door with no guarantee that it will open. Then again, how many of us are really seeking the unknown? Before his accident, Strange certainly wasn't. He might have been saving lives and advancing medical knowledge, but like the physician Kierkegaard describes in his journal, Strange saved people's lives because it was fun, out of a sort of vanity.[42] It was only Strange's change of fortune that elicited the search for the unknown.

Like Strange, many of us don't seek the impossible until we have become unhappy and existence has become painful, for such journeys are often undertaken out of a sense of profound need and despair.[43] None of us like having our normal lives and expectations turned upside down, if we can help it. If there is an unknown to discover, however, hopefully we have a willingness to find it without needing to get our hands—and our egos—crushed.

Notes

1. Jayson D. Bradley, "The Complex Faith of 'Doctor Strange' Director Scott Derrickson: Why He's Hollywood's Most Interesting Filmmaker," *Relevant Magazine*, issue 84, November/December 2016, available at http://archives.relevantmagazine.com/culture/film/director-strange
2. Ibid.
3. Søren Kierkegaard, *Philosophical Fragments*, ed. and trans. by Howard V. Hong and Edna H. Hong (Princeton, NJ: Princeton University Press, 1985), 37. (Actually it was his pseudonym Johannes Climacus who said this, which is an important distinction to make in Kierkegaard scholarship, but we're not going to worry about the significance of that right now… or at all.)
4. All the dialogue quotations in this chapter are from the 2016 film *Doctor Strange*.
5. Kierkegaard, *Philosophical Fragments*, 37.
6. Ibid.
7. Ibid.
8. Søren Kierkegaard, *Søren Kierkegaard's Journals and Papers*, Vol. 3.1, L–P, ed. and trans. Howard V. Hong and Edna H. Hong (Bloomington, IN: Indiana University Press, 1975), 241.
9. Ibid.
10. Ibid.
11. Ibid., 247.
12. Ibid., 406.
13. Kierkegaard, *Philosophical Fragments*, 44.
14. Ibid.
15. Ibid., 45.
16. Ibid., 9.
17. Ibid.
18. This relates to Socrates's belief in the pre-existence of the soul, as Kierkegaard points out in ibid., 10.
19. Ibid.
20. Ibid., 11.

21. Ibid.
22. While Kierkegaard's literary project does have an overarching Christian orientation, in *Philosophical Fragments*, his description of the god is meant to be a "pre-Christian" thought experiment.
23. Kierkegaard, *Philosophical Fragments*, 13.
24. Ibid., 14.
25. Ibid.
26. Ibid.
27. Ibid., 15.
28. Ibid., 49.
29. Ibid., 50.
30. Ibid., 51.
31. Ibid.
32. Ibid.
33. Ibid., 52.
34. Ibid., 50.
35. Kierkegaard, *Søren Kierkegaard's Journals and Papers*, vol. 3.1, 366.
36. Ibid., 54.
37. Søren Kierkegaard, *Søren Kierkegaard's Journals and Papers*, vol. 2, F–K, ed. and trans. Howard V. Hong and Edna H. Hong (Bloomington, IN: Indiana University Press, 1970), 9–10.
38. Ibid., 14.
39. Ibid.
40. Ibid., 22.
41. Ibid.
42. Kierkegaard, *Søren Kierkegaard's Journals and Papers*, vol. 3.1, 246.
43. Kierkegaard, *Søren Kierkegaard's Journals and Papers*, vol. 2, 8, 24.

Part V
"IT'S NOT ABOUT YOU"

16
The Otherworldly Burden of Being *the* Sorcerer Supreme

Mark D. White

Stephen Strange is a lonely man. As the Sorcerer Supreme, he is Earth's sole protector from mystical forces that threaten its very existence. Only he can see the various ghouls, interdimensional demons, and evil sorcerers that conspire to destroy humanity, and only he can fight back against them using the deep secrets of magic, which he learned at the feet of his master and the previous Sorcerer Supreme, the Ancient One. As he reflects in a recent comic, "I have a unique position in the realm of magic. A burden and responsibility so great it cannot be shared with any living entity."[1]

Strange's sense of isolation was present in Stan Lee and Steve Ditko's original stories in *Strange Tales* beginning in 1963, and was illustrated spectacularly by artist Chris Bachalo in his recent run of *Doctor Strange* with writer Jason Aaron.[2] In many pages throughout this run, Bachalo shows Doctor Strange walking the streets of Manhattan with the world that everyone else sees in black and white, while mystical threats of all shapes and sizes swirl around them in dazzling color, visible only to Strange (even without using the Eye of Agamotto). Doctor Strange thus shoulders the unique and solitary burden of protecting others in their blissful ignorance.[3]

The fact that he assumes this burden voluntarily and without complaint is part of what makes him a hero. However, like many heroes, Doctor Strange goes too far sometimes. In this chapter, we'll explore several ways in which Strange fails to operate with the proper balance

Doctor Strange and Philosophy: The Other Book of Forbidden Knowledge,
First Edition. Edited by Mark D. White.
© 2018 John Wiley & Sons Ltd. Published 2018 by John Wiley & Sons Ltd.

between extremes, what moral philosophers in the tradition of virtue ethics call the "golden mean."

A Strange Doctor Indeed

As fans of his adventures in the comics and movies know, before Stephen Strange was Sorcerer Supreme, he was a world-famous neurosurgeon. Some would say he was the world's best neurosurgeon—especially Strange himself. He chose the surgeries he performed, not to do the most good or save the most lives, but to make the most money or achieve the most fame. He bragged about his skill, flaunted his wealth, and treated women as a means to an end. Essentially, he was Tony Stark with a scalpel, showing that these "awesome facial hair bros," as Tony calls them, have more in common than goatees.[4]

As a medical doctor, Strange was living his life at the extremes. He possessed tremendous skill which, to be fair, he did use to help others, but not for that reason. As Stan Lee would put it in another great comic he created with Steve Ditko, Strange neglected the great responsibility that came with his great power as an expert neurosurgeon.[5] Outside the operating room he lived as a hedonistic man-child flitting from one temporary pleasure to another, never contemplating the deeper nature of being or life and never attaining true happiness or flourishing, which the ancient philosophers called *eudaimonia*.

Those same philosophers would also argue that Doctor Strange, M.D., was not living a life of virtue. *Virtue ethics* is the oldest of the three major schools of ethics, originating with Aristotle and the Stoics over two thousand years ago. The other two, *deontology* and *utilitarianism*, are far more recent, their current versions dating from the eighteenth and nineteenth centuries. Aristotle is the best known and influential of the virtue ethicists, and it is his understanding of virtue, laid out primarily in his *Nicomachean Ethics*, that we will use throughout this chapter.[6]

Virtues are positive character traits, such as courage, honesty, and generosity, which contribute to a good life and *eudaimonia* for those who possess them as well as others they interact with. The specific traits that are considered virtuous are hardly controversial—any ethical system worth the name would agree that honesty is generally moral.[7] Aristotle's unique contribution to our understanding of virtues lies in the concept of the "golden mean," the idea that virtues are found in the middle (or "mean") between two extremes. For example, the virtue of courage is between cowardice at one extreme and foolhardiness at the other; similarly, honesty is found between the extremes of deceitfulness (outright lying) and forthrightness (complete, unfiltered openness). In theory, the golden mean is easy to define, but in practice it is difficult to achieve, changing with each situation and the person facing it. Returning to the example of courage, Aristotle wrote that the brave person is one "who faces and who fears the right things and from the right motive, in the right way and from the right time."[8] This is not a simple idea of virtue but a multifaceted one, which demands *judgment*, honed by experience, to put into practice in each unique circumstance.[9]

In his early life as a doctor, Strange was anything but virtuous. You can say he did the right thing by developing and refining his talents to become a premier neurosurgeon and save lives. But he did not practice medicine in the right way or for the right reason; instead, he chose the cases he would take based on their potential to bring him fame and fortune. Rather than finding the golden mean of generosity between selflessness and greed, he chose the extreme of greed. He followed a similar pattern in his private life: rather than finding the golden mean of temperance between self-denial and gluttony, he embraced the extreme of gluttony. Strange may have been a fine doctor as far as skill and knowledge are concerned, but he was not a virtuous person.

The Sorcerer Extreme

Strange's carefree and reckless lifestyle helped contribute to the automobile accident that crushed his hands, ending his medical career and leading him to seek out the mystical healing powers of the Ancient One. After initially doubting magic as "hocus pocus," Strange ultimately accepted that there is another world beyond what he can see (as gloriously depicted in the 2016 film). He renounces his arrogant, self-centered ways and submits to the Ancient One's tutelage, pledging to help protect the Earth from mystical threats. Once his training is complete, Doctor Strange returns to New York City, taking up residence in his Sanctum Sanctorum with his servant Wong and his assortment of magical trinkets. Ultimately, after the Ancient One ascends to become one with the universe—as you do—Strange assumes the mantle of this dimension's Sorcerer Supreme.[10]

Is the mystical Doctor Strange more virtuous than the medical Doctor Strange? "By the Hoary Hosts of Hoggoth," you shout, "of course he is! He's a selfless hero now, not the narcissistic surgeon he was." Not so fast, young disciple. Virtue is found not just in what a person does but also how he or she does it. We saw earlier that, as a medical doctor, Strange did much good, saving lives with his matchless surgical skills. But he was not virtuous in how he practiced medicine or conducted his life in general, operating (no pun intended) at the extremes and never even trying to find the golden mean. After his mystical education, though, he did not become less extreme—merely extreme in a different way.

As the narration in the 1986 graphic novel *Doctor Strange: Into Shamballa* reads, when Stephen first climbed the Himalayan mountains in search of the Ancient One,

> he was a mere man then: bitter, spiteful, avaricious—and grim as Death. Now, so the whispered legends would have us believe, you are far more. Now you are called—Master of the Mystic Arts. Since assuming this majestic title, you appear to have ripped bile, malice, and greed from your heart. A pity you have not yet learned to smile.[11]

To be fair, Stephen Strange did go from one extreme to a very different one when he experienced his spiritual epiphany. Specifically, he went from being a self-centered individual to an utterly selfless one, devoted to protecting humanity rather than serving his own narrow interests. "I was a wreck of a man: a selfish cold-hearted fat-walleted S.O.B.—then a miserable alcoholic bum—and my master the Ancient One showed the way, the way of disciple, dedication—self-denial!"[12] And while it is reasonable to say that the extreme of excessive generosity is better than the extreme of no generosity at all, it is better yet, from the viewpoint of virtue ethics, for Strange to find the middle between the two extremes where he is practicing the *best* kind of generosity, helping others while not ignoring his own well-being.

Time and time again, though, Doctor Strange fails to find this golden mean, instead operating at an extreme level of generosity and selflessness. From his earliest tales, he had already assumed responsibility for protecting all of humanity from all mystical threats, saying things like "where mankind is menaced by magic... there must Dr. Strange go to combat it!"[13] Later, he lamented: "Many things there are that mankind must not know—not until the human race stands ready to accept that which is, but can never be seen! A nameless menace threatens the world—and I must face it alone!"[14] The narration at the end of another early adventure reads:

> Dawn is breaking over the city—the city which cannot suspect the strange forces lurking beyond the border of man's imagination! But, so long as they exist, just so long will Dr. Strange be here to battle them, in the name of humanity![15]

I could go on—trust me—but the key point is that Doctor Strange has assumed sole responsibility for all life on Earth, and indeed in its entire dimension, whatever the cost.[16]

The Sorcerer Solitary

And the cost is high, especially the way Strange conducts himself. For example, he does not rest. Even early on, he acknowledges the mental and physical toll of being the Earth's mystical protector: "I am exceedingly weary! For days I have gone without sleep in my unending battle against the supernatural forces which menace mankind!"[17] Others know it as well: as his disciple and lover Clea muses, "He tires, he hungers, he makes mistakes... yet he has chosen to protect the rest of unsuspecting mankind from evil—to stand alone against the unknown dangers that lurk in the kingdoms of magic."[18] During the recent destruction of the Marvel Universe, Doctor Strange even sells his soul (or what remained of it) to gain absolute mystical power to try to prevent the end of the world.[19]

Of course, no one knows this better than Wong, who tells Clea that "for many years now, he has borne the weight of the world upon his shoulders... and by temperament and avocation, he is a solitary man!"[20] Solitude is an extreme that Stephen Strange practiced as both a surgeon and a sorcerer, although for different reasons. Before his accident, Strange made few close connections with other people because of his oversized ego; he had few friends because he regarded most people as beneath him, and he treated women as playthings rather than partners. To Doctor Strange, M.D., people were just like things, money, and even his own skill, to be used for his pleasure and then discarded.

After his accident, Strange gained humility and perspective, appreciating the value of life and dedicating his own to protecting humanity. However, he continued to keep other people at arm's length, but now it was because he felt his mission took precedence over relationships, another element of his excessive practice of generosity and selflessness. As he tells Clea when she questioned his love for her, "I have my promises to the Ancient One to keep. You understand as I do that the balances of good and evil must be maintained. I have little time for anything else."[21] During a similar conversation later, he tells her, "I must deny myself! I have to be pure and undistracted to do what must be done! I can't—I can not—I can not love another!"[22] As a result of this self-imposed isolation, none of his relationships with other people were truly reciprocal, which virtue ethicists such as Aristotle feel is a necessary component of any true friendship.[23]

Consider three of Strange's most important relationships: with his mentor, the Ancient One, with his servant, Wong, and with his love interests, most important among them Clea. Obviously, his relationship with the Ancient One was one-sided, as befits a master and disciple, and continued in that fashion long after the Ancient One's ascension (and occasional return to human form, only to ascend again once he finished his Netflix queue). This relationship was mirrored in the ongoing one between Strange and Wong, even though they have had time to grow much closer as friends than Strange and the Ancient One ever did. (One can imagine that Wong's father, Hamid, may have been as close with the Ancient One, whom he served for many years.) Strange and Wong obviously care strongly for each other, but theirs is still, at its heart, a dynamic between master and servant, not a friendship among equals that Aristotle described as the ideal.

Strange Romance

Most interesting are Strange's relationships with women he has cared for since he became Earth's mystical protector. While he has eschewed the laddishness of his earlier days, Strange still keeps an emotional distance between himself and women he cares for. As the narration reads while he reflected on a recent adventure: "Every woman he has known... he has held them at arm's length. And when the woman Topaz kissed him with unexpected fervor—he recoiled! Recoiled both in body and spirit!"[24] This is true even with his longest-lasting relationship, with the extradimensional sorceress Clea. Initially appearing as a stereotypical "damsel in distress," Clea quickly became Strange's disciple and lover—and wife, albeit in a mystical, extradimensional sense—and developed her own magical abilities, eventually becoming ruler of the Dark Dimension, succeeding her mother Umar and before her, Umar's brother the dread Dormammu. (Imagine their holiday dinners!)

Thrown together by circumstance and then adopting a teacher-student relationship, it is no wonder that Strange and Clea never seemed to form the loving, romantic bond of other classic comics couples such as Superman and Lois Lane, Spider-Man and Mary Jane Watson, or Tony Stark and Tony Stark. Instead, the dual nature of their relationship interfered with the equality of status necessary for true friendship and romantic love to prosper. Strange realizes this when he thinks to himself, "Perhaps I should never have made Clea my disciple. The duality of our relationship was always an impediment to our love. Perhaps... if I had not been the master, and she the disciple... we might still be lovers."[25] Clea has acknowledged the problems with their asymmetric relationship, as seen when she gives up being his disciple to devote herself to their love. In time she comes to doubt her love for him, realizing it may have been merely admiration, and decides to leave for the Dark Dimension.[26] Stephen and Clea's relationship has never been a settled one, as this essential imbalance has never been resolved.[27]

So when it comes to his close relationships with other people, Stephen Strange seems to be doomed to be separate and alone. This is somewhat understandable given Aristotle's requirement that true friendships be among equals: after all, Strange is *the* Sorcerer Supreme and, as such, literally has no equal. However, friends need not be exact equals, but just comparable in ways that ensure their compatibility. While it may be difficult for Strange to form close relationships with ordinary humans, he could bond with other superheroes, even if they're not mystical in nature. Despite his self-proclaimed lone wolf status, Strange can be a team player, occasionally working with the Avengers or the Illuminati, and more regularly with the Defenders and most recently other Sorcerers Supreme from throughout history. But even his closest colleagues in the Defenders—Namor the Sub-Mariner, the Silver Surfer, and the Incredible Hulk—are not the most sociable heroes in the Marvel Universe, which may indicate that Strange's issues with relationships run deeper than simply having trouble finding pals.[28]

"I Must Save Humanity. Or Most of Them.
At Least One of Them"

Even though Doctor Strange is overly zealous in how he prioritizes his mission as Earth's mystical defender over his personal life, the choices he makes in pursuit of that mission are nuanced. While he talks a lot about how he must protect all of humanity on Earth (or all life in this dimension), he often shows preference for some lives over others, whether that means favoring those in this world or dimension over others, or even one life close to him over countless others.

The examples are many. In one of his earliest adventures, Strange realizes that, to save the lives of everyone on Earth from Dormammu, he must endanger the inhabitants of the Dark Dimension whom Dormammu protects from the Mindless Ones. Even though Clea pleads for her people, Strange bows his head and says, "I wish to bring no harm to this fantastic world... and yet my first duty is to Earth... and the ones who inhabit it! I have no choice... I must be true to my oath!"[29] In a much more recent adventure, Strange and the rest of the Illuminati—a secretive cabal of genius superheroes who have appointed themselves protectors of the world—became aware of repeated "incursions" of parallel Earths that must be destroyed to save their own.[30] While Strange's old Defenders colleague Namor is the one who pushes the button to destroy the first alternate Earth, Strange acknowledges that they all have played a role in the outcome, asking (and answering), "If the road I have traveled always led me here, were the choices still all mine? I think they were. I'm not a victim. I'm not a pawn. I chose this," even if the outcome of that choice was as unacceptable as the alternative.[31]

Such decisions, where any choice leads to catastrophic consequences and the decision-maker cannot escape "with clean hands," are what philosophers call *tragic dilemmas*, and they lie at the core of many superhero stories. After all, what is more dramatic than our hero being forced to decide between saving two planets from destruction, necessarily condemning the inhabitants of one to death? Ideally, our hero finds a way to save both worlds, but as in the real world, this isn't always possible. In the debate among the Illuminati once they became aware of the incursions, Captain America is the sole voice urging the rest not to accept a fatal solution, arguing that "I believe we'll find a way to stop it. And we'll do it without sacrificing who we're supposed to be." Doctor Strange speaks for the rest when he says, "That's just another way of saying, *I hope*, and today—after what we've seen—how could I possibly find comfort in that?"[32] Tragic dilemmas demand that some action be taken even though none is acceptable, and in this way they highlight the need for judgment in choosing what action to take when simple ethical rules don't provide the answer, which virtue ethicists have emphasized for thousands of years.[33]

But not all of the dilemmas Strange faces are this evenly balanced, with billions of lives on each side of the equation. Sometimes, his choices show a shocking degree of partiality in that they favor the lives of a select few people close to him—or even just one—over the lives of many anonymous souls who depend on him. In one adventure, Strange is forced to destroy the Sanctum Sanctorum to save the lives of Wong and Topaz (she of the recoiling kiss) from an alien sorcerer named Urthona to prevent him from obtaining the power of all the magical artifacts and instruments stored there. Just before he casts the final spell, Strange asks himself,

> But what are my choices? I who was chosen guardian of these objects of power—can I destroy these that guard and aid me against all the dark powers that would prey on my world? But if I leave them in Urthona's hands... I must strike at the most immediate threat and trust in my abilities to deal with the consequences! Or am I letting my concern for the safety of personal friends override what's best in the long run?[34]

In effect, this resembles several others times that Strange has relinquished some of his mystical power or retired altogether.[35] Ironically, these may be indications that Doctor Strange is introducing some moderation into his life, being more willing to balance his role as Earth's protector with his life as Stephen Strange. This is not usually the case, though: when he retires it doesn't last long, and when he sacrifices some power, he doesn't seem to relinquish any responsibility (showing that even when heroes give up great power, their sense of great responsibility never goes away).

For the Life of Wong

More recently, Strange chose to sacrifice the lives of countless people to save the life of one: Wong. In an adventure combining his mystical and medical lives, Doctor Strange fought a corrupt pharmaceutical CEO named Nicodemus West who had come into possession of the legendary "panacea," an elixir that could cure any disease.[36] During the search, Wong reveals that he has been suffering from an inoperable brain tumor. By the end of the story, most of the panacea is lost, with only a single drop remaining. Strange faces a very personal tragic dilemma: duplicate the drop of panacea and use it to save countless lives around the world, but in the meantime letting Wong die, or use the last drop to save Wong. "It's not fair," he says. "I can't condemn the world to save my friend." West invokes the particular (and very partial) duties of the physician when he replies, "And yet, you took an oath never to withhold treatment from patients under your care ... All you do is ask which choice will allow you to look yourself in the mirror come morning."[37]

In the end, Strange chose to use the last drop of the panacea to save Wong, telling his servant and friend that it was "the very least I owed you" for saving his life recently and presumably many times to come. The Night Nurse, who joined Strange and Wong on this adventure, helps Strange feel better about his choice: "Look, you and I both know we can't save everyone. The best that doctors can do is take care of the people who entrust their lives to us. Leave the search for new cures to the drug companies."[38]

Was it selfish for Strange to favor the lives of those close to him over anonymous others? It seems unethical on the surface: if we take every life to be equally valuable, then there would seem to be no good reason to favor the life of someone who happens to be close to you over someone who is not so lucky to know you! Surprisingly, perhaps, philosophers are often supportive of a certain degree of partiality. Virtue ethicists, in particular, who emphasize both friendship and judgment, often acknowledge that people will favor those close to them when there is a choice of whom to help: a person who has the chance to save either her friend or a stranger is within her rights to save her friend, given that she could only save one.[39]

But Strange went much further than this: he saved Wong at the expense of saving countless others stretching into the future. A normal allowance for partiality in ethical behavior would have to stretch awfully far to cover a choice to save one person close to you over potentially billions of strangers.[40] While this affirms the closeness of the friendship between Strange and Wong, possibly even countering the unequal nature of it, it does call into question Doctor Strange's moral judgment—and at the same time confirms the imperfect and partial humanity at his core.

The Sorcerer So Human

The bright side of Doctor Strange's partiality to his friends is that it shows a crack in his extreme, ascetic façade. While he is still not operating at the golden mean by any stretch of the Ditko-inspired imagination, Strange does have his moments. For example, he refused ascension when the Ancient One offered it to him. With Clea at his side, he tells his mentor that "I am still searching for answers. I can't raise myself above asking questions. I'm still young. My life and loves are still before me."[41] He also occasionally opens himself to romantic attachments, such as when he tells Morganna Blessing that he's "achieved a high level of mastery over many things—and taken on responsibilities. But by doing that, I've lost something—the ability to be human." When she argues that saving the world from mystical destruction is more important, Strange responds, "the love and fear in the human heart is just as important as the power of the Vishanti and the Hosts of Hoggoth combined!"[42] Unfortunately, Doctor Strange can't seem to maintain his balanced and virtuous perspective for long—even the Eye of Agamatto can't help the good doctor see this truth for very long.

Notes

1. *Doctor Strange and the Sorcerers Supreme* #1 (December 2016), collected in *Doctor Strange and the Sorcerers Supreme: Out of Time* (2017).
2. For the original stories by Lee and Ditko, see *Marvel Masterworks: Doctor Strange, Volume 1* (2003) and *Volume 2* (2005). Aaron and Bachalo's run starts with *Doctor Strange: The Way of the Weird* (2016).
3. However, he does want to educate the public as well. As Devin Grayson wrote in her novel *Doctor Strange: The Fate of Dreams* (New York: Marvel Worldwide, 2016):

   [Strange] often found himself wishing there were better ways to share the more wondrous, inspiring facets of magic with the general population while continuing to shield them from the terrors that lurked in the shadows. As it was, he endeavored to drip-feed knowledge of the paranormal to them, hoping to slowly raise the consciousness of the general population at a speed they could tolerate.

   (pp. 27–28)

4. *Invincible Iron Man*, vol. 2, #3 (January 2016), collected in *Invincible Iron Man: Reboot* (2016). Strange hates it when Tony says this… or does he? (See issue #5, March 2016, in the same collection.)

5. Even though Strange met Spider‑Man soon after their respective introductions, Spidey never had the chance to tell him about his Uncle Ben. (Oh Uncle Ben!) See *Amazing Spider‑Man Annual*, vol. 1, #2 (October 1965), "The Wondrous World of Dr. Strange," reprinted in *Doctor Strange*, vol. 1, #179 (April 1969) and collected in *Marvel Masterworks: Doctor Strange, Volume 1* and *Spider‑Man/Doctor Strange: The Way to Dusty Death* (2017).

6. Aristotle, *Nicomachean Ethics* (350 BCE), available at http://classics. mit.edu/Aristotle/nicomachaen.html. For an overview and comparison of these three schools of ethics, see my chapter "Superhuman Ethics Class with the Avengers Prime," in Mark D. White (ed.), *The Avengers and Philosophy: Earth's Mightiest Thinkers* (Hoboken, NJ: Wiley, 2012), 5–17.

7. For more examples of virtues, see the Chapters 2, 6, and 7 by Lee, Manninen, and Timm, respectively, in this volume.

8. Aristotle, *Nicomachean Ethics*, Book III.7.15–20.

9. For more on judgment in the context of superheroes, see my chapter "Moral Judgment: The Power That Makes Superman Human," in Mark D. White (ed.), *Superman and Philosophy: What Would the Man of Steel Do?* (Hoboken, NJ: Wiley, 2013), 5–15, and Chapter 5 in Mark D. White, *The Virtues of Captain America: Modern‑Day Lessons on Character from a World War II Superhero* (Hoboken, NJ: Wiley, 2014).

10. This short history is based on the comics, though the film followed the main beats very closely.

11. *Doctor Strange: Into Shamballa* (1986).

12. *Strange Tales*, vol. 2, #1 (April 1987), "And Have Not Charity…," collected in *Doctor Strange: Strange Tales* (2011).

13. *Strange Tales*, vol. 1, #118 (March 1964), "The Possessed!", collected in *Marvel Masterworks: Doctor Strange, Volume 1*.

14. *Marvel Premiere* #3 (July 1972), collected in *Doctor Strange Epic Collection: A Separate Reality* (2016).

15. *Strange Tales*, vol. 1, 122 (July 1964), "The World Beyond," collected in *Marvel Masterworks: Doctor Strange, Volume 1*.

16. In one tale, he cries out, "I have failed my galaxy!", recalling yet another successful Marvel franchise! See *Doctor Strange*, vol. 2, #25, (October 1977), collected in *Essential Doctor Strange, Volume 3* (2007).

17. *Strange Tales*, vol. 1, #122.

18. *Doctor Strange*, vol. 2, #1 (June 1974), collected in *Doctor Strange Epic Collection: A Separate Reality*.

19. See *New Avengers*, vol. 3, #14 (April 2014), #20 (August 2014), and *Annual* #1 (August 2014), the first two collected in *New Avengers:*

Other Worlds (2014) and *New Avengers: A Perfect World* (2014), respectively.

20. *Doctor Strange*, vol. 2, #15 (June 1976), collected in *Essential Doctor Strange, Volume 3*.

21. *Doctor Strange Annual*, vol. 1, #1 (December 1976), collected in *Essential Doctor Strange, Volume 3*.

22. *Strange Tales*, vol. 2, #1.

23. Aristotle, *Nicomachean Ethics*, Books VIII and IX.

24. *Doctor Strange*, vol. 2, #77 (June 1986), collected in *Doctor Strange: Don't Pay the Ferryman* (2015).

25. *Doctor Strange*, vol. 2, #54 (August 1982), collected in *Essential Doctor Strange, Volume 4* (2009).

26. *Doctor Strange*, vol. 2, #45–53 (February 1981–June 1982), collected in *Essential Doctor Strange, Volume 4*.

27. Strange and Clea were joined in "mystical union" in *Doctor Strange, Sorcerer Supreme* #3 (March 1989), collected in *Doctor Strange, Sorcerer Supreme Omnibus, Volume 1* (2017), but continued to drift together and apart over the years. Recently, they agreed not to sever their mystical union, but resolved to remain, as Stephen says: "Friends. Nothing more" (*Doctor Strange Annual*, vol. 2, #1, November 2016, "To Get Her. Forever," collected in *Doctor Strange: Mr. Misery*, 2017).

28. For more on Strange's issues with love and friendship, see Chapter 3 by Cleary in this volume.

29. *Strange Tales*, vol. 1, #127, "Duel with Dread Dormammu!", collected in *Marvel Masterworks: Doctor Strange, Volume 1*.

30. Beginning with *New Avengers*, vol. 3, #1 (March 2013), collected in *New Avengers: Everything Dies* (2013).

31. *New Avengers*, vol. 3, #22 (October 2014), collected in *New Avengers: A Perfect World*.

32. *New Avengers*, vol. 3, #3 (April 2013), collected in *New Avengers: Everything Dies*. After the rest of the Illuminati overrule Cap, Tony Stark signals Strange to wipe Cap's mind of the memory of what they did—which is something Strange does an awful lot when civilians catch sight of the mystical realm that he decides they "shouldn't" see.

33. For instance, see Rosalind Hursthouse, *On Virtue Ethics* (Oxford: Oxford University Press, 1999), Chapter 3, as well as the popular accounts in note 9 above.

34. *Doctor Strange*, vol. 2, #81 (February 1987), collected in *Doctor Strange: Don't Pay the Ferryman*.

35. Strange first "retires" in *Incredible Hulk*, vol. 1, #126 (April 1970), but returns in *Marvel Feature*, vol. 1, #1 (December 1971), "The Day of the Defenders!", both collected in *Doctor Strange Epic Collection: A Separate Reality*. Later, he rejects the Ancient One's offer of "completeness," to "rise above the flesh and to become a spirit in the

universe," after which his former mentor revokes the title of Sorcerer Supreme from him. As he tells Clea, "I became a man again... that is all" (*Doctor Strange*, vol. 2, #19, October 1976, collected in *Essential Doctor Strange, Volume 3*),

36. *Doctor Strange: The Oath*, #1–5 (December 2006–April 2007), collected in *Doctor Strange: The Oath* (2007).
37. *Doctor Strange: The Oath* #5 (April 2007).
38. Ibid. For more on the responsibilities of doctors (even Strange ones), see Chapter 19 by Wright and Zehr in this volume.
39. For example, see John Cottingham, "Partiality and the Virtues," in Roger Crisp (ed.), *How Should One Live? Essays on the Virtues* (Oxford: Oxford University Press, 1996), 58–76.
40. This is an interesting reversal of Batman's refusal to kill the Joker even though it would save untold numbers of innocent citizens the Joker will inevitably kill: Strange endangered innocent lives to save his closest friend, while Batman did the same to avoid killing his worst enemy. For more on the former, see my chapter "Why Doesn't Batman Kill the Joker?" in Mark D. White and Robert Arp (eds), *Batman and Philosophy: The Dark Knight of the Soul* (Hoboken, NJ: Wiley Blackwell, 2008), 5–16.
41. *Doctor Strange*, vol. 2, #19 (October 1976), collected in *Essential Doctor Strange, Volume 3*.
42. *Doctor Strange*, vol. 2, #79 (October 1986), collected in *Doctor Strange: Don't Pay the Ferryman*. If the Vishanti are reading this, I'm only the messenger.

17
The Ancient One and the Problem of Dirty Hands

Michael Lyons

Stephen Strange was skeptical about the Ancient One almost immediately upon his arrival in Kamar-Taj. Nevertheless, even he was surprised to discover that she had been tapping into the very dark magic she had forbidden him to use. And Strange wasn't alone: This discovery also shattered Mordo's idealized image of her, and marked the beginning of the end of Mordo's fervent commitment to the Ancient One and Kamar-Taj.

If it was genuinely wrong to use dark magic, as the Ancient One taught her disciples, how can she justify her decision to use it herself? Are the benefits from using dark magic enough to overcome the fact that she broke an important rule to do it? In general, does adhering to a rule justify foregoing the benefits of breaking it, especially if counted in human lives? Philosophers call this type of moral conflict the Problem of Dirty Hands, and it's a mainstay of superhero stories, especially given the stakes that Doctor Strange and his compatriots encounter on daily basis.

The Problem of Dirty Hands: "It's Not About You"

Contemporary philosopher Michael Walzer described the Problem of Dirty Hands as the choice between achieving a morally good end by violating one's own moral principles and sticking to one's moral principles without achieving this end.[1] Walzer specifically explored this

Doctor Strange and Philosophy: The Other Book of Forbidden Knowledge, First Edition. Edited by Mark D. White.
© 2018 John Wiley & Sons Ltd. Published 2018 by John Wiley & Sons Ltd.

problem in the context of someone in the position of political power who can make a significant impact on the greater good but only through performing morally problematic deeds.

In the 2016 film *Doctor Strange*, there are three characters who see themselves as presented with this problem: the Ancient One, Kaecilius, and Strange himself. The Ancient One chooses to use forbidden dark magic to prolong her lifespan and continue to defend Earth from mystical threats. Kaecilius wants to unleash Dormammu upon Earth as a way to avoid death, not only for himself, but for all the inhabitants of Earth. As he tells Strange, "We don't seek to rule this world. We seek to save it!"[2] Even if Kaecilius' justification is less convincing than the Ancient One's, Strange seems struck by the parallels and he finds himself forced into the conflict between them.

We can frame such a choice as placing the higher value on either the consequences of one's actions, following the school of ethics known as *consequentialism*, or on the principles behind one's actions, following the school of ethics known as *deontology*.[3] If you put more value on the consequences of your actions, then getting one's hands dirty will be less important to you than the good that can be achieved as a result. On the other hand, if you put more value on the principles behind your actions, then you believe that by getting your hands dirty, you're crossing certain moral lines that should never be crossed, no matter what good could be achieved as a result. A third option would be to refuse to place an absolute priority on either principles or consequences. For example, you might think that principles should be the primary guide for your actions, except in extreme circumstances where the costs of sticking to your principles would be too high. Strange himself seems to take this perspective, generally following the rules of Kamar-Taj until he breaks them to use the Eye of Agamotto to negotiate the fate of Earth with Dormammu.

It is natural to ask whether there is any problem here at all. In Strange's case, for instance, he is able to come up with a way to force Dormammu to leave Earth—which is obviously praiseworthy, right? Does it really matter that he broke the Ancient One's rules or violated the "natural law"? You might think that the lesson to learn from Strange's example is that consequences should act as our moral guide rather than moral principles—unless that is, in fact, your guiding moral principle. However, if we look more closely at Kaecilius and the Ancient One, the genuinely problematic nature of this strategy becomes clearer, because in their cases, we have significant reason to say that the actions they took for "the greater good" were in fact morally wrong.

Does Dark Magic Get a Bad Rap?

Kaecilius may see himself as using dark magic for the ultimate benefit of Earth and all life on it, but there's a lot more to his choices that makes them seem deeply immoral in a deontological sense. Consider, for example, his betrayal of the Ancient One, his theft of pages from the Book of Cagliostro, and his intent to murder... well, anyone in his way. If his goal in summoning Dormammu were a genuinely moral one, then Kaecilius would have been faced with a genuine moral dilemma: either stick to his principles and refuse to summon Dormammu, or summon him and violate those principles. However, one could fairly argue that summoning Dormammu was not at all a moral goal, so Kaecilius was not faced with a moral problem at all. Rather, he was engaging in immoral acts to pursue an immoral end.

The Ancient One's situation provides us with a more plausible version of the Problem of Dirty Hands in that she performs ostensibly immoral acts for truly good reasons. But we still have to answer one question: why is the use of dark magic considered wrong in the first place? The most obvious reason is that, as Strange is told, dark magic is "volatile" and "dangerous," suggesting that it's forbidden chiefly on the basis of its extremely negative consequences. This would explain why it's not simply a matter of requiring sorcerers to be skilled enough to use it, or explaining that its use can only be permitted in extreme circumstances. This is not the case, however. Dark magic is one of those things that are so dangerous that they're simply forbidden, even by the most adept of users, such as the Ancient One.

This objection is not deontological in nature, though. It doesn't explain why using dark magic is wrong in an intrinsic way. We often consider murder, theft, or lying to be wrong in an intrinsic way, but why would it be just plain wrong to use dark magic? There does not seem to be an answer. Instead, the justification for the prohibition is consequentialist: using dark magic is bad because it usually leads to negative consequences that outweigh any possible benefits. Sometimes actions are so harmful that we want general rules against them. For example, *rule utilitarians* argue that we should not lie, not because it's morally wrong in and of itself, but because it almost always ends up hurting people. Even though we can imagine cases in which lying might be beneficial, we should develop and follow a rule against it because such a rule will lead to better outcomes in the long run than making decisions about lying on a case-by-case basis.

In this sense, then, we can see how the use of dark magic is so dangerous that sorcerers adopted rules forbidding it, rules that took on a deontological life of their own, even if they were originally based on consequentialist reasoning. Furthermore, it explains why the Ancient One is so firmly against it that she regrets breaking this rule even for clearly good consequentialist reasons, such as saving the Earth's dimension from Dormammu.

The Ancient One's Real Problem

If we accept that it was wrong for the Ancient One to use dark magic, her situation would be an example of the Problem of Dirty Hands, one in which she justified her violation of a principle by appealing to the tremendous costs of upholding the principle. But this reasoning relies on the assumption that these tremendous costs could be avoided only by using dark magic—that there were no other options. The Ancient One presents herself as being stuck between wrongfully using dark magic and failing to save the Earth. She believed she had no choice, given that saving the Earth was more important to her than her principles.

If the Ancient One did have other options, though, particularly ones that did not involve violating her moral principles, then her justification for that violation goes out the window (or sling-ring portal, if you will). Indeed, there may have been other options. For example, she claimed that she had to extend her life because only she could fight Dormammu. But she had acolytes, including the surprisingly adept Doctor Strange, as well as the acceptably competent Mordo and Wong (and those are just the ones we saw). Even if they didn't have all the necessary skills or abilities, she could have taught them or other qualified students in the time she naturally had left, rather than resort to drawing energy from the Dark Dimension as her "only choice."

But maybe she indeed was the only sorcerer who had the skill to fight Dormammu, and there was no time to find or train a successor (at least when she first started extending her life). Even then, however, it would have been to her benefit to come clean with others, particularly Mordo, who became so disillusioned he ended up turning on the sorcerers as a result. If the Ancient One had confided in him, perhaps Mordo would have understood her decision even if he still might have disagreed with it. This could have prevented not only his disillusionment, but his corruption and betrayal as well.

Knock Knock...

When explaining his dismay about the Ancient One to Strange, Mordo says, "The bill comes due. Don't you see? Her transgressions led to the Zealots to Dormammu. Kaecilius... was her fault! And here we are... in the consequence of her deception. A world on fire." Here, Mordo highlights another aspect of the Ancient One's Problem of Dirty Hands: her responsibility for any negative consequences arising from her wrongful use of the forbidden dark magic, even though it was done for the sake of the greater good.

The deontologist Immanuel Kant (1724–1804) made just this point in his infamous example of "the murderer at the door."[4] A Stranger version of it might go like so: Wong knocks at the Ancient One's door and asks her to hide him from a man trying to kill him. She does, and then she answers a second knock at the door. It's a minion of Dormammu with a huge bloody axe, asking if Wong is there. The question is: should the Ancient One lie to the murderer to protect Wong? Kant said no, the duty not to lie is paramount, and it will keep the Ancient One's hands clean, regardless of what happens to Wong. If she did lie to protect Wong, according to Kant's argument, she would bear the responsibility for whatever happened as a result: maybe the evil minion would become frustrated and go on a killing spree. By lying, the Ancient One inserted herself into the chain of events with a wrongful act, and can be considered responsible for the consequences. If she had told the truth—or, at least, kept her mouth shut, which is not the same as lying—she would have been in the right and would not bear responsibility for anything that happened as a result, including Wong's death.

Though Kant's argument about the importance of not lying relative to protecting a friend's life has been widely disputed, his point about bearing responsibility for the consequences of bad acts lives on. Even a simple white lie told to spare someone's feelings—like telling Strange his white temples don't make him look old when they really do—can backfire, and the liar is responsible for what happens. If we accept that the use of dark magic is wrong, then it makes sense that the Ancient One is responsible for what happens after she uses it, including Mordo's disillusionment and rebellion, as well as the positive consequences of saving the world.

The Bill Comes Due

Of the three characters we've considered, the Ancient One most obviously faced the Problem of Dirty Hands. Doctor Strange said that "she did what she thought was right," but at the same time it is clear that she did what she knew was *wrong*, even if she did it for the right reasons. This kind of dilemma is not unique to Sorcerers Supreme or Marvel superhero movies: all of us, from time to time, face situations in which we are inclined to do something we feel is wrong to promote a greater good. We must be careful not to abandon our moral principles outright, nor should we dismiss consequences altogether. Instead, we have to keep both in mind and make the choice that we think is the right one, taking into account all the practical circumstances and moral factors. Unfortunately, sometimes there is no clear "best" or "right" decision. Doctor Strange is admirable, though, for showing that he can break the rules when he feels it's necessary while accepting responsibility for the consequences. He stands ready to pay the bill when it comes due—and that is what makes him a hero.

Notes

1. Michael Walzer, "The Problem of Dirty Hands," *Philosophy & Public Affairs* 2(1973): 160–180.
2. All quoted dialogue is from the 2016 film *Doctor Strange*.
3. The prototypical example of consequentialism is classical utilitarianism, defended most famously by Jeremy Bentham (1748–1832) and John Stuart Mill (1806–1873), where morally good actions are those that cause pleasure and morally bad actions cause pain. Deontology is most often associated with Immanuel Kant (1724–1804), who wrote that actions are right or wrong depending on whether they adhere to or violate duties that apply unconditionally rather than by their consequences.
4. Immanuel Kant, "On a Supposed Right to Lie Because of Philanthropic Concerns," in *Grounding for the Metaphysics of Morals*, trans. James W. Ellington (Indianapolis, IN: Hackett Publishing, 1993), 63–67.

18

They Also Serve Who Only Stand and Wong

Daniel P. Malloy

Doctor Stephen Strange is a noted eccentric and loner, even among the superhero community. The Sorcerer Supreme generally doesn't function well in a group. Even his one extended membership, in the Defenders, was with a loosely connected group of loners and outcasts like himself.

But throughout all of Strange's battles with hoary hosts, demon gods, and wicked wizards, there has been one constant presence by his side: his loyal manservant Wong. Some look at Wong and see a servile underling, who is as lacking in self-respect as he is in magical ability. They think Wong should stand up for himself, stop kowtowing to the whims of an arrogant magician, and be his own man. In living his life as he does, Wong seems to them to be doing something wrong: He is letting himself down by being content with the life of a servant.

This chapter examines the concepts of respect, self-respect, and mastery and servitude to show that Wong does nothing wrong, and in fact something exceedingly noble, in dedicating his life to the service of Doctor Strange. Wong and Doctor Strange may not exactly be equals, but their relationship is far more complicated than the titles master and servant imply. While Strange may be able to give commands, in some ways he is completely dependent on Wong. This dependence makes his authority over Wong illusory at best. Far from simple master and servant, Strange and Wong are partners.

Doctor Strange and Philosophy: The Other Book of Forbidden Knowledge,
First Edition. Edited by Mark D. White.
© 2018 John Wiley & Sons Ltd. Published 2018 by John Wiley & Sons Ltd.

Alfred, Jarvis, and Wong

Manservants and butlers are a notable element of comic book stories. Batman has Alfred, Iron Man and the Avengers have Jarvis, and of course, Doctor Strange has Wong. Their primary duties seem to be the same: maintain the residence, cook, clean, act as a sort of gatekeeper, keep schedules of appointments (of both the mundane and the extraordinary variety), and generally manage the household. These are all standard duties for manservants or butlers, but they are a bit exaggerated in comics. In actuality, a team of servants would be tasked with all of these duties—poor Alfred could no more manage stately Wayne Manor by his lonesome than he could arm-wrestle Superman. Alfred Pennyworth, being the house's butler, would really be a sort of general manager, overseeing a large staff (as Mr. Carson does in *Downton Abbey*).

On top of those fairly normal duties, each of these servants has duties associated with the extraordinary lives their masters lead. Alfred has to clean the Batcave—did you think all the guano just evaporated?—and help maintain Batman's equipment and secret double life. Jarvis is the last line of defense at the Avengers' mansion, as well as the only person who knows where everything and everyone is. And Wong is quite literally Doctor Strange's bodyguard, protecting his physical form when the Sorcerer Supreme has to be away from it for whatever reason, jaunting about the astral plane. After one such journey, Strange returns to see Wong fighting gruesome mystical creatures, about which he merely says, "Doctor… you'll have to forgive me for lunch being late."[1]

Their formal duties are extensive, but the most essential service these men provide is emotional support to their employers. Alfred is an odd kind of father figure for Bruce Wayne, Jarvis serves as a sort of den mother for the Avengers, and Wong is really the closest thing Stephen Strange has to a friend on this plane of existence. Each represents an anchor point for their respective employers, the bedrock that supports the whole superhero enterprise. With that in mind, maybe it shouldn't be surprising that some superheroes have these kinds of servants—we might rather wonder why more of them don't (aside from that pesky issue of money).

Second-Rate Jarvis

Still, it's a thankless kind of life, waiting on a superhero's every need and whim. It leaves very little, if any, time for yourself. In fact, Alfred, Jarvis, and Wong seem to have no real life outside of their jobs.

We might ask why Wong or Alfred or Jarvis would accept the job in the first place. In fairness, Alfred and Jarvis just kind of fell into the position: they were butlers for wealthy, respectable families whose scions opted to become superheroes, thus "expanding" their workload enormously. Wong, on the other hand, was raised and groomed to be the manservant/bodyguard for the Sorcerer Supreme. He announces as much to Strange at their first meeting in the comics: "I am to be your man-servant, to see after your care and comfort! As my father, and my fathers before him, cared for the Ancient One! That is my destiny!"[2]

Does this make Wong a slave? Based on his duties and attitude, he certainly seems to be slave-ish, but he's not a slave. Slaves are intelligent beings who are literally owned by other intelligent beings. Wong may call Strange his master, but he isn't Strange's property. At the same time, though, Wong doesn't seem to completely own himself. His life, his skills, his labors are all dedicated to the maintenance and upkeep of Stephen Strange, which can lead us to suspect that Wong undervalues himself.

In other words, Wong lacks self-respect. A self-respecting person stands up for herself and doesn't just take commands. He certainly doesn't neglect his own affairs, especially important ones, to look after even the tiniest details of another person's life. And yet, Wong does. He may not be a slave, but he certainly seems servile.

World Saved, Lunch Delayed

We may say that's fine. If he wants to live his life as a servant, well… it's his life, right? Every person has the right to be a spineless worm if that's what he or she wants. Another line of thinking, though, has more intuitive appeal. According to this approach, there's something wrong about being servile, because the servile are letting everyone down, not just themselves.

Contemporary philosopher Thomas E. Hill, Jr., building on the thought of Immanuel Kant (1724–1804), has argued that the trouble with servility is that the servile person fails to demand his or her rights as a person possessed of dignity.[3] As Kant put it, "one who makes himself a worm cannot complain afterwards if people step on him."[4] Fundamentally, servility means a lack of self-respect. Self-respect is a complex idea, but we must be careful not to make the easy mistake of confusing it with self-esteem, which has to do with the particular traits a person has. For example, Wong might have high self-esteem because he is very good at his job, while in his former life, Doctor

Strange esteemed himself (perhaps a bit too much) for his skill as a surgeon. Self-respect, on the other hand, has to do with what makes a person a person. As a person, Wong is a rational being with free will. Self-respect means valuing that fact by, for instance, not surrendering his will to his master.

In this sense, there's nothing inherently servile about being a servant, which is just a job like any other. Servility refers to how the servant conducts him- or herself, expressing an attitude toward oneself in which one lacks self-respect or denies one's worth. Consider Alfred Pennyworth again. He is an excellent butler, performing his duties with both skill and dedication, and is by no means servile in how he does it. Alfred maintains his self-respect quite clearly by deploying his sharp wit in a somewhat paternal relationship with Bruce Wayne to establish his equal moral standing with his employer. Alfred knows his worth, and he makes sure that "Master Wayne" knows it as well.

Wong, however, may actually be a servile servant. He rarely challenges Strange on anything, even when his proposed course of action is plainly insane. When Wong does question one of Strange's plans, it's usually to protect Strange or his mission, not out of any concern for himself. When, for example, Strange embarks on a mission to find a cure for Wong's cancer, Wong begs him not to, telling him that the risk to Strange is too great, and the rewards—Wong's own survival—too small. After all, he's already arranged for his replacement![5] From his childhood on, Wong's entire life, his very being, has been dedicated to the service of the Sorcerer Supreme.

Let's be clear: what Wong does is important, and he knows it. Doctor Strange is our realm's sole defender against a vast variety of occult threats, and he needs Wong's help to be successful. Wong is well aware of this fact. That awareness, along with the knowledge that he performs his duties well, doubtless provides Wong with a degree of self-esteem—and rightly so. We should all have such meaningful tasks! But the question is whether Wong has self-respect. Does he value himself independently of the job he performs? If not, then Hill's argument about servility applies, which would mean that Wong is in the wrong.

Wong Matters Too

There are two ways we could defend Wong. One would be to argue that he is not, in fact, servile, and the other would be to argue that one can be servile yet retain self-respect. I want to make a case that, while

Wong is a servant and seems to act in a servile manner, he is not servile in the sense that Kant and Hill criticize.

Defending servility in one form or another will take some doing, but let's start by considering the kind of character trait servility is. The servile person is someone who denies or neglects their own interests in favor of someone else's. Note the two parts of this statement, detailing *what* servile people do and *why* they do it. To be servile is to deny or neglect one's own interests, and the reason a servile person sets their own interests aside is to focus on those of another person, typically someone of higher rank or status. One who behaves servilely to someone of lower rank or status isn't usually thought of as being servile. They might be called generous or kind-hearted, or they might be considered disingenuous, patronizing, or condescending.

Let's look at the two parts of servility separately. Is it wrong to neglect your interests? It can be, if doing so puts your health or well-being in danger, especially for no good reason. But it can also be permissible or even good to neglect your interests—it all depends on why you do it. Like all heroes, Doctor Strange neglects his own interests on a regular basis, and that's one reason he needs Wong. Without Wong there to remind him of his needs, Strange can get so caught up in defending our realm from otherworldly threats that he forgets more trivial things that are in his interest—such as eating and sleeping.

If there's anything wrong with being servile, then, it must be based on the second component of servility: neglecting one's own interests in favor of another's, usually someone of higher rank or status. Exactly whose interests you favor over your own is more important for defining servility than we've let on so far, but so are the reasons for doing so. In order for an act to be servile, it must be done for someone of higher status, but there's even more to it than that. I would argue that a key component of servility is that the difference in status between the servile and the served is either illusory or unearned, but the servile person accepts it wholeheartedly nonetheless.

Consider, for instance, the apparent servility Mordo displayed to the Ancient One during his studies. Mordo put on every appearance of servility, placing the Ancient One's every interest ahead of his own. But Mordo was never truly servile, because he never accepted that the Ancient One was his better. He acknowledged, of course, that the Ancient One was powerful and skilled in ways Mordo wasn't, but that's a matter of esteem. In terms of respect, Mordo always saw the Ancient One as his equal, if not his inferior. To be truly servile is to internalize a difference in status: to believe that the object of your servility is inherently better or worthier than yourself. That wasn't the case with Mordo, so he wasn't servile in spite of appearances. The truly servile person, however, would embrace the imbalance in status. This is the core of the moral argument against servility: the servile deny their own value as equal beings. There's nothing inherently wrong with servile behavior itself. Rather, it is this attitude toward oneself that is wrong, resembling a kind of self-enslavement and unjustified self-denial.

Occult Studies and Clean Socks

In spite of appearances, I don't think Wong is any more servile than Mordo. One possible argument in support of this is that he and Strange are genuinely not equals. As the Sorcerer Supreme, Strange is the superior being, and therefore is truly entitled to the sort of deferential treatment he receives from Wong. But this isn't satisfactory, for a couple of reasons. I think both Strange and Wong would object to it, both believing in a basic moral equality between persons that makes this line of reasoning repulsive. Also, it confuses esteem with respect: Strange may be worthy of more esteem than Wong because he is the Sorcerer Supreme, but that doesn't make him worthy of greater respect. As Wong tells some guys who accost him on the street for lowering himself to serve another man, "in the land of my birth, wisdom was respected, and to be of service to a man of wisdom was a high estate indeed!"[6] Wong acknowledges and values Strange's greater wisdom and skill, but this doesn't elevate him—or lower Wong—in terms of basic human respect or dignity.

Happily, there's a better argument in defense of Wong against the charge of servility. Though Wong doesn't regard Strange as better than him or of greater moral status, he is more central or important to the battle they both fight. Wong, no less than Strange, is a protector of our earthly realm. They share a mission, but have different roles to play in it. Wong can't be the Sorcerer Supreme, but nor can Strange do Wong's job. Understood this way, Wong doesn't elevate Strange above himself—he elevates their shared mission above both of them. Wong is no mere servant; he's a partner, dealing with all the earthly matters so that Strange can take care of the otherworldly stuff.

Theirs is an odd sort of partnership, and not one that many people would choose to take on. Imagine starting a business with someone, and having the partnership drawn up in such a way that partner A made all the decisions, had all the fun, and kept all the profits, while partner B did all the hard work, toil, and drudgery. When you look at it this way, it seems like Wong's been Tom Sawyered.[7] But that's a very narrow view of the partnership and what each man gets out of it. A broader, and I think more accurate, perspective on this unusual partnership is inspired by philosopher G.W.F. Hegel (1770–1831), who analyzes the relationship between masters and servants in his influential 1807 work, *Phenomenology of Spirit*.[8]

What the master gets out of the arrangement is obvious: Doctor Strange is free from a lot of the petty concerns that bother the rest of us. He doesn't have to pay bills, go grocery shopping, or clean the Sanctum Sanctorum—all that stuff is taken care of by Wong. Strange can focus on all the occult matters that interest him (including his extradimensional protégé and lover, Clea). Thanks to the ever-present Wong, Strange gets freedom from mundane concerns, as well as an expanded freedom to choose what he's going to do with his time and talents.

It seems like a great deal for the Sorcerer Supreme, but we shouldn't jump to the conclusion that it's all upside for him. It's not that Strange is making sacrifices to have Wong as his servant; it isn't a hardship to have someone like Wong looking after your every need. The problem for Strange is that, as Hegel would predict, the master becomes dependent on the servant. In one story, as Strange browses some arcane tomes, he and Wong are approached by a group of would-be muggers. While Strange remains oblivious to the whole affair, Wong easily dispatches the thugs. When Strange comes out of his reverie and notices the unconscious men on the ground and asks where they came from, Wong tells him, "Leave worldly matters to me, master."[9] So long as Wong is there, Strange's dependence isn't a problem—Wong is dependable and efficient. But the realities of life being what they are, Wong won't always be there. When that happens, the Sorcerer Supreme is going to be in the awkward position of being one of the most powerful beings on the planet and yet being utterly incapable of finding a pair of clean socks. Keeping Wong around provides Strange with a great deal of freedom, but it also deprives him of any incentive to develop the skills needed to manage his own life.

Worldly Matters

By that logic, at least, Wong comes off the better in his partnership with Doctor Strange. Imagine, for example, Wong and Strange competing for a job. Wong has years of experience managing a household, taking care of a wide variety of relatable matters, and developing skills that can translate well to any number of workplaces. Strange, on the other hand, walks in wearing a cape with a collar higher than his own head and starts babbling about the Eye of Agamotto and the hoary hosts of Hoggoth. Which person do you hire? If your answer is Strange, well, have fun in bankruptcy. Wong is the obvious choice, and not just because he's an ideal employee—he'd also make a better manager than Dr. Strange. Dealing with the mundane affairs of the Sanctum Sanctorum means that Wong delegates and negotiates with living, breathing people from Earth, whereas his master spends most of his time engaging beings like Dormammu and Nightmare.

The drawbacks of Wong's side of the partnership are more obvious than the ones on Strange's side, of course. The life of a servant is not a great one. Many of us hate doing our own cooking, cleaning, and laundry, which is the whole reason the position of servant was created to begin with. Managing your own life can be difficult enough without the added burden of having to manage your boss's.

But there's another benefit to Wong's side of the partnership, one that Hegel brings out well. In developing the skills to keep himself and his master alive and comfortable, Wong also develops a better understanding of himself and the world. Think about it this way: if Strange, as both a magician and a master, wants something, he merely has to say a few words, whether it's a command to Wong or some mystic incantation. If Wong wants something, he has to consider his environment, what it contains and what it doesn't, and his place in it. He needs to know what materials he has available, what his own abilities are, and how he can acquire any materials or skills that he needs but doesn't have. As such, Wong develops a better understanding of himself, his master, the world, and their places in it than Strange does. Hegel argues that this kind of reflection is the key to developing self-consciousness: "Through work, the servant becomes conscious of what he truly is."[10]

You can see expanded consciousness in the form Wong's supposed servility takes. His devotion is not to Doctor Strange as a person or even the Sorcerer Supreme as a title or office, but to the mission. Being somewhat removed from the day-to-day mystical activity, and having to deal with both the mystical and the mundane realms, Wong understands the mission and its importance better than anyone—even his master. Wong's understanding of his role is clear when his services are donated to the Avengers, diverting him from his mission of helping Doctor Strange. After being reunited with his master, Wong quips,

"When I dedicated my life in service to you as Sorcerer Supreme... I remember I closed my eyes and I prayed that one day I would grow up to be a second-rate Jarvis for a second-rate pile of Avengers."[11] He keenly appreciates his role in the mission he shares with Strange... and wants to keep it that way!

Power Behind the Cloak

Ultimately, Wong is not servile in how he performs his duties as servant to the Sorcerer Supreme. Rather it is through his servitude that Wong gets the better part of the bargain in their partnership. Wong's servitude leads to a more robust self-consciousness and awareness of the world, and self-consciousness is an important foundation for self-respect, which defeats any accusation of servility. Through his work for Doctor Strange, Wong better understands himself and the role he plays in protecting the world, which in turn makes him more aware of why he is worthy of respect and why the world is worth saving. It turns out that Wong's servitude is not a symptom of a lack of self-respect. Quite the contrary, it is a condition of a deep and abiding knowledge of his own value.

Notes

1. *Doctor Strange*, vol. 4, #3 (December 2015), collected in *Doctor Strange: The Way of the Weird* (2016).
2. *Doctor Strange*, vol. 2, #56 (December 1982), collected in *Essential Doctor Strange, Volume 4* (2009).
3. Thomas E. Hill, Jr., "Servility and Self-Respect" and "Self-Respect Reconsidered," in Thomas E. Hill, Jr., *Autonomy and Self-Respect* (Cambridge: Cambridge University Press, 1992), 4–24.
4. Immanuel Kant, *The Metaphysics of Morals*, trans. Mary Gregor (Cambridge: Cambridge University Press, 1797/1996), 437.
5. *Doctor Strange: The Oath* #1 (December 2006), collected in *Doctor Strange: The Oath* (2007).
6. *Doctor Strange*, vol. 2, #15 (June 1976), collected in *Essential Doctor Strange, Volume 4* and *Marvel Masterworks: Doctor Strange, Volume 6* (2013). Wong's early portrayal has been rightly criticized as offensively stereotypical; the bulk of this discussion will focus on Wong's more recent appearances, which reveal a richer and more complex character.
7. In Mark Twain's 1876 novel, *The Adventures of Tom Sawyer*, young Tom tricks his friends into doing one of his chores for him. Forced to

paint a fence, Tom acts like it is the most fun he's ever had in his life. When his friends offer to help out, he charges them for the privilege.

8. G.W.F. Hegel, *Phenomenology of Spirit*, trans. A. V. Miller (New York: Oxford University Press, 1807/1977).

9. *Doctor Strange: The Oath* #1.

10. Hegel, *Phenomenology of Spirit*, 118.

11. *New Avengers*, vol. 2, #7 (February 2011), collected in *New Avengers by Brian Michael Bendis: The Complete Collection, Volume 6* (2017).

19
Doctor Strange, Master of the Medical and Martial Arts

Bruce Wright and E. Paul Zehr

When you think of Doctor Strange, you may think of his flashy costume, psychedelic magical battles, and some of the funkiest foes in film. But what about his medicine, mayhem… and martial arts? *Primum non nocere*—more commonly known as the dictate "first, do no harm"—is embedded in the Hippocratic Oath that physicians adhere to as part of their code of conduct. Perhaps surprisingly, this is also found in many martial arts practices; the principle of "hurt, rather than harm" means that hurting an opponent, or causing temporary discomfort, is preferable to harming, or causing lasting damage.

Stephen Strange was a renowned neurosurgeon in his "previous life," but after his time in Kamar-Taj he is mostly associated with his mastery of the mystic arts. As we'll see, Strange's skills and ethics in this area are reminiscent of both medical and traditional martial arts training.

Doctor Strange, M.D.

The 2006–2007 comic book miniseries *Doctor Strange: The Oath* shows our hero behaving as both physician and sorcerer. When Strange discovers that Wong, his long-time companion, martial arts teacher, and friend, is suffering from an inoperable brain tumor, Strange travels to an alternate dimension to find the mysterious Otkid's elixir. Only later does Strange discover that the elixir can do

Doctor Strange and Philosophy: The Other Book of Forbidden Knowledge, First Edition. Edited by Mark D. White.
© 2018 John Wiley & Sons Ltd. Published 2018 by John Wiley & Sons Ltd.

more than cure Wong's brain tumor; it literally has the potential to cure humanity of all diseases. After most of the elixir is lost in the battle, Strange has two options. Option one is to use the tiny amount of Otkid's elixir left to save his companion Wong, who needs it right away. Option two is to give the remaining elixir to scientists to replicate in the hopes of curing every disease known to mankind. Doctor Strange chooses to save Wong.

Is this the moral choice that a self-respecting physician—or sorcerer, for that matter—would make? There are a few problems with this rather strange (pun intended) choice. First, there is the trade-off between the inestimable number of current and future lives the elixir could have saved and the one, personally important life, that it did save. Even though Wong is Strange's closest friend, there is no medically grounded moral argument that would justify giving the last drop of this miracle elixir to save his life alone versus (literally) countless others. The only justification Strange offers is that "you cannot withhold treatment from patients under your care," implying that the rest of humanity must suffer because they were not lucky enough to be one of his patients. While allowing Wong to die in front of his eyes would have been tragic and personally heart-wrenching for Strange, the principle of "first, do no harm" would have been better served had he let one person die to save billions of others. And we imagine that's what Wong would have wanted as well.

By the Hoary Hosts of Hippocrates!

Ironically, the reason that Strange originally gave for seeking the elixir is that he swore the Hippocratic Oath, which requires him to prescribe medical treatments for the good of his patients. The oath we now associate with Hippocrates has a long history predating its namesake and has evolved over time.[1] When distilled to its essential components, the key passages include:

> I will use my power to help the sick to the best of my ability and judgment.
> I will abstain from harming or wronging any man by it.
> I will not give a deadly medicament to anyone, if I am asked, nor will I suggest any such a thing.

Whenever I go into a house, I will go to help the sick and never with the intention of doing harm or injury. I will not abuse my position to indulge in sexual contacts with the bodies of women or of men, whether they are freemen or slaves.

Whatever I see or hear, professionally or privately, which ought not to be divulged, I will keep secret and tell no one.

Strange's decision conflicts with some of these precepts. More strikingly, he has the power to help the sick—all of them in the world—yet he chooses to help only one—hardly an example of "best judgment."

One problem with applying the Hippocratic Oath to Strange's choice is that it's meant to apply to the doctor-patient relationship, and Strange is not Wong's physician. They are friends, and in fact Doctor Strange behaves more as his friend than a physician throughout the entire story—until he justifies his choice to save Wong's life, when he invokes the "cannot withhold treatment" logic as Wong's doctor. Also, because they are friends, Strange should not be Wong's doctor because, as a rule, physicians do not give medical care to friends or family to avoid conflicts of interest.

Maybe we shouldn't be too surprised at Strange's haphazard application of Hippocrates in *The Oath*. After all, he wasn't a particularly "good" doctor before his life-altering automobile accident that ended his surgical career. There is no question that he had superior technical skills and talents as a surgeon, maybe the best in the world. But he used them only to further his own interests and career trajectory, and made no apology for doing so. There is more to being a good doctor than being good at what one does, however—one also has to do it in a good way. In the broadest sense, a good physician always guides her or his actions according to the social contract that binds them to putting the interests of their patients before their own.

There are many examples where Strange's choices prior to his accident put him in breach of the social contract, such as turning down life-saving surgeries that wouldn't bring him enough money or fame, as seen in the 2016 film *Doctor Strange*. But after his transformation to Sorcerer Supreme, most of his choices are heroic, acting solely for the benefit of others, often at great risk to himself. Ironically, after he loses his ability to perform surgery, Strange becomes a better doctor in the ethical sense, even if he wields the Eye of Agamotto rather than a scalpel. Perhaps Stan Lee and Steve Ditko, the creators of Doctor Strange, meant to show that, by losing his skill as a surgeon, Strange finally learned what it means to be a good physician.

I Swear by the Vishanti!

An oath is a public proclamation of a promise, ethically binding the person swearing the oath to certain behavior regarding those to whom they make it. As such, oaths are usually specific to certain relationships, such as a trial witness's promise to tell the truth, the whole truth, and nothing but the truth; the sentimental vows that people make to each other in weddings; and of course, doctors' oaths to serve their patients.

Once Strange lost the use of his hands for complicated surgery, he effectively stopped being a physician. True, he is still referred to as "Doctor Strange" and not "Mr. Strange" (although the Ancient One does call him that when she first meets him in the film), but this may be just the kind of courtesy whereby judges, coaches, and presidents are still called by their titles long after they retire. Nonetheless, if Strange has moved on from medical practice, then the oath he took as a physician should no longer be considered binding, and a new oath related to becoming a sorcerer may take precedence.

When Strange uses the Hippocratic Oath, it is more as a way to remind himself, and others, of what he used to be—and in his heart, maybe he still is. He continues to identify as a physician, and there is certainly some merit in using the oath as a moral barometer to measure the good he does as a sorcerer (keeping in mind the irony that he rarely did so as a medical doctor). In the film, after he is forced to take a life in a mystical battle, Strange invokes the Hippocratic Oath, telling the Ancient One, "When I became a doctor, I swore an oath to do no harm, and I have just killed a man. I'm not doing that again. I became a doctor to save lives, not take them." But in his new role as a sorcerer, he may find himself in a position where he must take one life to save many others, and the Hippocratic Oath is more hindrance than help. Because he's no longer a physician, it's neither necessary nor appropriate to explain or justify his actions with reference to the Hippocratic Oath—especially when, in cases such as *The Oath*, it doesn't work very well anyway.

Enter the Doctor Strange

Perhaps we should see Strange's new practice as guided by a martial arts ethic more than a medical one. It's fairly clear that Stephen Strange needs physical skills to go along with his mystical ones.

In *Doctor Strange* we see many initiates training in physical disciplines at Kamar-Taj in scenes that could have come right out of a Bruce Lee film such as *Enter the Dragon*. We also learn that mastery of physical skills is critical for mastery as a mystic. Indeed, Mordo says that "mastery of the sling ring is essential to mastery of the mystic arts... all you need to do is focus." In *The Oath*, Strange explains why he learned martial arts from Wong:

> After I left the Ancient One, I realized that my education was only beginning. And so I decided to study the martial arts along with the dark ones. I won't be besting Iron Fist in any challenges... but it gets the job done.[2]

Even the Official Handbook of the Marvel Universe states that "Doctor Strange has a good knowledge of various ... martial arts."[3]

But why should Doctor Strange be a martial artist? One reason is that magic, like any tool, can be misplaced and leave us otherwise defenseless. As Motokatsu Inoue, the Japanese grandmaster and founder of several martial arts systems (including Yuishinkai), wrote: "You must be able to use weapons, but never depend on them."[4] This is clearly shown in a recent run of the *Doctor Strange* comic in which Strange's magic is greatly weakened and he must find other ways to defend himself and save the world. In a fight with Dormammu—nothing like a challenge when you're magically depleted—Strange loses his knife, and Dormammu taunts him by saying, "You have no weapons left, Doctor Strange." Never one to give up, Strange replies, "You're wrong. I've still got one. The most dangerous one of all. Me."[5] Earlier in the same run we see Strange using a bow and arrow to fight a foe, and he comments, "It's a good thing I took all those archery classes Hawkeye taught at Avengers Mansion" (after missing his target he adds, "too bad I never passed one").[6]

Examples of Doctor Strange as a martial artist abound in the comics. In one story, we see a flashback of Strange training with the Ancient One, his wizened teacher admonishing him to "concentrate if you are to become a sorcerer ... you must learn discipline of both the mind and body," against a panel showing an athletic Stephen Strange doing a flying side kick into a heavy bag.[7] Even the Punisher is impressed by the martial skill of Doctor Strange, commenting that "the man knows how to swing an ax."[8] In his earliest adventures in *Strange Tales*, Strange engages in hand-to-hand combat with Dormammu—his favorite sparring partner—and proclaims that "we humans, whom you mock and scorn, have a science called Judo...! A science which teaches us how to turn the very strength a foe possesses against him!"[9] In another early story, Strange says to assassins he's fighting, "sorcery is more than the learning of ancient spells! It also stresses muscle power and fighting skill!"[10] To the extent that mystical spells take physical exertion, anything that gets sorcerers in better shape makes them better at it—and being able to handle yourself when magic fails is an added bonus.

A Strange Meld of Magic and Medicine by the Moons of Munnopor!

In addition to the physical skills of martial arts, the portrayal of Doctor Strange is reminiscent of many aspects of Eastern philosophical traditions. In Japan, Zen Buddhism had a major influence on the martial code of the samurai, *bushido*. This "martial arts warrior way" was manifested in extreme self-control and could be distilled into seven virtues articulated in 1900 by Inazo Nitobe: righteousness and justice; heroic courage; compassion and benevolence; respect, politeness, and courtesy; integrity, veracity, sincerity; honour; and duty and loyalty.[11]

The concept of preserving lives seems at first glance to be far removed from the techniques of most martial arts, whose practices instead seem to be aimed at taking lives, rather than saving them. This is a popular misconception, yet one that is part of the paradox of martial arts training: truly learning deadly skills includes learning to use them sparingly and in the way that does the least damage possible. When Strange told the Ancient One in the film that "I have just killed a man. I'm not doing that again," he could have been referring to the martial arts warrior way (rather than the Hippocratic Oath).

Readers of a certain age will no doubt remember this concept from the 1970s television show *Kung Fu*, which journalist Alex Gillis said "merged martial arts mayhem with Eastern philosophy in the American Wild West."[12] In flashbacks, Master Kan instructs the main character, Kwai Chang Caine, on masterful moves as well as the essential philosophy of martial arts. In the pilot movie, Kan gives Caine the following advice:

> Perceive the way of nature and no force of man can harm you. Do not meet a wave head on: avoid it. You do not have to stop force: it is easier to redirect it. Learn more ways to preserve rather than destroy. Avoid

rather than check. Check rather than hurt. Hurt rather than maim. Maim rather than kill. For all life is precious nor can any be replaced.[13]

A critical concept here is that of "hurt rather than maim," or "hurt rather than harm."

Like many of the concepts in the show, this quote from *Kung Fu* is firmly grounded in principles found in many traditional martial arts. The introductory form taught in the Yuishinkai karate system, for example, is one of a series called *Pinan*, meaning "peaceful and safe." The initial movement of the form involves a strike, not a so-called "defensive" movement. Yet, the initial striking movement is meant not to attack the body of the aggressor to harm them, but rather to hurt the attacker's attacking limb mildly to give them an opportunity to quit the fight, as in the Japanese proverb taught with the form: "Itami ku ji ku," or "pain removes fighting spirit." Contemporary philosopher and martial artist Barry Allen wrote about something similar when he said that "martial arts techniques are designed for compulsory compliance, destroying an opponent's will to fight," which provides a way to achieve victory without causing serious injury or death.[14]

Martial and Medical Mastery by the Omnipotent Oshtur!

Before his car accident, after losing three patients in one night, Strange commiserates with his surgical colleague, Doctor Robinson, telling him, "I can't do it, Robinson—I can't watch any more people die under my hands. I can't bring myself… Robinson, I can't care any more… and I can't take the responsibility."[15] The dissonance Stephen Strange experiences here is well captured an important ideal espoused by the philosopher Confucius (551–479 BCE): personal responsibility. As contemporary philosopher Damon Young writes, "Confucius wanted to cultivate individuals who cared for one another and their society."[16] These characteristics obviously permeate medicine, but they are found in many martial arts as well.

Buddhism expert and aikido master John Stevens writes that the founder of aikido, Morihei Ueshiba, thought martial arts could be a way that "human beings are harmonized" and that the martial arts empower "one to cut through and destroy all evil, thereby restoring this beautiful world to its innate purity."[17] Further, Grandmaster

Inoue called his empty hand system Yuishinkai, which means "society for those of good hearts and minds." Inoue emphasized that martial skills can unite right actions in the world. The philosophical link between the use of the mind for magic, medicine, and martial arts is highlighted when Stephen Strange is shown engaging in some staff fighting with Grem, a "master of the mystic arts." After Strange is defeated, he learns that "your mind is the tool … you need only let it do its work for you to succeed."[18] Easier said than done!

Medicine and martial arts also share an essential ethos of constant practice and training—and a sense of humor helps in both. Early in his training, Strange is described as "pathetic," to which he responds "Come on! I just started!"[19] This resonates with the idea of ongoing practice and discovery, as in the famous words from the *Tao Te Ching* by Taoist philosopher Lao Tzu (sixth century BCE): "a journey of a thousand miles begins with a single step."[20] Another important Taoist principle, balance, is emphasized in the narration to a training montage found in a tie-in comic to the recent film:

> The novices train diligently. They force their bodies to the brink of ruin. Such practice takes great discipline … in body as well as mind. And as such it takes a great toll on the spirit. So, as with everything in existence, it is about balance.[21]

This passage could easily describe training in either the mystic or martial arts—or medical school!

By the Crimson Bands of Cyttorak… We Conclude!

Doctor Strange gives voice to the resonance with martial arts and medical training when he proclaims: "Impossible? I've learned never to use that word in my line of work."[22] He represents a truly integrated fusion of the Western Hippocratic and Eastern warrior spirits, with dashes of New York cynicism and strong hints of human kindness. Stephen Strange may fail to fully articulate each of these elements taken independently, but he manages to combine them in a manner worthy of a superhero. His evolution shows us a traveler on an inspiring journey from flawed physician to true master of mystic, medical, and martial arts. All the while, he remains grounded in candor, wit, and humor—garbed in a cool, sixties psychedelic outfit. 'Nuff said!

Notes

1. George K. Daikos, "History of Medicine: Our Hippocratic Heritage," *International Journal of Antimicrobial Agents* 29(2007): 617–620; Larry Smith, "A Brief History of Medicine's Hippocratic Oath, or How Times Have Changed," *Otolaryngology–Head and Neck Surgery* 139(2008): 1–4.

2. *Doctor Strange: The Oath* #1 (December 2006), collected in *Doctor Strange: The Oath* (2007).

3. *The Official Handbook of the Marvel Universe: Deluxe Edition* #4 (March 1986), reprinted in *Doctor Strange: Don't Pay the Ferryman* (2015).

4. Motokatsu Inoue, *Bo, Sai, Tonfa, and Nunchaku: Ancient Martial Arts of the Ryukyu Islands* (Tokyo: Seitosha Co., 1987), 6.

5. *Doctor Strange*, vol. 4, #16 (March 2017), collected in *Doctor Strange: Blood in the Aether* (2017).

6. *Doctor Strange*, vol. 4, #8 (July 2016), collected in *Doctor Strange: The Last Days of Magic* (2016).

7. *Doctor Strange: From the Marvel Vault* #1 (April 2011).

8. *Doctor Strange/Punisher: Magic Bullets Infinite Comic* #3 (December 2016), reprinted in *Doctor Strange/Punisher: Magic Bullets* #2 (March 2017) and collected in *Doctor Strange/Punisher: Magic Bullets* (2017).

9. *Strange Tales*, vol. 1, #140 (January 1966), "The Pincers of Power!", collected in *Marvel Masterworks: Doctor Strange, Volume 1* (2010).

10. *Strange Tales*, vol. 1, #131 (April 1965), "The Hunter and the Hunted!", collected in *Marvel Masterworks: Doctor Strange, Volume 1*.

11. Inazo Nitobe, *The Way of the Samurai* (London: Arcturus Publishing Limited, 2011), 128.

12. Alex Gillis, *A Killing Art: The Untold History of Tae Kwon Do* (Toronto: ECW Press, 2016), 264.

13. Pilot movie, *Kung Fu: The Way of the Tiger, The Sign of the Dragon*, aired February 22, 1972.

14. Barry Allen, *Striking Beauty: A Philosophical Look at the Asian Martial Arts* (New York: Columbia University Press, 2015), 252.

15. *Doctor Strange*, vol. 2, #77 (June 1986), collected in *Doctor Strange: Don't Pay the Ferryman*.

16. Damon Young, "Pleased to Beat You," in *Martial Arts and Philosophy: Beating and Nothingness*, ed. Graham Priest and Damon Young (Chicago: Open Court, 2010), 3–14, at p. 11.

17. John Stevens, *Abundant Peace: The Biography of Morihei Ueshiba, Founder of Aikido*. (Boston: Shambhala Publications, 1987), 129.

18. *Doctor Strange: Mystic Apprentice* #1 (December 2016).

19. From the graphic novel *Doctor Strange: Season One* (2012).
20. Lao Tzu, *Tao Te Ching*, Chapter 64, available at http://classics.mit. edu/Lao/taote.html
21. *Marvel's Doctor Strange Prelude* #2 (October 2016), collected in *Marvel's Doctor Strange Prelude* (2016).
22. *Doctor Strange*, vol. 4, #5 (April 2016), collected in *Doctor Strange: The Way of the Weird* (2016).

Part VI
"I'VE COME TO BARGAIN"

Is Dormammu Evil?
St. Augustine and the Dark Dimension

Andrew T. Vink

Heroes are often defined by their villains: Captain America and the Red Skull, Daredevil and the Kingpin, Spider-Man and the Green Goblin, and the X-Men and Magneto. Each relationship sets the stage for that greatest of all clashes: good versus evil. In the comics and the 2016 film, Doctor Strange has a number of foes, including Baron Mordo and Nightmare, but his most powerful nemesis is Dormammu, master of the Dark Dimension. We naturally see Dormammu as evil, set against the heroic Doctor Strange. Yet we could also understand Dormammu, a being without concept of time or other elements of our reality, as a force of nature that is inherently without a concept of morality. To determine whether Dormammu is indeed evil, we first need to understand what evil is. That's where Saint Augustine of Hippo (354–430) can help us with his classification of three different types of evil.

A Dread Understanding

Introduced in the comics in 1964, the "Dread Dormammu" is the ruler of the Dark Dimension and its magicks, with power comparable to the Vishanti, the mystical beings from whom Doctor Strange summons his own mystical energy.[1] While not the Marvel Universe's version of the devil or ultimate evil—that description is usually reserved for Mephisto—Dormammu soon became synonymous

Doctor Strange and Philosophy: The Other Book of Forbidden Knowledge,
First Edition. Edited by Mark D. White.
© 2018 John Wiley & Sons Ltd. Published 2018 by John Wiley & Sons Ltd.

with dark and destructive magic. With the goal of absorbing "our" universe into the Dark Dimension to expand his power, Dormammu has been a consistent nemesis of Doctor Strange over the last seven decades, requiring all of the Sorcerer Supreme's skill and wit to defeat.

In the film, however, Dormammu is given a much more limited role, and we know much less about him (assuming Dormammu goes by "him"). As in the comics, we know that Dormammu exists in the Dark Dimension, one of the "dark places where powers older than time lie ravenous and waiting," according to the Ancient One. Wong tells Doctor Strange that Dormammu is a cosmic conqueror with an endless hunger, desiring to conquer Earth most of all. We see for ourselves that Dormammu has great power, granting Kaecilius extraordinary mystical energies beyond that of the other sorcerers (as he often does for Mordo in the comics). Only by manipulating the power of the Eye of Agamotto was Strange able to force Dormammu to abandon his conquest of Earth. Finally, given the conversation between Dormammu and Strange in the third act of the film, we can say that Dormammu is a sentient being, and not a mindless force. This isn't much information, compared to the long history from the comics, but it is enough to give us a good start on determining whether Dormammu is truly evil.

St. Augustine and Doctor Strange, Not So Different?

St. Augustine's journey was not too different from that of Stephen Strange: a man of secular culture who eventually is awakened to his higher calling from forces beyond the physical realm. Augustine began as an oratory teacher, living for beautiful women and his own glory. Eventually, his intellect drove him to study the works of Neoplatonist philosophers, which started him on the path to becoming one of the greatest thinkers in human history. This journey culminated, as he wrote in his autobiographical *Confessions*, in a garden in Milan, where he heard a voice telling him to read the text next to him, a copy of St. Paul's Epistle to the Romans.[2] This discovery of Paul brought him to Christianity; he subsequently served as bishop and, in general, as an intellectual defender of the faith. He wrote many sermons, letters, and books, and these works still contribute to philosophical discussions on topics ranging from human nature to the philosophy of religion to ethics.

For Augustine, the question of evil is intimately connected with the question of sin, so the way he writes about evil is religious, with mention of God, angels, and the like. Though we can't assume Augustine's Christian worldview for a discussion of Dormammu, we can establish important similarities that help. The world of Doctor Strange does not necessarily deal with sin as the separation from God, but it is clear from the film that the questions of human flaws and brokenness do exist. We see these flaws in various characters, ranging from Strange's arrogance and selfishness to the Ancient One's desire for unnaturally long life. Another shared aspect of the Strange world and Augustine's world is a well-defined difference between good and evil. While some methods, such as using the Eye of Agamotto to reverse time and interfere with the natural order, are morally ambiguous, the intent—to save the world as we know it—is clear. Finally, the issue of suffering is real in both contexts. Strange suffers throughout the film, just as would any person Augustine met in the late fourth century.

To bring this back to Dormammu, there are three different ways we can use Augustine to try to understand what Dormammu is. Specifically, we will discuss three types of evil: (1) metaphysical evil as privation; (2) natural evil, such as a tornado that destroys farms and homes throughout the American Midwest or the deadly tsunamis of southeast Asia; and (3) moral evil, which fits most of the villains in the Marvel Universe.

What Is Not But What Should Be

One of Augustine's key insights into the realities of the human person is an understanding of evil. His definition of metaphysical evil is a standard that still dominates conversations among philosophers centuries after his death. According to Augustine, evil is a *privation*, or an absence. In *Concerning the City of God Against the Pagans*, Augustine's extensive work on political philosophy and other topics, he describes evil in the following way:

> If an angel turns away from God he becomes impure: and such are all those who are called "impure spirits." They are no longer "light in the Lord"; they have become in themselves darkness, deprived of participation in the eternal light. For evil is not a positive substance: the loss of good has been given the name of "evil."[3]

For Augustine, privation is when something that should be present is missing. In his example, all of creation, including angels, are supposed to stand in the light of God. When an angel turns away, something is not as it should be; a fundamental relationship is missing, and that absence is called evil.

Augustine's explanation isn't especially concrete, so let's use an example. It's not a privation that Doctor Strange's gloves don't have eyes; gloves, even magical ones, aren't supposed to have eyes. If Wong accidentally burned a hole through one of Strange's gloves, it would be a privation, because gloves should not have holes other than the ones sewn into them. A hole in a glove might create friction by rubbing against the hand, causing discomfort or pain. More generally, metaphysical evil is the lack of something that should be there, and this lack generates suffering for the people who experience this lack.

The major problem with applying this definition of evil to Dormammu is that he is clearly not a giant hole in the fabric of space and time. Dormammu is a being: he manifests himself as a body with a face, has consciousness, and communicates with Doctor Strange during their fated meeting at the climax of the film. From this, Dormammu is by definition not a privation; he does not represent anything missing in the world. Augustine would affirm this; he states in *Confessions* that evil in creatures comes from the absence of a goodness that should be there.[4] This means we must keeping look for another definition of evil to apply to the Dread Dormammu.

A Dread Force of Nature

The next type of evil we'll explore is natural evil; examples are typically natural disasters, like tornados and tsunamis. For philosophers, the distinction between natural evil and moral evil (to be discussed next) is an important one, especially when dealing with questions of the goodness of God. Natural evils are those events that lack goodness and have no agent or actor to commit them (or blame for them). For example, when a hurricane comes up the eastern coast of the United States and destroys lives and property along the shoreline in Florida, Georgia, and the Carolinas, there is no responsible agent causing this destruction. No evil villain is willing the destruction— only forces of nature coming together in a way that unfortunately harms humans and other living creatures.

Augustine's conception of natural evil is rooted in his understanding that evil was brought into the natural world by sin. In *Confessions*, he follows the Christian doctrine of Original Sin—by which the first human beings disobeyed God's explicit commands and, as a result, brought suffering into the world—and offers the idea that evil is caused by free will.[5] This aspect of sin corrupts the natural world just as it corrupted human beings, leading to the possibility of natural disasters that destroy cities and illnesses that even gifted doctors like Stephen Strange can't cure.

This conception of natural evil is problematic for our purposes because Augustine's Christian assumptions, rooted in our world (and the heavens), make evil difficult to square with Dormammu's home in the Dark Dimension. However, while Augustine's thinking on the source of evil is problematic, his conclusion about nature is something we can work with. Things happen in the natural order without an agent; no one acts to create something beautiful like a rainbow, and no one acts to create an earthquake either. This means that the defining attribute of natural evil is the lack of an agent who is responsible for the harmful or wrongful action.

Does this fit Dormammu's situation as depicted in the film? Given the cosmic power associated with the Dark Dimension, it would seem as though the natural evil aspect might fit. However, we have already established that Dormammu is a sentient being, with intentions and goals, meaning he would be an agent acting by his own will. Again, this doesn't fit with the understanding of natural evil discussed above, so this type of evil is out too.

Is Dormammu Morally Evil?

The final category we have to consider is moral evil. As understood by Augustine, moral evil applies when a being chooses of its own free will to commit an act that deprives someone or something of a goodness that should be there. In *On Free Choice of the Will*, he offers the following reflection on one example of an evil act, adultery: "Then perhaps what makes adultery evil is inordinate desire, whereas so long as you look for the evil in the external, visible act, you are bound to encounter difficulties."[6] The key point here is that the existence of a desire to deprive someone one of goodness, the motivation for performing an evil act, differentiates it from natural evil. Murder is considered an evil act because it deprives the victim of the goodness that is life, and is motivated by some desire on the part of the murderer to take that life away. We can have one person kill another without that desire, such as in the case of manslaughter, but it lacks the status of moral evil due to a lack of desire and intent.

From this definition, we need to show three things to prove Dormammu is morally evil: that he possesses free will, has a victim in mind, and intends to deprive his victim of a good. As discussed above, Dormammu is an intelligent, sentient being of some kind, so we can reasonably assume that he also has free will.[7] Also, given Wong's exposition in the gateway between the three Sanctums, we know that Dormammu plans to absorb Earth and the rest of its dimension, and deprive everyone in it of independent existence, which gives us his victim and intention. The three elements of moral evil have been clearly met, and it seems as though Dormammu cleanly fits in the moral evil category.

But... there is one problem. Most of our information about Dormammu comes from the Ancient One (or Wong, who probably got it from her). As we discover in the film, the information the Ancient One shared about Dormammu is incomplete, opening the possibility that some of that information may not be true. This is an *epistemological* issue about the reliability of knowledge, which is beyond the scope of this chapter. However, we only need to focus on the fact that we have no information about Dormammu that is unbiased or beyond doubt. This means we should consider alternative explanations about why Dormammu wants to consume the Earth.

As Benedict Cumberbatch undoubtedly asked before voicing him in the film, what's Dormammu's motivation? We're assuming that his intent is malevolent; the traditional frame of "good versus evil" for superhero stories predisposes us to see Dormammu as the scheming villain. What if, instead, Dormammu lacked a concept of morality, and consumed worlds for sustenance? This is the way that Galactus, the Devourer of Worlds, operates in the comics. Galactus is another Marvel cosmic entity, normally associated with the Fantastic Four, and he travels the universe consuming planets, not out of anger or animus but necessity. When Galactus first appears above the Earth, planning to absorb its energies, he does not appear malicious, seeking to do harm out of hatred for the human race. Rather, he is dispassionately preparing to "eat."[8] As the Asgardian All-Father Odin describes him, he is a "natural force ... like the solar wind, like the super-nova," and Reed Richards goes as far as to argue that Galactus is a necessary part of the "order of things in our universe."[9] Even the very embodiment of the universe, Eternity—introduced in a Doctor Strange comic—confirms that Galactus serves a greater purpose.[10] Galactus is not a villain by intent, but only by perception. He sees no difference between consuming a world of warring Chitauri or a peaceful world like Xandar—it's all just food for him. Yet, to the inhabitants of these planets, he appears to be a villain most foul.

What about Survival?

To bring things down to earth, we can look to the animal kingdom for an analogy. We don't consider the lion evil for hunting and eating the gazelle in the wilderness; it's simply a part of the circle of life. There is a moral neutrality to actions necessary for survival. For example, if Mordo were to break the hands of an attacking assassin, it would be acceptable because of self-defense. Things change, however, if Mordo were to kill the assassin and then cannibalize the remains. Western culture generally frowns upon cannibalism since there are other ways for people to feed themselves.

What if Dormammu, like Galactus, is merely trying to consume Earth's dimension out of the need to survive? It's difficult to make moral judgments when a creature does something necessary for its existence. Can we make the same accommodation we gave to Galactus (and the beasts of our world) to Dormammu?

This interpretation of Dormammu's nature is undermined, however, by what he says and does in the final confrontation of the film. Dormammu is filled with malice and rage against Strange, especially after the sorcerer traps them both in an endless time loop. The threats of doom and destruction strongly suggest that Dormammu has a clear intent to end the goodness that is Strange's existence, and willingly does it time and time again, until Dormammu realizes that the loop cannot be broken without agreeing to Strange's deal. The anger- and malice-filled lines, such as "your world is mine, like all worlds," indicate a purpose far beyond a mere need for sustenance and a desire to survive. Rather, a drive for power and domination lies under those words, supporting our initial conclusion that Dormammu fits best in the category of moral evil.

One more thing: is the issue of scale relevant to declaring Dormammu morally evil? Let's say Mordo is trying to meditate in his room, but a horsefly keeps buzzing around his head. Mordo tries to ignore the horsefly, but it makes too much noise. After several minutes, the fly lands on Mordo's face and bites him, and in irritation, Mordo kills the fly. The fly isn't attempting to accomplish any great mischief; it's just looking to feed. By analogy, the battle between Dormammu and Strange in the time loop is very similar: Dormammu simply wants to consume his meal, and this annoying pest is distracting him from it. By most estimations (other than the fly's), swatting a fly is no great moral event, just a part of the natural order of things.

The difference between these two situations doesn't have to do with scale, but with the nature of the "pests." We're pretty sure flies aren't intelligent, whereas human beings are, which is a major reason that killing humans, but not flies, is usually considered wrong. Dormammu and Strange carried out a conversation, so we can assume Dormammu realizes that Strange, and by proxy all of humanity, is intelligent. If Dormammu seeks to consume the Earth and kill all its inhabitants, while acknowledging their intelligence, this marks him as morally evil.

The Dread Conclusion!

It seems that, being morally evil, Dormammu fits the mold of a classic Marvel villain. But he did accomplish one good thing: he allowed us to think through the various kinds of evil that create suffering in our world. While Dormammu's evil is a matter of fiction, there are similar evils in our world. Throughout the film, both Christine Palmer and the Ancient One challenge Strange to find ways to save lives in new ways beyond the work his broken hands could no longer accomplish. I offer a similar challenge to you: now that you can reflect on the evils of the world using philosophy, can you find a response that fills the void?

Notes

1. *Strange Tales*, vol. 1, #126 (November 1964), "The Domain of the Dread Dormammu!," collected in *Marvel Masterworks: Doctor Strange, Volume 1* (2010).
2. Augustine, *Confessions*, trans. F.J. Sheed (Indianapolis: Hackett Publishing Company, 2006).
3. Augustine, *Concerning the City of God Against the Pagans*, trans. Henry Bettenson (New York: Penguin Books, 1984), 440.
4. Augustine, *Confessions*, 44.
5. Ibid., 119.

6. Augustine, *On Free Choice of the Will*, trans. Thomas Williams (Indianapolis: Hackett Publishing Company, 1993), 5.
7. Insomuch as anyone does, which is an entirely different discussion.
8. *Fantastic Four*, vol. 1, #48 (March 1966), collected in *Marvel Masterworks: Fantastic Four, Volume 5* (2011).
9. *Fantastic Four*, vol. 1, #262 (January 1984), collected in *Fantastic Four Visionaries – John Byrne, Volume 4* (2005).
10. Ibid. Eternity, one of Stan Lee and Steve Ditko's most mind-blowing creations, was introduced in *Strange Tales*, vol. 1, #138 (November 1965), "If Eternity Should Fail!," collected in *Marvel Masterworks: Doctor Strange, Volume 1*.

Doctor Strange and Leo Tolstoy: Brothers in Nonviolence?

Konstantin Pavliouts

Meet Stephen Strange, egotistical neurosurgeon, his life based on wealth and fame, master of his fate. In the 2016 film *Doctor Strange*, Stephen invites fellow doctor Christine Palmer to a dinner of the Neurological Society, where he has been invited to speak. Christine demurs, telling him that his speaking engagements aren't about the audience or medicine: "Stephen. Everything is about you." Similarly, in the 2007 animated movie *Doctor Strange and the Sorcerers Supreme*, Dr. Gina Atwater tells Strange, "I am sick of this hospital feeding your monster ego. It's time you start giving back!"

On this score, Strange was not that different from the Russian author and philosopher Leo Tolstoy (1828–1910). A rich and successful writer who also distinguished himself at military campaigns as an officer, Tolstoy had respect among his peers, was popular with women, and spent his life at balls and endless celebrations. Understandably, he was proud of his accomplishments and felt his successes were deserved and sufficient for a full life.

Strange and Tolstoy both experienced significant changes in midlife, though, that affected their worldviews and led them to reconsider the meaning of life. For his part, Tolstoy developed a strong opposition to violence, even when used in resistance to evil. This would seem to condemn the actions of Strange as he battles mystical threats to the Earth. But maybe there is something unique about Doctor Strange's world that can avoid Tolstoy's condemnation.

Doctor Strange and Philosophy: The Other Book of Forbidden Knowledge, First Edition. Edited by Mark D. White.
© 2018 John Wiley & Sons Ltd. Published 2018 by John Wiley & Sons Ltd.

Strange Transformations

The changes that Strange and Tolstoy experienced led to transformations in the ways they thought about themselves and their roles in the world. For Strange, the turning point was his car accident, after which he lost his ability to perform surgery, thus also losing the way he defined himself and the way he achieved the fame and wealth. Strange quickly and radically changed the way he looked at the meaning of this life after he traveled to Kamar-Taj and began his mystical training with the Ancient One.

Tolstoy had more of a continuous change throughout his life, but by age 50 he had come to realize that "one can only live while one is intoxicated with life; as soon as one is sober it is impossible not to see that it is all a mere fraud and a stupid fraud!"[1] He clearly realized the futility of continuing to live a vapid life seeking glory and wealth: "I had, as it were lived, lived, and walked, walked, till I had come to a precipice and saw clearly that there was nothing ahead of me but destruction."[2] Eventually, every person will cease to exist, so any common, physical act of living has no meaning at all: "sickness and death will come (they had come already) to those I love or to me; nothing will remain but stench and worms."[3]

Tolstoy clearly described the state of Strange's mind after the accident when he wrote:

> I now no longer care for the things that I had prized, and I have begun to desire things concerning which I had formerly been indifferent. Like a man who, going out on business, on his way suddenly becomes convinced of the futility of that business and turns back; and all that stood to the right now stands to the left, and all that was to the left is now to the right.[4]

However, Strange needed more than just a horrific car accident to reveal the transcendental nature of the world beyond the physical. While he was seeking Western medical treatment, he remained haughty and arrogant with people, and even after his introduction to the Ancient One these attitudes were still displayed. In the film, the Ancient One tells Strange that "arrogance and fear still keep you from learning the simplest and most significant lesson of all: it's not about you," and Mordo recommends that he "forget everything you think you know." It seems Tolstoy and the Ancient One, though from two very different worlds, would have the same lessons for Stephen Strange to help him comprehend the final, absolute meaning of life.

Tolstoy relates an Eastern fable in his autobiographical *Confession*. A traveler dives into a dry well to hide from a tiger. He discovers, however, that a hungry dragon lives at the bottom of the well. So he clings to a branch growing out of a crack in the wall—but there are two mice gnawing at the root of the branch. In the midst of all this danger, the man notices honey dripping down from a beehive on the branch, and the honey is so delicious he shakes the branch to get more, endangering his life even further. Tolstoy wrote:

> I too clung to the twig of life, knowing that the dragon of death was inevitably awaiting me, ready to tear me to pieces; and I could not understand why I had fallen into such torment. I tried to lick the honey which formerly consoled me, but the honey no longer gave me pleasure.[5]

Stephen Strange is in the same situation, "licking the honey" of Western medicine in a vain and futile attempt to heal his hands in order to continue his egoistic and glorious life. Tolstoy used this fable to show that people, including himself, need to find a deeper sense of reality and meaning, each in his or her own way. Thankfully, Strange starts to do this in Kamar-Taj.

The Evil of Violence

A central focus of Tolstoy's newfound philosophy is the evil of the violence practiced by humans throughout history. As he sees it, evil destroys the meaning of life itself: "to understand the meaning of life it is necessary first that life should not be meaningless and evil."[6] While he was skeptical of life centered on material pursuits, Tolstoy realized the importance of survival, which implies the evil of causing harm or death:

> Thus, it is clear that life for oneself can never have any meaning. If there is a rational life, it must be some other kind of life; it must be one, the purpose of which does not consist in securing one's own future. To live rationally, we must live so that death cannot destroy our life.[7]

In this spirit, Tolstoy regards violence as evil. In the broadest sense, violence makes others act against their will, and "consists in forcing others, by threats of suffering or death, to do what they refuse to do."[8]

Naturally, then, the worst manifestation of violence is killing, because it denies the sacred status of every human life. This includes violence as practiced by the state as well. In "Memoirs of a Soldier's Court-Martial," included in his diaries from 1908, Tolstoy writes that the death penalty is an act that is impossible if you truly think about what it means, but is possible only if done mindlessly or mechanically, such as by a soulless state mechanism. This extends to state violence against other nations and peoples:

> Not a single general, not a single soldier, would kill hundreds of Turks or Germans, and devastate their villages—no, not one of them would consent to wound a single man, were it not in war, and in obedience to discipline and the oath of allegiance. Cruelty is only exercised (thanks to our complicated social machinery) when it can be so divided among a number that none shall bear the sole responsibility, or recognize how unnatural all cruelty is.⁹

Therefore, every person should adopt a position of nonresistance to evil that rejects all violence against the will of others. "Do you not see that if you claim and exercise the right to resist by an act of violence what you regard as evil," Tolstoy asked,

> every other man will insist upon his right to resist in the same way what he regards as evil, and the world will continue to be filled with violence? It is your duty to show that there is a better way.¹⁰

Evil in this World and Others

Tolstoy's profound and heartfelt views concerning evil and violence lead to more essential questions. What is the nature of evil? What are the foundations of violence? And where is the metaphysical "root" of evil in the world? Happily for us, the world of Doctor Strange provides a way to look at these questions from another angle.

In the 2016 film, the Ancient One sends Strange on a mental journey across numerous dimensions of the multiverse, and explains that there are "dark places where powers older than time lie ravenous … and waiting. Who are you in this vast multiverse, Mr. Strange?" But these worlds and dimensions are not available to most men; they are metaphysical by nature, and by extension, so is the evil they produce. Over time, Strange will become a sorcerer-defender of his world from this supernatural evil. As Wong tells him, "While heroes like the

Avengers protect the world from physical dangers, we sorcerers safeguard it against more mystical threats." Like all the sorcerers, Strange acquires and develops the power to fight against "negativistic, nihilistic force."[11]

Tolstoy maintained that metaphysical evil is much more dreadful than physical acts of violence. In one of his later articles, he wrote mainly of state politics, but we can easily extend this to a metaphysical sphere of reality:

> In general, the government has allowed killing as a means of obtaining its ends. As a result, miserable people who have been perverted by that example now consider all crimes, robbery, theft, lies, tortures, and murders to be quite natural deeds, proper to a man. Yes! Terrible as the deeds are themselves, the moral, spiritual, unseen evil they produce is incomparably more terrible.[12]

Ideally, eliminating the metaphysical "root" of evil and violence would free humankind from the force of violence.

The metaphysical nature of evil is reflected in the amount of time Doctor Strange spends in such realms as the Dream Dimension, fighting the darkness that tries to take over human minds and souls. Bending people to evil's will is possible through control of the mind and, through that, the soul, as we see in the case of mind-controlled children in the animated film. In the comics, personifications of evil such as Dormammu and Satannish the Supreme seek to conquer human souls. As another evil being Xandu says, "Silence! When Xandu commands, others obey! My will is your will! Thus speaks Xandu!"[13] In many of these cases, Strange leaves his physical body behind to engage in battle in his astral form against shapeless metaphysical evil.

Tolstoy dramatizes the conflict between good and evil with the metaphor of light and dark, writing that "we shall see in it one phase of the awful struggle between good and evil, light and darkness."[14] In Strange's world, the sorcerers' mission is to use "the light" of goodness to stop the dark or black magic from destroying the world. As Strange says in one of his mystic incantations,

> Now let the rising tide of power/From birth of stars to final doom/ Reveal the place, the form, the hour/Where light's salvation forth may bloom/Where seen and unseen twine and blend—and darkness end![15]

Evil comes not only in the form of creatures from the other worlds, but also in the form of men who are willing to trade their souls to demons to get power to control other people's wills. In the film, it is the "fallen" sorcerer Kaecilius, and in the comics it is Mordo, who work with the dread Dormammu to get what they want while sacrificing part of their world to the Dark Dimension. Both rejected their mission as sorcerers to defend the world from evil and instead became the part of evil themselves. As Strange tells Kaecilius, "Look at your face. Dormammu made you a murderer. Just how good can his kingdom be?"

Tolstoy wrote that society itself is violent because of people who trade their freedom and morality for power: "What supports the present order of society is the selfishness and stupefaction of the people, who sell their freedom and honor for insignificant material advantages."[16] Even though the types of power are different—metaphysical and mystical in Strange's world, political and social in Tolstoy's and ours—the principle is the same. And when people who choose evil band together, evil becomes concentrated, not unlike the metaphysical Dark Dimension in the world of Doctor Strange. As Tolstoy wrote, "Men linked together by deception form, we might say, a compact body. In the compactness of this body lies all the evil of the world."[17]

No Violence Means *No Violence!*

Tolstoy goes even further, arguing that we should not use violence to fight evil because every act of violence creates, multiplies, and strengthens evil: "'Do not resist evil' means never to resist evil, i.e., never offer violence to anyone."[18] It is necessary to end violence in all its forms, for only then we can rid our souls of evil. Tolstoy once again turns to social reality as an example of this metaphysical conclusion, citing

> the erroneous idea that my welfare can be secured by defending my property and myself against others. I now know that the greater part of the evil men suffer from arises from this. Instead of working for others, each tries to work as little as possible, and forcibly makes others work for him. And on recalling to mind all the evil done by others and myself, I see that it proceeded, for the most part, from our considering it possible to secure and better our conditions by violence.[19]

As we know, Doctor Strange trained to become a master of the mystical arts to fight evil, even if he relied more on metaphysical or magical tools than physical ones. In the animated film, Mordo asked Strange if he had ever held a blade, to which the former neurosurgeon answered, "To save lives, yes. But not to take them." In his physical form he was generally nonviolent, but that changed on the astral plane, where he didn't fight evil creatures physically, but rather eliminated them meta-physically, by destroying their essence or banishing them to other dimensions.[20] Often in the comics, Strange and other sorcerers repeat the phrase "We shall have no violence here."[21] In the animated film, Wong says to Mordo that they are sorcerers, not warriors, to which Mordo replies, "Yet, we fight a war." They are both correct: it is a war, but a metaphysical war against evil that can be waged only by sorcerers.

Tolstoy's position on nonviolent resistance was successfully adapted in the twentieth century by Mahatma Gandhi (1869–1948) in his campaign for Indian independence from Britain. Some philosophers, such as the great Russian thinker Nikolai Berdyaev (1874–1948), called Tolstoy's philosophy "religious anarchism."[22] This label fits because in his later works Tolstoy attacks state and private property as the primary sources of evil in the world:

> All that I had formerly prized – such things as riches, property, honor, and self-dignity – have grown worthless in my eyes … I dare not use violence of any kind against my fellow-creatures … nor can I now take part in any act of authority, the purpose of which is to protect men's property by violence. I can neither be a judge, nor take part in judging and condemning.[23]

Tolstoy expressed the practical side of his "anarchism" in calls to stop paying taxes, serving in the army, or working in every part of state administration. As he wrote,

> Do not resist the evil-doer and take no part in doing so, either in the violent deeds of the administration, in the law courts, in the collection of taxes, or above all in soldiering, and no one in the world will be able to enslave you.[24]

However, we can't understand this specific kind of anarchism without his fundamental metaphysical beliefs about the real essence of evil that appears in human souls.

But What about Doctor Strange…?

Nevertheless, violent resistance to evil, at least in a mystical or meta-physical sense, is regarded as necessary in Doctor Strange's world. What would Tolstoy have thought about Strange's situation in which evil could be defeated only by the use of magic force? Could he have accepted this idea, or was it simply inconsistent with his teaching?

The key is to recognize that Tolstoy protested only against the violence of man against man. So, what if the root of evil lies in some other form of reality? Might Tolstoy find it acceptable to use violence against acts of personified metaphysical evil to save humankind?

We can find a clue in a conversation between Tolstoy and the American journalist and explorer George Kennan (1845–1924), in which Tolstoy challenged the American policy of "forbidding the Chinese immigration" as a betrayal of their principles of freedom.

KENNAN: Suppose the Chinese should come to California at the rate of a hundred thousand a year; they would simply crush our civilization on the Pacific coast.

TOLSTOY: Well, what of it? The Chinese have as much right there as you have.

KENNAN: But would you not allow a people to protect itself against that sort of alien invasion?

TOLSTOY: Why alien? Why do you make a distinction between foreigners and countrymen? To me all men are brothers, no matter whether they are Russians or Mexicans, Americans or Chinese.[25]

From this, we clearly see that Tolstoy forbids violence against people, regardless of nationality.

Kennan then asked Tolstoy what he would do if a criminal attacks somebody. Tolstoy answered first in the context of his nonviolent philosophy, but then made an analogy with another vital form: an animal. Kennan wrote:

I asked him the direct question whether he would kill a highwayman who was about to murder an innocent traveler, provided there were no other way to save the traveler's life. He replied, "If I should see a bear about to kill a peasant in the forest, I would sink an axe in the bear's head; but I would not kill a man who was about to do the same thing."[26]

If Tolstoy would kill a bear to save human's life, perhaps he would endorse Strange's use of magic violence against the dread Dormammu—especially considering that the bear is not morally responsible for his actions but Dormammu certainly is.[27] In his opposition to the evil of violence, Tolstoy was primarily concerned with the souls of humans, not other beings—and certainly not evil incarnate!

Leo Tolstoy, Sorcerer-Defender Supreme

Both Stephen Strange and Leo Tolstoy suppose that evil and violence are the main threats to humankind. In addition, both believe that evil and violence have metaphysical essence, and they regard violence against humans as unacceptable. They differ mainly in their methods and means of nonviolent resistance: Tolstoy chooses moral, social, and political methods, while Strange uses magical ones. If Tolstoy were in the world of Doctor Strange, he might open the sacred Book of Vishanti, don the Eye of Agamotto, and become a sorcerer-defender of our planet from demonic evil. In multiple realities, everything is possible!

Notes

1. Leo Tolstoy, *A Confession* (1882), trans. Louise and Aylmer Maude, Chapter 4, available at https://en.wikisource.org/wiki/A_Confession_ (Maudes_translation).
2. Ibid.
3. Ibid.
4. Leo Tolstoy, *What I Believe* (1886), trans. Constantine Popoff, Introduction, available at https://en.wikisource.org/wiki/What_I_ Believe_(Tolstoy)
5. Tolstoy, *Confession*, Chapter 4.
6. Ibid., Chapter 11.
7. Tolstoy, *What I Believe*, Chapter 8.
8. Leo Tolstoy, *The Law of Love and The Law of Violence* (1908), trans. Mary Koutouzow Tolstoy, Chapter 3, available at http://www. nonresistance.org/docs_pdf/Tolstoy/Law_of_Love.pdf
9. Tolstoy, *What I Believe*, Chapter 4.
10. George Kennan, "A Visit to Count Tolstoi," *The Century Magazine*, June 1887, 252–265, at p. 259, available at https://www.unz.org/Pub/ Century-1887jun-00252
11. *Doctor Strange*, vol. 1, #175 (December 1968), collected in *Essential Doctor Strange, Volume 2* (2007).
12. Leo Tolstoy, "I Cannot Be Silent" (1908), available at https://www. nonresistance.org/docs_pdf/Tolstoy/I_Cannot_Be_Silent.pdf
13. *Amazing Spider-Man Annual*, vol. 1, #2 (October 1965), "The Wondrous World of Dr. Strange," reprinted in *Doctor Strange*, vol. 1, #179 (April 1969) and collected in *Marvel Masterworks: Doctor Strange, Volume 1* (2003) and *Spider-Man/Doctor Strange: The Way to Dusty Death* (2017).

14. Tolstoy, *What I Believe*, Chapter 5.
15. *Doctor Strange, Sorcerer Supreme* #3 (March 1989), collected in *Doctor Strange, Sorcerer Supreme Omnibus, Volume 1* (2017).
16. Leo Tolstoy, "Thou Shalt Not Kill" (1900), available at http://www. nonresistance.org/docs_pdf/Tolstoy/Thou_Shalt_Not_Kill.pdf
17. Tolstoy, *What I Believe*, Chapter 12.
18. Ibid., Chapter 2.
19. Ibid., Chapter 12.
20. For more on Stephen Strange's limited and restrained use of physical violence, see Chapter 19 by Wright and Zehr in this volume.
21. *Defenders*, vol. 1, #27 (September 1975), collected in *Essential Defenders, Volume 2* (2006).
22. Nicolai Berdyaev, *The Russian Idea* (New York: Macmillan, 1948).
23. Tolstoy, *What I Believe*, Chapter 12.
24. Leo Tolstoy, "A Letter to a Hindu" (1908), available at http://www. online-literature.com/tolstoy/2733/
25. Adapted from George Kennan, "A Visit to Count Tolstoi," 263.
26. Ibid., 256.
27. For more on whether Dormammu is truly evil, see Chapter 20 by Vink in this volume.

Doctor Strange, Moral Responsibility, and the God Question

Christopher P. Klofft

What does it take to become Sorcerer Supreme? Mastery of the mystic arts, to be sure, and maybe also a tragic accident and years of hard searching and harder education. It also involves a special kind of relationship with the fundamental powers of the universe. After all, the Sorcerer Supreme must contend with other-dimensional rulers such as Dormammu and personified cosmic concepts like Eternity. But what about the concept of God—not "gods," as are often invoked in Strange's adventures as well as the broader Marvel Universe, but rather the one Creator God of all that is? And is this God merely the "god of the philosophers," or is this a God who is also a person?

As Sorcerer Supreme, Doctor Strange has had several occasions in which he's had to deal specifically with the concept of a personal God. In his early career, he recognized that God was a power above all other powers with which he dealt. Later on, however, he ignored this God and gave in to powers that were forbidden to him—and as a result, he lost nearly everything. By reflecting on the concepts of God and the idea of an objective order to the universe as presented by some for the world's wisest philosophers, we'll see that Doctor Strange can only be the guardian and hero he is meant to be by acknowledging the place of the Source of All That Is.

God Among the Gods

In his *Metaphysics*, the ancient Greek philosopher Aristotle (384–322 BCE) presents the idea of God, or more specifically a god among the gods, who is responsible for the origin and operation of the whole universe. This god is the "first cause" and the "prime mover," responsible for the existence of everything and for setting everything in the universe in motion. This concept of God isn't very relevant to Doctor Strange's experiences, though, because this god is not a person. It therefore has no relational engagement with creation. In other words, Aristotle's god is merely a mechanistic force, not a being to whom one could appeal for help, and not one Doctor Strange could interact with.

A more helpful image of God can be found in the writing of Saint Thomas Aquinas (1225–1274), who formed a theological synthesis of Aristotelian philosophy and Christian revelation. In his *Summa Theologiae*, Aquinas gives us his five proofs for the existence of God, relying on conclusions that can be attained by reason alone, but which are further developed and understood by what God has revealed (through the Hebrew and Christian Scriptures).[1] In addition to the Aristotelian notions of the prime mover and first cause, Aquinas also notes that God is the reason for everything's existence, the possessor of all perfections, and the intelligence that governs the movement of all things in the universe. He demonstrates that God is the origin of all goodness, because he himself is all good. The same being that is behind the creation of the objective order of the universe in Aristotle's philosophy is also benevolent—and this has important ramifications for understanding morality.

According to Aquinas, the all-good Creator of the universe is the author of the moral law. In this sense, the moral law is not a relative construct existing separately from the physical laws of the universe: just as God is the architect that creates scientific law, God is also the architect of immutable objective laws that govern the way rational beings should live. The entirety of God's law is contained in Aquinas' description of the eternal law, all the laws of creation as they exist in the mind of God in eternity.[2] This law in its totality cannot be understood by our limited mortal intellects, so God makes his law known through natural law and divine law. Divine law is given through revelation, but the natural law is that which we can know through reason alone. So it makes sense that what can be known about nature and the world around us is accessible by reason.[3] The law of nature also applies to the objective moral order created by an all-good Lawgiver, and thus, moral precepts are also accessible by reason.

We see no evidence in the comics that Doctor Strange follows the thought of Aquinas. However, we do see a strongly consistent presentation of an objective order to reality and the moral obligations that arise from it, especially when the Sorcerer Supreme must interact most directly with the concept of the Creator God, the Source of All That Is.

Strange Religion

Some characters in the Marvel Universe are noted for—and in some rare cases, even defined by—their faith or relationship with God (setting aside, of course, those characters that actually *are* gods). For example, Kamala Khan, the latest Ms. Marvel, is constantly informed by her Islamic faith; Nightcrawler and Daredevil make frequent reference to their Catholicism; and Kitty Pryde and the ever-lovin' blue-eyed Thing occasionally refer to their Judaism.

By contrast, Stephen Strange doesn't fit into any category of traditional faith. We get the impression that he's simply a secular scientist who must be dragged into a transcendent understanding of reality. After his training in the mystic arts, Strange meets god-like beings, but we still don't see any sign of "faith" in the traditional sense.[4] He does, though, have a special relationship with the Vishanti, three quasi-divine beings who evidently empower his magic and protect him. They also seem to have been the source of power for Strange's mentor, the Ancient One, who was a member of a Vishanti "order" (without much more detail). One would be hard-pressed to call Strange's relationship with the Vishanti "religious," though. Most of his invocations to them are not actually magical intonations but mere exclamations.

Despite his lack of traditional faith, there are important instances in which Doctor Strange explicitly acknowledges the Creator God using expressions drawn from the Western monotheistic traditions. On these occasions, Strange either makes an appeal to a "highest power" to achieve some purpose, or he shows respect for this highest power in relation to his own role in the cosmos, thereby acknowledging Aristotle's concept of a prime mover. Also, despite a metaphysical mélange of competing higher powers and authorities, there does seem to be an objective sense of good and evil in Strange's universe. This is especially important when one sees the consequences of his deliberate invocation of "evil powers," which would make no sense if the creator of the universe had not also defined the concepts of good and evil.

In order to shed light on Doctor Strange's relationship with the Creator God and why acknowledgment of that being is necessary for him to effectively fulfill his role as Sorcerer Supreme, we look at three specific adventures, beginning with a most unlikely opponent...

The Lord Versus the Lord of Vampires

In one memorable case, Doctor Strange encountered Dracula, the Lord of Vampires, who attacked and killed Strange's faithful man-servant Wong, prompting the sorcerer to investigate the murder and try to bring Wong's killer to justice.[5] When he finally encounters the vampire, Strange implores him to restore life to Wong, and holds himself back in their battle so as not to destroy him. This proves to be Strange's undoing, as Dracula is a more powerful foe than he anticipated. Dracula compels Strange to stop fighting, and then drinks the sorcerer's blood and kills him.

After the death of Strange, Dracula ponders in the night. The narration reads, "Only two things on all the earth does he fear: the cross—and sorcery, which to him is much the same!"[6] Yet, as we will see, they are not really the same at all. The Sorcerer Supreme already brought sorcery to bear against Dracula and it was unsuccessful. Strange would need a different approach to defeat this enemy.

Strange's dead body is cast into a tomb, waiting for the time it would rise again as a vampire under Dracula's control. However, Strange's spirit lives on in his astral form, allowing him to continue thinking of a way to prevail against his vampiric foe. When Strange's now-undead body rises, his two warring natures as vampire and sorcerer prevent him from mounting much of a fight against Dracula... that is, until Dracula taunts Strange by saying, "I am your lord!"

This gives Doctor Strange the insight he needed to do something that he implies he had never done before: call on the one God of the universe. He realizes, "That's—who holds power—here I've called on—many gods—in my life! Never—have I needed strength—more than now! In the name of the Tetragrammaton, Jehovah! O great Unmanifest, hear my plea!"[7] Doctor Strange calls on the one Creator God, invoking the name Yahweh (the "tetragrammaton" that are the four consonants that make up the name of God in Exodus) as the power responsible for all other powers. At this point, Strange's touch burns Dracula and the resulting blast that kills the vampire takes on a distinctly cross-shaped flash of light. Still infused with divine power,

Strange heals Wong and himself and concludes, "Thank God, Dracula will menace man no more!"[8]

In the light of imminent defeat, in a conflict in which his created body fails to cooperate with his magical power, the Sorcerer Supreme calls upon a God stronger than all other gods, and finds victory through the cross, Dracula's one weakness. Had Strange not taken this approach, he would have fallen to the lord of the undead. Taking the approach he does, Strange accepts Aquinas' belief in an all-good, objectively higher power in the universe.

Back to the Start

In a lengthier adventure, Doctor Strange engaged in a protracted battle against the cosmic horror Shuma-Gorath that culminated in the death of Strange's mentor, the Ancient One, leaving his spirit to become one with the universe—a universe Strange had to protect by himself as Sorcerer Supreme.[9] Afterwards, in a bout of introspection, Strange explains to his beloved Clea,

> To live means to influence the cosmos! One's actions—one's presence— changes every being he meets! The cosmos is everything! To affect any part of the cosmos is to affect the totality! Life is the most precious gift the cosmos can bestow ... and it is the lot of Dr. Strange to preserve the gift.[10]

While we should not too readily equate "the cosmos" and "God," there is still a vivid sense of Strange's responsibility to an objective order, the eternal law, that he has come to perceive.

Strange then finds Mordo, his oldest foe and his rival for their master's attention, to tell him that he has taken the Ancient One's place. Before he does, though, he comes across a gypsy woman seeking vengeance on Mordo for stealing a magic book. The stolen book, the ancient Book of Cagliostro (which also plays an important role in the film), gives its possessor the power to travel through time and change reality. Once they are united, Strange and Mordo travel separately back to eighteenth-century Paris to meet the author, who proves to be less than charming. More important, Cagliostro reveals himself to be a thirty-first-century time traveler named Sise-Neg, which, not at all coincidentally, is "Genesis" backwards.[11]

Sise-Neg explains his plan to return to the dawn of creation when there is more "ambient magic" for him to control and manipulate for himself, with the ultimate goal of becoming God: "And what is another term for an all-powerful being at the dawn of creation? I shall tell you, as I leave you, gentlemen—it is God!"[12] There's some sketchy metaphysics involved with his statement: evidently, Sise-Neg's definition of "God" simply means an "all-powerful" being that happens to exist at the beginning of time. This is not Aristotle or Aquinas' concept of God as first cause or unmoved mover, and no explanation is given for the beginning of time itself—a failure of understanding that Sise-neg will come to realize before long.

Thus begins an epic backwards journey to the dawn of time, though there are only three stops shown on the way. The first occurs when Sise-Neg detects a huge amount of magical energy. Needing "all possible knowledge" to become God, he investigates the source of the energy, which turns out to be the legendary wizard Merlin. Sise-Neg uses his magic to summon a dragon to fight a knight who happens to be in the area. Doctor Strange implores his opponent to have mercy: "Does the God you wish to be care nothing for humans?" Sise-Neg responds, "I am above humans."[13] This is not really an answer to Strange's question about the nature of God who, as Strange implies and Aquinas asserts, is all-good, and thus should care for all humans. The Sorcerer Supreme engages the dragon in battle and helps the knight to defeat it—a knight who turns out to be Lancelot du Lac, on his way to the court of King Arthur.

Mordo takes this incident as an occasion to give Sise-Neg a reflection on freedom, consequence, and morality:

Strange's compassion for humanity has saved the life of Lancelot—he whose oh-so human love for Queen Guinevere will soon destroy Camelot, one of humanity's most noble dreams! Humans sow the seeds of their own destruction through their willful natures! People cannot control themselves! They need to be controlled by someone strong!

A couple of points are worth noting here. First, Camelot is described as one of humanity's most noble dreams. Many views could be offered as to what exactly is the "dream" of Camelot, but it isn't out of the question to see it as the image of Christian virtue lived through pure and noble lives or, as Aquinas would put it, a life lived according to the eternal law as revealed in natural and divine law. True, Mordo is suggesting that Strange's heroic action will lead to the death of this dream, but it's more important that he recognizes it as objectively noble in the first place. Mordo then goes on to effectively summarize the Christian doctrine of original sin when he says that humans fall as a result of their own free will and cannot control themselves. This only makes sense in the context of an objective order to reality within which all three players are operating, which will become especially important in the climactic conclusion of the story.

A Strange Tale of Biblical Proportions

The second stop on their journey is an ancient city whose people are lost in "sin and degradation." Mordo suggests this is sufficient reason to kill them all, while Strange pleads that "sin is no excuse for murder." Taken literally, sin is a violation of God's law, even if that is only understood as a violation of right reason perceived in the law of nature, making Strange's choice of words another invocation of an objective order and its implied author.

Sise-Neg is willing to entertain Mordo and Strange's philosophical disagreement and takes on a human appearance to speak to the people. What results is a parallel to the story of Sodom and Gomorrah from Genesis 19, in which two angels are threatened by the wicked townspeople. The scene in Strange's adventure is not quite so sordid, with a threat of "Let's show him what happens to strangers here!" At this point, there is a dramatic change from the biblical text: the "priests of death" are summoned, who command the people to tear the strangers apart with their bare hands. Sise-Neg has seen enough and informs the townspeople that they have angered God. With the pronouncement of his divine name, the town is destroyed. A handful of survivors escape, and it is only then that the names of the Biblical cities are heard on the survivors' lips, horrifying Doctor Strange.

The third stop before they reach the beginning of time is the prehistoric past where, in true comic book fashion, dinosaurs exist alongside proto-humans. It is also the dwelling place of the cosmic horror Shuma-Gorath. The primitive humans are no match for Shuma-Gorath, so Strange pleads to Sise-Neg: "Those are your ancestors... They are responsible for your existence! When all is said and done, you and they are one!" This awakens something in Sise-Neg and he intervenes on their behalf; he is unable to destroy Shuma-Gorath, but he is able to put it to sleep for millennia. Then the would-be god says, "Now only one act remains for me here—an act, this time, not of destruction, but of creation—the creation of a haven—a garden—for the two surviving apes! They should not know fear again…" And so, Sise-Neg creates the Garden of Eden.

Finally, the neonate god and his two traveling companions arrive at the beginning of time. Strange and Mordo witness the creation of the universe in reverse, culminating in "stark darkness," from which Sise-Neg speaks out. But now, he is now no longer the cosmic conqueror, having been enlightened by his experience of apotheosis.

> I have been wrong! My plan to re-create the universe in my image was truly pitiable! I have achieved my godhood, but in doing so, I have learned the truth—that everything is as it should be, if only one can see it! Reality is always in harmony. Man is imperfect—but he is this dimension's closest approximation of perfection! I cannot improve upon that, so I shall recreate the universe—exactly as it was before! Time turns and begins again with me! When you remember this, think not of the man called Sise-Neg—but the god called—Genesis!

After this, the story wraps up quickly. Strange and Mordo are propelled back to the present. Mordo is catatonic as a result of what he has seen, but Strange is unaffected.

The obvious question is: Did Sise-Neg actually become God? I would say no. The wizard possessed extraordinary "god-like" power, but in the end, he metaphorically knelt in submission before a higher power that had to have already existed—a first cause—who had founded the order of creation according to goodness, not power. By setting everything back to the way it was before his plan began, Sise-Neg undid everything that appeared to be his hand in history, including the destruction of Sodom and Gomorrah or the creation of the Garden of Eden. The universe continued to exist, not because of Sise-Neg, but because of the One who first set it into motion.

A deeper reflection on who was really "god-like" can instead be seen in the characters of Mordo and Doctor Strange. Mordo, hungry with a will to rule over others, experiences the beginning of all that is and becomes catatonic as a result. In abusing his will, he lost his freedom, which is only properly exercised in conformity with the eternal law of God. Strange, on the other hand, never strays from his observation to Clea about the goodness of creation. He holds on to the notion of both a physical order and a moral order that cannot be ignored or violated without serious consequence. He implies that the nature of God is to benevolently rule and protect creation. According to Aquinas, Doctor Strange's conformity to this vocation demonstrates that he is the most god-like of them all.

Pride Goeth Before the Zom

The nature of the demonic is never fully explained in the Marvel Universe, but there is little question that it exists and that it is objectively opposed to the concept of the good as understood by Aquinas. Surprisingly, these cosmological moral perspectives can be seen in an encounter between Doctor Strange and everyone's favorite green behemoth, the Incredible Hulk. Earlier, a group of Hulk's supposed friends (including Strange) expelled him to a far-away planet to prevent him for harming anyone else on Earth. Away from Earth, Hulk found purpose, love, and a family, all of which was stolen from him by an explosion—also caused by his friends back home. The Hulk returned to Earth on a mission of vengeance, blaming his friends for stealing his freedom and his newfound happiness.[14]

Upon meeting his old friend, Doctor Strange first spoke to Bruce Banner in a mindscape in Hulk's head and asked to hear the story from Bruce's point of view. Strange reacts with mercy, promising to help make things right, and offers his hand to lift Bruce up. As he does so, however, Bruce becomes the Hulk again, crushing all the bones in Strange's hands, which has the same effect in the real world. Unable to work magic to defend himself against the approach of Hulk's minions, Strange resorts to an infernal nuclear option. Despite his servant Wong's protest, Strange opens a box and intones, "In the name of the Eternal... by the Rings of Raggador... though his spirit be infernal... Zom must live once more."[15] Zom is a powerful being of chaos and destruction, with strength so great that the cosmic forces of the universe are the only beings previously able to stop him.[16]

Once possessed by the power of Zom, Doctor Strange is able to face the Hulk in combat. But Strange is no longer the articulate, urbane sorcerer; rather, he talks like an enraged Hulk (while the Hulk of this story is calm and intelligent). There is no reason or art left in Strange, just destructive, demonic power. He loses his freedom and his humanity when he violates the moral order of the cosmic lawgiver as explained by Aquinas. But even with the power of Zom, Strange is defeated.

Zom becomes dormant within Strange, but manifests later in an Avengers battle, which ends brutally thanks to Zom's influence on the sorcerer. It is only then that Strange realizes the full extent of what he's done:

I have had to call upon darker forces than I normally would use… forces I thought I could control, but I can't. It was arrogance. The same arrogance that led me down the path I'm on in the first place… and I have failed at my task as Sorcerer Supreme of this dimension… I need to atone for what I have done.[17]

He realizes that his mystical practice has to conform with the law of the universe as established by God, for that was the way he was able to persevere against Dracula and Sise-Neg. In penance, Strange relinquishes his title as Sorcerer Supreme. This atonement is short-lived, however; he eventually regains his title, not because he has returned to the way of thinking seen in the Sise-Neg story, but merely because he remains heroic in his intentions despite his use of forbidden magic. A purely subjective understanding of the moral law has replaced the objective one established by God.[18]

Magic and Deep Magic

In the classic fantasy series *Chronicles of Narnia,* author and English professor C.S. Lewis (1898–1963) refers to the eternal law of God as the "deep magic" that comes from the "Emperor Beyond the Sea."[19] There is a magic inherent in creation itself. One can choose to conform to the magic and experience happiness as a result. Or one can seek control over the magic, a choice that will bring about suffering for oneself and others. This seems to be the meaning of magic in the Marvel Universe as well, even if the theistic implications of this are rarely drawn out explicitly. The two sides of this equation can be seen in the stories of Doctor Strange, whose magic is sometimes seen as a manifestation of this deep magic that requires a responsible cooperation between human freedom and the order of nature established by the Creator.

While none of us are sorcerers like Doctor Strange, we too are called to engage the magic of our lives in accordance with the deep magic of the universe. As humans, we have the gift of free will to decide whether we will acknowledge the connectedness and value of all life and strive to protect it, or we can turn to the dark magic that seeks power at any price and tries to enforce one's will over the wills of others. Doctor Strange learned the price of such hubris, both in the beginning of his story and in events much later in his life. May we find his early examples edifying and his later examples a warning to us all.

Notes

1. Saint Thomas Aquinas, *Summa Theologiae*, available at http://www. newadvent.org/summa/, I.2.3.
2. Ibid., I-II.91.1.
3. Ibid., I-II.91.2.
4. However, Vision describes him as one with an "attitude that might be categorized as religious" in *Infinity Crusade* #1 (June 1993), collected in *Infinity Crusade Volume 1* (2008).
5. The two-part story began in *Tomb of Dracula*, vol. 1, #44 (May 1976) and concluded in *Doctor Strange*, vol. 2, #14 (May 1976); both are collected in *Essential Doctor Strange, Volume 3* (2007).
6. *Doctor Strange*, vol. 2, #14.
7. Ibid.
8. Ibid.
9. The horror-themed confrontation, inspired by Robert E. Howard, occurs in *Marvel Premiere* #3–10 (July 1972–September 1973), collected in *Doctor Strange Epic Collection: A Separate Reality* (2016).
10. *Marvel Premiere* #12 (November 1973), collected in *Doctor Strange Epic Collection: A Separate Reality*.
11. The story of Sise-Neg is presented in *Marvel Premiere* #12–14 (November 1973–March 1974), collected in *Doctor Strange Epic Collection: A Separate Reality*.
12. *Marvel Premiere* #13 (January 1974).
13. This and the rest of the quotations from the Sise-Neg saga are from *Marvel Premiere* #14 (March 1974).
14. These events took place in various comics from 2005-2007 and are collected in *Hulk: Planet Hulk Prelude* (2010), *Hulk: Planet Hulk* (2007), and *World War Hulk* (2008).
15. *World War Hulk* #3 (August 2007), collected in *World War Hulk*.
16. Zom's first appearance was in *Strange Tales*, vol. 1, #156 (May 1967), collected in *Marvel Masterworks: Doctor Strange, Volume 2* (2013).
17. *New Avengers Annual*, vol. 1, #2 (Febuary 2008), collected in *New Avengers: The Trust* (2008) and *New Avengers by Brian Michael Bendis: The Complete Collection, Volume 3* (2017).
18. While there isn't room to discuss it in detail, Doctor Strange's role in the 2015 multiverse-shaking *Secret Wars* event is also relevant to this chapter. We see that he has not stopped his practice of using dark magic: "If I am to be damned by these decisions, let it be by using all the resources at the disposal of a sorcerer supreme" (*New Avengers*, vol. 3, #14, February 2014, collected in *New Avengers: Other Worlds*, 2015). He claims that there is no difference between the black arts and the white arts, only the price paid to use them. This means then that there is no truth or order or goodness in the universe, merely the

enforcement of one's will over a purely mechanistic creation. Wielding this rationale and the power he gains from selling his soul (literally), he participates in the deaths of whole worlds, culminating in the megalo-maniacal Doctor Doom recreating the whole universe with himself as God. Strange becomes one of Doom's lieutenants, but when he works with the remnant of Earth's heroes that remain to stop Doom, Doom kills Strange (*Secret Wars* #4, September 2015, collected in *Secret Wars*, 2016). If the penance he had sworn earlier had been more sincere, perhaps things would have been different. Instead, Strange succumbed to a relativistic understanding of reality and lost sight of the whole he had previously witnessed: the eternal law of God.

19. C.S. Lewis, *The Chronicles of Narnia* (New York: HarperCollins, 2010), made up of seven novels written published between 1950 and 1956.

The Index of the All-Seeing Eye of Agamotto

Doctor Strange and Philosophy: The Other Book of Forbidden Knowledge,
First Edition. Edited by Mark D. White.
© 2018 John Wiley & Sons Ltd. Published 2018 by John Wiley & Sons Ltd.